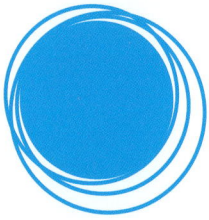

Contents

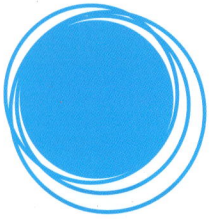

Introduction

About this book

Computer science is the study of computers, computing **hardware** and **software**, **computer networks** and the design of **computer programs**. It also includes the study of the way humans interact with computers and computing technology.

Computer science is linked to all areas of the world you live in today. It helps you to make positive changes to the world you live in, and provides important tools and applications to help you solve a wide range of problems. Computer science is continually **evolving** to provide new and valuable ways of improving your life and your interactions with the world around you.

This Student's Book will help you to understand some of the key areas of computer science, such as:

- How computing devices operate and communicate
- How computing devices store and process different types of data
- How to develop a program to solve a specific problem
- How computer systems and artificial intelligence are used to model and simulate real-life situations to help with task completion and decision-making.

This book also supports the learning objectives within the five strands of the Cambridge Lower Secondary Computing framework:

- **Computational thinking** is built into the tasks in this book. It looks at how computing can be used to explore and analyse **data** collected from the world around you. It is also about the development of skills to support problem-solving, for example how to describe a problem, and the data needed to solve that problem, in a way that a computer can understand.
- **Programming** explores the steps involved in designing and creating a computer program that can be used to carry out a particular task. In this book, you will be moving from **block-based** to **text-based programming** languages and explore how to program a **physical device** to solve a problem.
- **Managing data** looks at how computers and computer programs can be used to store, organise and manage different types of data. It also explores how that data can be used to support problem-solving. In this book, you will learn how to use, edit and create **databases** and **spreadsheets** to help with managing different types of data.
- **Networks and digital communication** focuses on the methods used to transfer digital data between different computing devices, and how these devices are used to support communication. In this book, you will explore how different computing devices can be linked together to support data transfer.
- **Computer systems** is about how computer hardware devices and computer programs work together to support users in solving problems. It involves considering how the hardware and software and the data input is processed, stored and then output, to help a user solve a problem. In this book, you will explore the network and communications devices used to transmit data and information around a computer network, and the world, in the process of solving a problem.

This Student Book has six units:

7.1 Block it out: Moving from blocks to text provides a transition from block-based programming to programming in Python, which is a text-based language. It focuses on the key concepts that underpin programming, enabling you to develop a series of programs in Python to be used in an educational environment.

7.2 Decomposing problems: Creating a smart solution provides an introduction to the text-based programming language MicroPython. You will learn how to program a physical device, the micro:bit, using its sensors to design a software solution for a smart device.

7.3 Connections are made: Accessing the internet explores how devices interact and send data between each other. It focuses on how data can be kept safe and looks at how artificial intelligence is changing the way in which computers function, enabling you to understand, collect and explain how connectivity technologies work.

7.4 The power of data: Using data modelling examines how applications, such as databases and spreadsheets, can be used to model data for real-life situations. You will explore how to use some of the key features of these applications, in addition to evaluating forms used to collect data for input into data models.

7.5 Living with AI: Digital data looks at the key differences between application and systems software. You will revisit the concept of artificial intelligence and how it is used in different industries. You'll also examine the methods used to store data and learn how image recognition is used in a range of applications.

7.6 Sequencing and pattern recognition: Getting the message across continues to explore programming the micro:bit using the text-based programming language MicroPython. You will learn to create a light sequence to convey a message, and you'll discover how to look for and use patterns to design and develop a prototype for a visual alarm.

How to use this book

In each unit, you will learn new skills by completing a series of tasks.

These features appear in each unit:

Get started!

This box introduces the unit and asks you some questions to discuss in pairs or a small group.

Learning outcomes

This box lists the learning outcomes that you will achieve in the unit.

Warm up

This box provides a task to do in pairs or a small group to get the learning started.

SCENARIO

This box contains a scenario that puts the tasks in the unit into a real-world context.

Do you remember?

This box lists the skills you should already have before starting the unit.

Learn

This box introduces new concepts and skills.

Practise

This box contains tasks to apply and practise the new skills and knowledge from the 'Learn' box.

Go further

This box contains tasks to enhance and develop the skills previously learned in the unit.

DID YOU KNOW?
This box provides an interesting or important fact about the task or theme.

Challenge yourself

This box provides challenging tasks with additional instructions to support new skills.

Final project

This box contains a final project that encompasses all the skills developed over the unit, in the context of the Scenario. The tasks in this box can be used to support teacher assessment of the learning objectives from the 'Learning outcomes' box.

Evaluation

This box provides guidance on how to evaluate and, if necessary, test the final project tasks.

What can you do?

This box provides a summary of the skills you have learned in the unit and can be used to support self/peer assessment of the learning objectives.

KEYWORDS
Important words are shown in **emboldened orange font** and are defined in this box. They also appear in the glossary at the back of the book.

Computational thinking

Most computational thinking skills are embedded into the 'Practise' tasks. However, where you see this box, an individual computational thinking skill is highlighted for your attention.

These speech bubbles provide hints and tips as you complete the tasks.

Student resource files, used in some of the Practise boxes, are available at **www.hoddereducation.com/cambridgeextras**

Get started!

Have you ever considered how a calculator actually works?

Examine a calculator. Discuss the following with a partner:

- What do you have to enter into a calculator for it to work?
- Are there any buttons that will automatically perform certain calculations? If so, what do these buttons calculate?
- How does a calculator display the results of calculations?

A calculator is like a computer program. The user enters numbers and presses certain buttons to perform a calculation. We assume calculators work correctly because they have been extensively tested before being released for sale.

In this unit, you will learn how **text-based programming** can be used to develop programs that perform calculations and allow the user to interact with programs to solve problems. You will use a text-based programming language, called Python, to create your own programs to solve a variety of mathematical problems.

> **KEYWORD**
>
> **text-based programming:** programming that requires the programmer to type text, e.g. Python

Learning outcomes

In this unit, you will learn to:

- identify and describe different data types that are used in Python
- create programs in Python that use different data types
- develop programs in Python that uses input and output
- develop programs in Python that use variables to perform calculations
- develop programs that use different arithmetic operators
- apply a test plan to a program in Python to ensure it works correctly
- understand how errors can occur in Python
- identify errors and debug programs in Python
- create algorithms using flowchart symbols
- predict the outcome of flowcharts that use selection
- understand and use selection statements and sequences in flowcharts
- select and use appropriate comparison operators when creating flowcharts
- follow, understand, edit and correct algorithms that use sub-routines.

Warm up

In pairs, read the following Scenario and write down the steps to calculate the answers to the questions below. You should not use a calculator to complete this task.

There are 13 Ashoka trees currently in the park. Park workers will plant 28 more Ashoka trees today and 36 more Ashoka trees tomorrow. It will take 10 workers 8 hours to finish the project.

1 How many Ashoka trees will the park have when the workers are finished?

2 How many trees were planted in 1 hour?

3 6 of the workers planted 8 trees each. The other workers each planted an equal number of trees. How many trees did each of the other 4 workers plant?

4 Check your answers in a small group. Did others break down the calculations in the same way? What problems did others have? Were the problems the same as yours?

In this unit, you will see how Python can be used to break large problems down into small problems, like you did in the calculations above. You will also learn how to test programs to ensure that the calculations are being performed correctly and giving the correct answers.

SCENARIO

The mathematics department at school want you to develop some programs that generate the answer to various calculation problems. Their current program uses Scratch, a **block-based programming** language. Students enter two **values** and the program generates the answer. Currently it allows for addition, subtraction, multiplication or division to be used.

To make it more appropriate for older students, they want the current program to be converted into Python (a **text-based programming** language). The mathematics department want you to create a series of programs that students could use depending on what calculation they want to complete. The programs should be able to complete the following calculations:

- Addition
- Subtraction
- Multiplication
- Division
- Area of a square
- Area of a triangle
- Perimeter of a rectangle
- Average of three numbers

The new programs should allow students to enter the values that are required and then calculate an answer.

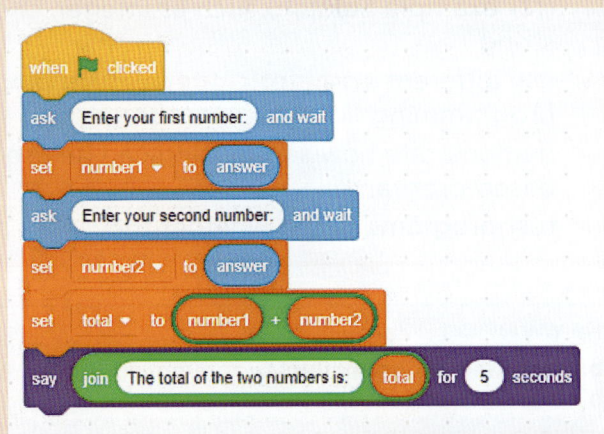

You will first create a **flowchart** to represent part of the problem. You will then need to create a series of programs to complete the different calculations and finally test the programs to ensure they work correctly.

DID YOU KNOW?

Python is one of the most popular text-based programming languages in the world, but how did it get its name? The person who created Python, Guido van Rossum, was reading the scripts from a popular UK comedy series called *Monty Python's Flying Circus*. He wanted a name that was short and unique, so he called the programming language Python!

Guido van Rossum

Do you remember?

Before starting this unit, you should be able to:
- ✔ describe what a flowchart is and understand the use of the start/stop, process and decision symbols
- ✔ describe what an algorithm is and read and interpret algorithms using flowcharts
- ✔ create block-based programs that use multiple variables
- ✔ use different data types in block-based programming (for example Scratch) such as integer, character and string
- ✔ use different **arithmetic operators** in block-based programming
- ✔ demonstrate how sequencing can be used in block-based programming
- ✔ test programs to see whether they work as intended.

KEYWORDS

block-based programming: programming using drag-and-drop blocks; a popular block-based language is Scratch

value: a number that can be used in a programming language

text-based programming: programming that requires the programmer to type text, e.g. Python

flowchart: a diagram showing the sequence of actions in a computer program; a graphical representation to show the steps to solve a problem

arithmetic operator: +, -, *, / and other symbols that can be used for arithmetic calculations

In this unit, you will use the following programming languages:
- Scratch
- Python

Scratch is web-based – find it at **https://scratch.mit.edu/**.

To install Python:

Python's Integrated Development and Learning Environment (IDLE) provides features for creating, editing and running programs. Before using Python you will need to install IDLE on your own personal device:

1 Go to **www.python.org/downloads**.
2 Select `Download Python`.
3 Once downloaded, double-click on the file to open it and then choose `Install Now`.
4 Once IDLE has installed, it should appear in your start menu.

For more information about IDLE see page 11.

Comparing Scratch and Python

Learn

There are hundreds of different types of programming languages used around the world. Most of these programming languages can be categorised into one of two types: block-based or text-based.

Previously you have learned how to program using a block-based programming language; the most common one that is used is Scratch. Block-based programming languages are a popular way to introduce people to programming. This is because you do not have to remember specific code and the different blocks click together like building bricks. To create programs using block-based programming, you use a **graphical user interface**, where you select the blocks you need and drag and drop, which makes it much easier to use.

Text-based programming requires you to remember the different **syntax** (code) that you will need and you have to type in the code that you require. There is no drag-and-drop option to build your programs and this can make it more challenging.

Python is normally installed on a computer with an **Integrated Development and Learning Environment (IDLE)**. IDLE provides lots of functions that are useful when writing Python code.

> Computers often make use of input and output to interact with those using it. Inputs are when data is entered into the computer, e.g. someone typing something in, or someone clicking on something. Outputs are when the computer displays something to the user after completing processing.

Regardless of whether you program using block-based or text-based programming languages, the key programming constructs remain the same, and this is why you can transfer from one type of programming language to the other.

The following image shows what the Scratch programming environment looks like:

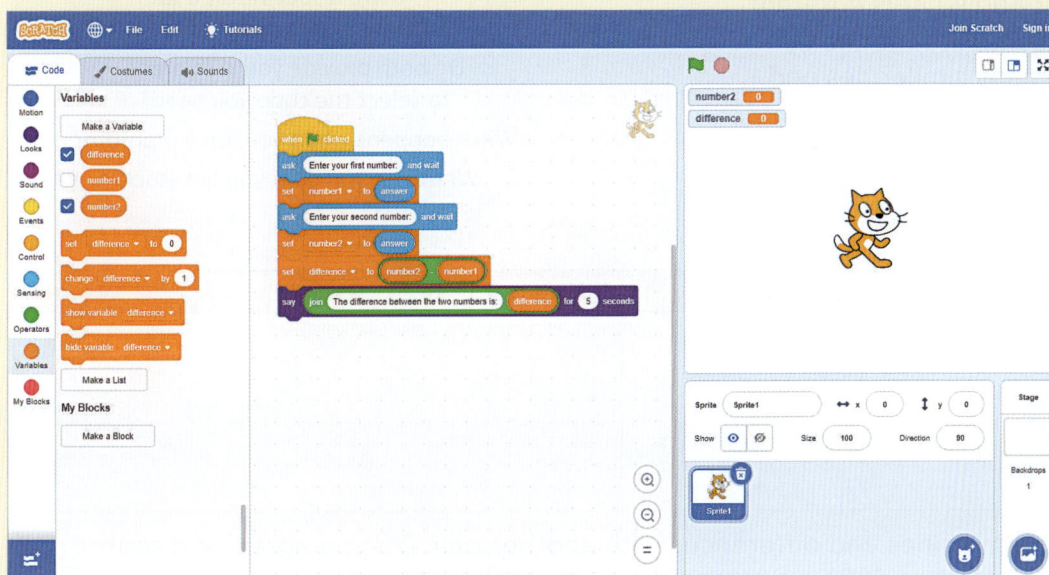

Below is an example of what a text-based programming environment looks like. This is IDLE, which is used to program in Python:

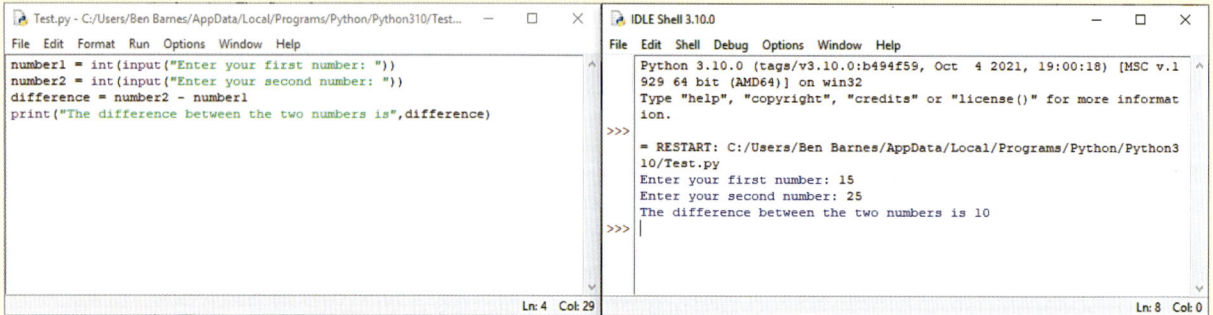

```
number1 = int(input("Enter your first number: "))
number2 = int(input("Enter your second number: "))
difference = number2 - number1
print("The difference between the two numbers is",difference)
```

```
Python 3.10.0 (tags/v3.10.0:b494f59, Oct  4 2021, 19:00:18) [MSC v.1
929 64 bit (AMD64)] on win32
Type "help", "copyright", "credits" or "license()" for more informat
ion.
>>>
= RESTART: C:/Users/Ben Barnes/AppData/Local/Programs/Python/Python3
10/Test.py
Enter your first number: 15
Enter your second number: 25
The difference between the two numbers is 10
>>>
```

These programming environments look very different. However, the examples given produce programs that do exactly the same thing. Can you work out the following questions:

- How many pieces of data need to be entered into the program?
- What calculation does the program do?

KEYWORDS

graphical user interface: also known as a *GUI*; used to interact with a computer using icons and menus

syntax: the structure of the code used in a programming language

Integrated Development and Learning Environment (IDLE): an environment used to program in Python

Practise

In pairs, take another look at the two screenshots of the Scratch and IDLE coding environments above. Identify what is similar and what is different.

- Copy and complete the table, adding as many similarities and differences as you can between the two types of programming language.

When looking for similarities and differences, think about:

Is there a specific area to do the programming in?

Do both provide you with areas to select the code you need?

What happens when you run a program?

What can you do if you get stuck?

Similarities	Differences

- Discuss the similarities and differences with another pair. Do you agree or disagree with their observations? Give a reason for your opinion.

Using Python

Learn

Using IDLE to program in Python makes it much easier to write, test and run your code. Click on the IDLE (Python) icon on your computer to launch the program.

Python can operate in two modes: the first is **interactive mode**.

When you launch Python IDLE, the prompt >>>, on the last line, shows that you are in the **Python shell**. This is the interactive mode, which allows individual Python commands to be typed directly and carried out.

```
Python 3.7.4 Shell                                          —    □    ×

File  Edit  Shell  Debug  Options  Window  Help
Python 3.7.4 (tags/v3.7.4:e09359112e, Jul  8 2019, 19:29:22) [MSC v.1916 32 bit
(Intel)] on win32
Type "help", "copyright", "credits" or "license()" for more information.
>>> print("Hello world")
Hello world
>>> (7+6)*2
26
>>>

                                                              Ln: 7  Col: 4
```

In the example above, you can see a print statement. The **print statement** is a Python command that outputs information onto the screen. This print statement will output the words 'Hello world' onto the screen.

The next line (7+6)*2 will output the result of the calculation. Notice that you do not need to use the print commands when performing calculations in the shell.

When using Python code you need to ensure that you type commands using lower-case letters.

Python can tell the difference between upper-case (capital) letters and lower-case (small) letters (it is **case sensitive**).

For example, if you enter `Print("Hello world")` an error should occur because 'Print' (with a capital 'P') is not the same as 'print' (with a small 'p'). You should always type Python commands in lower case.

Python can also help at the command prompt. You can type `help()` and find out how to use commands in a Python program, for example you can type `help(print)` to find out how to use the print command, such as how you can use it to display different data types on screen.

> Python can use arithmetic symbols such as + for adding, / for dividing and * for multiplying.

To close Python, type `exit()`.

When a command is typed, it must be 'translated' so that the computer can understand it. IDLE has an **interpreter** that does this. Each command is changed into a form of **machine code** so that the computer can carry out or *execute* the command.

Typing commands directly into the Python shell is called *programming in interactive mode*. One disadvantage of using interactive mode is that the code cannot be saved when using Python in this way.

> **KEYWORDS**
>
> **interactive mode:** the Python shell allows commands to be entered and run immediately
>
> **Python shell:** the Python interactive mode, where commands can be typed directly
>
> **print statement:** a Python statement used to output text or values onto the screen
>
> **case sensitive:** able to distinguish between capital and small letters
>
> **interpreter:** the feature of Python that translates the Python code into language that the computer can understand, line by line
>
> **machine code:** the language that a computer uses to carry out instructions

Practise

1. Open the Python IDLE. The Python shell will open as shown here:

   - Enter this command at the interactive prompt (>>>) and press ENTER:

     ```python
     print("Welcome to the Python Shell")
     ```
   - Now enter a command to print your name onto the screen and press ENTER:

     ```python
     print("Type your name here")
     ```
   - Now try this command:

     ```python
     print("Hello World)
     ```

   An error should occur because you have left out a set of quotation marks.

   Correct the error and execute the command again.

2. Try entering this calculation:

   ```python
   (7+3*2
   ```

   Look at what has happened this time. Why do think this is?

   Correct the error and execute the command again. The answer should be 20.

   - Try entering four of your own maths commands. Remember that the * (star symbol) is used for multiplying.
   - Get Python to add 150 and 23 together and then multiply the result by 3.

Using Python IDLE in Script mode

Learn

In the previous theme, you used Python Shell to enter single lines of Python code. These are translated and executed one at a time and they cannot be saved.

Most of the time, people write programs with many lines of code that they want to save.

To create and save a program, Python's IDLE is used in the second mode; this is called **script mode**.

You use a text editor (a bit like Notepad), which allows you to enter and save lines of code.

Create a program

Follow these steps to create a new program.
- From the Python shell, select 'File'.
- Then select 'New File'.
- A new window will open and you can enter lines of code into this text editor.

Type the command shown below into the new file.

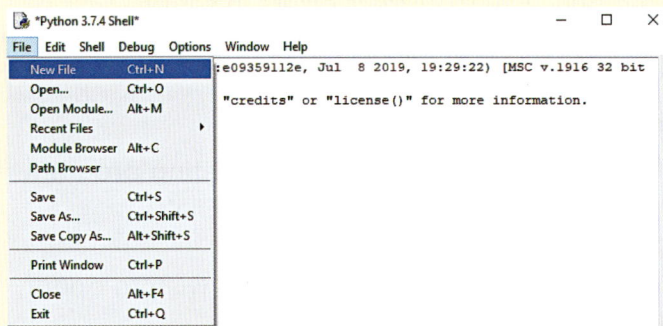

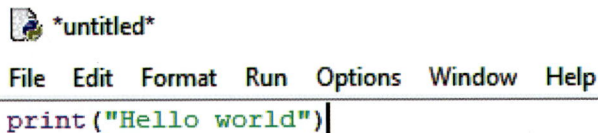

```
print("Hello world")
```

Save a program

Follow these steps to save a program.
- From the text editor menu, select 'File'.
- Then select 'Save as'.
- Call the program 'HelloWorld' and save it. (Note that all Python programs will have .py at the end to show that they are Python files.)

Run a program

Once you have completed the code, you can run the program.
- From the text editor menu, select 'Run'.
- Then select 'Run module' (or press F5). This will cause the Python interpreter to **execute** the program.
- The output from the program will appear in the window of the shell. In this case, you should see the words 'Hello world' in the shell window.

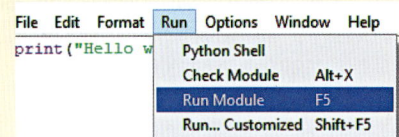

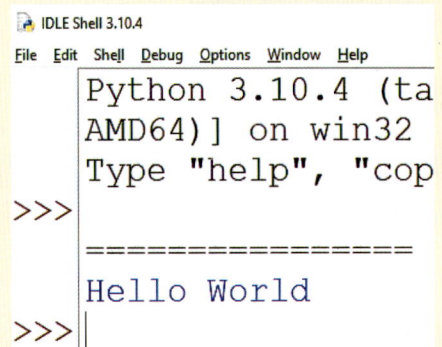

Correct errors

Here's how to correct errors in script mode.

Look at the code in the screenshot below. There is an error (remember that Python can tell the difference between capital and small letters).

```
HelloWorldWrong.py -                                    □    ×
File  Edit  Format  Run  Options  Window  Help
Print("Hello World")                                         ^
```

Can you see the error?

If there are errors in the code, they will be highlighted in red after you run or execute the program:

The only way to correct errors in script mode is to open the program and correct the mistakes in the code.

```
Print("Hello World")
NameError: name 'Print' is not defined
```

Open a program

Follow these steps to open an existing program.

1 From the Python shell, select 'File'.
2 Then select 'Open'.
3 Select the name of the file you wish to open.
4 Edit or correct the code.
5 Save the program.

Add comments

Here's how to add comments to a Python program:

Adding **comments** to code allows you to explain what the code does or to provide extra information about the code. In Python you can do this by starting the comment with a hash (#) symbol. Any text on a line after a # symbol will be ignored by the interpreter.

```
File  Edit  Format  Run  Options  Window  Help
#This is an Adventure Game about The Digital Sweet Shop
#The program was written by me
#
#
#
#The next few lines give the introduction


print("Welcome to The Digital Sweet Shop")
print()
print("You have been invited to take part in a competition in the shop.")
print("You must find the chocolate room where you will be asked a question.")
print("If you get it right you will receive letters which are part of a password and a clue.")
```

KEYWORDS

script mode: Python's text editor, which allows programmers to enter a list of commands and they are executed together

execute: another word for running a program

comments: text entered by a programmer to improve the readability of code; they start with the # symbol in Python

Practise

1   Open Python IDLE.
   - From the Python shell, select 'File'.
   - Then select 'New File'.
   - Enter the following code on line 1:
     ```
     print("Welcome to my first program in Python")
     ```
   - Now enter a command to print your favourite hobby onto the screen
     ```
     print("Add favourite hobby")
     ```
   - Save your program. Call it 'My First Program'.
   - Run the program and make sure it works correctly.

2   Now add the following programming code to your program:
    ```
    print("Did you know Python can do calculations? The line of code below
    will display the number 10")
    print(7+3)
    print("How about this? The calculation below should display the number 25")
    print(7+3*2+5)
    ```
   - Run the code. There should be an error that has occurred; can you correct the error so that the program runs?
   - The final number doesn't give the correct answer; it says 18 instead of 25. Correct the error and run the program again.
   - Add a comment on your programming code above the line you have just corrected explaining why it didn't work correctly to begin with.

3   Create a new program in IDLE and save the program, calling it 'Maths Favourites'.
   - Add code so that it prints out three different pieces of information; it should display your name, your favourite number and your favourite type of calculation, for example addition. An example of what your program could look like is shown below:
     ```
     Name: Adnan
     Favourite number: 7
     Favourite calculation: multiplication
     ```
   - Save and run your file.

4 Rewrite in Python the Scratch program shown below.

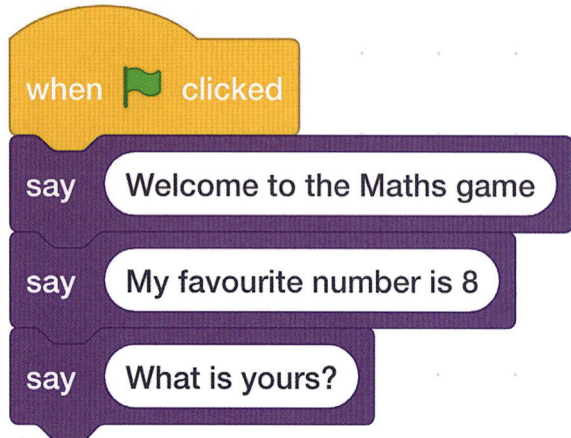

when 🏳 clicked

say Welcome to the Maths game

say My favourite number is 8

say What is yours?

- Create and save a new file first.
- Save and run your file to check it works.
- Correct any errors.

Variables

Learn

You have already seen how to output information onto the screen using the print statement. A computer should also be able to store values in a program so that they can be used at a later time.

Variables are used to store data in a program.

A variable is a named location in the computer's memory that stores data of a particular type. Data can either be assigned to a variable in the program itself, or it can be assigned from input from the user.

The code below shows four variables; these are the name, age, address and favourite colour of a student. All four variables are assigned a value.

```
name = "Ardeel"
age = 12
address = "Station Road"
colour = "Red"
```

If you wanted to print out the contents of the 'name' variable, you could use the following code:

```
print(name)
```

What if you wanted the message to display 'Your name is' followed by the name variable? You could adjust your print message as follows:

```
print("Your name is",name)
```

Notice how the variable is not inside quotation marks, and is joined to the other text that is in quotation marks by using a comma. This is what the program looks like when run:

```
Your name is Ardeel
```

You can continue to develop a print statement using variables, for example if you wanted the print message to say 'Your name is' followed by their name and then 'Nice to meet you', you could use this code:

```
print("Your name is",name,". Nice to meet you.")
```

> **KEYWORD**
>
> **variable:** a named memory location used to store data of a given type during program execution; a variable can change value as the program runs

Practise

1 Open the Python IDLE.
  - From the Python shell, select 'File'.
  - Then select 'New File'.
  - Type the following code:
    ```
    name = "Ardeel"
    age = 12
    address = "Station Road"
    colour = "Red"
    print("Your name is",name)
    ```
  - Now add the following code, so it displays the age:
    ```
    print("You are",age, "years old")
    ```
  - Complete the program by getting it to say:
    - 'You live at' and then the address
    - The colour and then 'is your favourite colour'.
  - The finished program should look like this:
    ```
    Your name is Ardeel
    You are 12 years old
    You live at Station Road
    Red is your favourite colour
    ```

2 Create a new program that shows your name, age, address and favourite colour. Save and run your file.

Adding more information to a program

Learn

The `input()` command allow users to enter information into the program and store it in a variable.

For example, `name = input("What is your name?")` displays the message 'What is your name?' on the screen and stores the input from the user in a variable called `name`.

Command	Description
`input()`	Used to take input from a user. If you wish to store this input you need to assign it to a variable.

Here is a comparison of what a Scratch program looks like in Python.

Scratch	Python
when ⚑ clicked ask What's your name? and wait set name ▾ to answer say join Hello name	`name = input("What's your name? ")` `print("Hello",name)`

Practise

1 Below are two different programs in Scratch. Rewrite each of these programs in Python.

Use the example in the Learn box above to help you.

Program 1	Program 2
when ⚑ clicked ask **Enter a word:** and wait set **word ▾** to **answer** say join **The word you entered was** **word**	when ⚑ clicked ask **How old are you?** and wait set **age ▾** to **answer** say join join **You are** **age** **years old** ask **Where do you live?** and wait set **live ▾** to **answer** say join **You live in** **live**

2 Create a new program in Python that:
   - asks the user to 'Enter your name' and stores it in a variable called `name`
   - asks the user to 'Enter a number between 1 and 10' and stores it in a variable called `number`
   - uses print to create an output that looks something like this when run:

```
Enter your name Khalil
Enter a number between 1 and 10 6
Your name is Khalil and the number you entered was 6
```

Run your program to check for errors.

Pair up with another student and review their solution. Check that the print message is in the same format as the example above.

Data types – string, integer and real

Learn

Variables can hold different **data types**. To store data you must decide on a name and a data type for the variable first, for example to store the player's age you will need to name a variable that can hold a whole number (also known as an **integer**).

> Remember: a variable is a named location in the computer's memory that stores data of a particular type. Data is often entered by the user while the program is running.

Variable name	Data type
playerage	integer

To store the player's name, you will need a variable that can hold letters – this is called a *string*.

Variable name	Data type
playername	string

The variable names have been chosen as **playerage** and **playername** but they could have been called anything we wanted.

Variables hold different data types. The table shows examples of each data type.

Data type	Example
String	Any textual characters, such as 'Hello World' or 'WE5694MC'
Integer	Any whole number, such as 24 or –10
Real	Any number with a decimal point, such as 6.98 or –0.045

In Python, the data type **real** is referred to as **float**. This is short for 'floating point number', which is a decimal number.

To capture data from the user, you use the **input function**.

The input function captures user input as a **string** data type. This contains numbers, letters and symbols, for example 'Robot', @password123' and '**WWW777' are all examples of a string data type.

Input is a built-in function in Python – it is part of the Python language.

```
playername=input("What is your name? ")
print("Welcome",playername)
```

KEYWORDS

data type: the different ways in which data can be stored, e.g. integer, string, decimal number

integer: whole number

real any number with a decimal point, such as 1.2 or 56.8

float: another name for the data type *real*; it is short for 'floating point number', which is a decimal number

input function: a function that Python uses to capture string data from users

string: data that is made up of letters, numbers or any characters on the keyboard

DID YOU KNOW?

Variables are not used just in computer programming; they are used in other applications as well.

Spreadsheets make use of variables too, but they are referred to as *cell references*.

Variables are extremely powerful as you can use them to store data and model different scenarios. A common method of modelling is taking historical data about weather conditions and using this to forecast the weather. Other examples of scenarios using variables for modelling include natural disasters, financial markets and aerodynamics.

Practise

1   Look at the Python code below. It shows a number of variables storing different pieces of data:

```
name = "Maryam"
cardNumber = "0012563943029845"
balance = 145.98
address = "Mall Road"
age = 11
```

Copy and complete the table below, identifying the data type for each variable and giving an explanation of the data type you have chosen.

Variable name	Variable name	Data type	Explanation
Name on bank card	name		
Bank card number	cardNumber		
Bank account balance	balance		
Address	address		
Age	age		

2   Open the **DataTypes.py** provided by your teacher.

Edit the code and finish the program so when it is run it looks like this:

```
Name: Maryam
Age: 13
Address: Station Road
Bank Card Number: 0012563943029845
Current Balance: 145.98
```

Casting

Learn

When using Scratch you did not have to worry about the data types as Scratch worked out the data type automatically. In Python, when the user inputs data and it is stored in a variable, you will need to inform the program what type of data it is. The process of ensuring data is set to the correct data type is known as **casting**.

It is very important when programming in Python that you always consider what data type the variable is and ensure it is set to the right type using casting. This is particularly important when using variables to perform calculations. If you do not inform Python of the data type of variables, it will not work correctly.

Consider the following example:

```
num1 = input("Enter a number: ")
answer = num1 * 2
print("The answer is",answer)
```

The program above should multiply the number entered by 2 and give an answer. If 5 was entered it should say 10, but this is not what happens:

```
Enter a number: 5
The answer is 55
```

The input function captures user input as a string data type. This means that if you want to perform a calculation using the input, you will need to cast it to either an integer (int) or decimal (float). Below shows an example of how you cast an input to a different data type:

Code	What it does
`num1 = int(input("Enter a number: "))`	The input statement is cast to an integer as it is wrapped in the code `int()`. This means that Python stores the value entered in the variable `num1` as an integer.
`num1 = float(input("Enter a number: "))`	This is exactly the same as the previous example, except the input statement is wrapped in the code `float()`. This means that Python stores the value entered in the variable `num1` as a decimal number.

If the original code is now amended to cast the input to an integer, it will look like this:

```
num1 = int(input("Enter a number: "))
answer = num1 * 2
print("The answer is",answer)
```

When the program is run, it now gives the correct answer:

```
Enter a number: 5
The answer is 10
```

> **KEYWORD**
>
> **casting:** the process of ensuring data is set to the correct data type

Practise

1 Open the file **MealCost.py** provided by your teacher:

```
money = input("How much money do you have? ")
meal = input("How much did the meal cost? ")
left = money - meal
print("After your meal you have,",left,"left")
```

   - Run the program; you will see it contains errors.
   - Make changes to the code so that the inputs are cast to the correct data type and the program runs.

2 A rabbit's age is approximately nine times the age of a human. Create a new program in Python using the Scratch program solution below, which calculates the age of a rabbit in rabbit years:

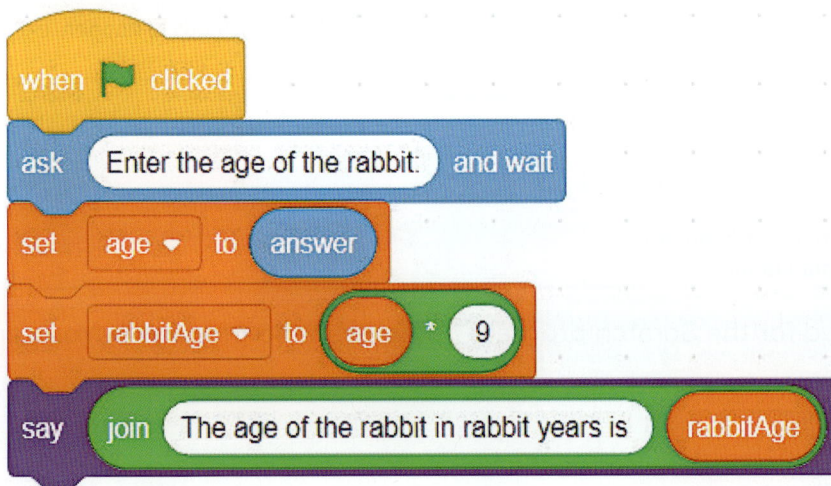

when ⚑ clicked

ask `Enter the age of the rabbit:` and wait

set `age ▾` to `answer`

set `rabbitAge ▾` to `age` * `9`

say join `The age of the rabbit in rabbit years is` `rabbitAge`

3 Create a new program in Python that:
   - asks the user to **"Enter the length of one side of a square"** and stores it in a variable called **length**; this should be cast as an integer
   - calculates the area of the square (HINT: this is the length multiplied by the length)
   - uses **print** to create an output; an example is given below:

   ```
   Enter the length of one side of a square: 7
   The area of the square is: 49
   ```

4 Create a new program in Python that calculates the speed of a moving car. The program should:
   - ask the user to enter the distance in meters; this should be cast to an integer
   - ask the user for the journey time in seconds; this should be cast to an integer
   - calculate the speed; this is the distance divided by time
   - use **print** to output the speed; an example is given below:

   ```
   Enter the distance in meters: 1500
   Enter the time in seconds: 40
   The car was travelling at a speed of 37.5 meters per second
   ```

Flowcharts and algorithms

Learn

To code a new calculation program in Python, you first need to complete some planning. This allows you to break down the problem and work through a solution. This applies whether you are using block-based programming or text-based programming. To do this you create the **algorithm**.

A common method of planning using algorithms is to create a **flowchart**. Here is a reminder of the key symbols and what they are used for:

Start/Stop **Purpose:** Used at the start and the end of the flowchart to signify the start and the end	**Process** **Purpose:** Used when something needs to happen, e.g. Add two numbers together
Input/Output **Purpose:** Used when data needs to be input and/or output from the program, e.g. Input number 1	

The flowchart below is used for the Scratch program in the Scenario on page 9. You can clearly see:

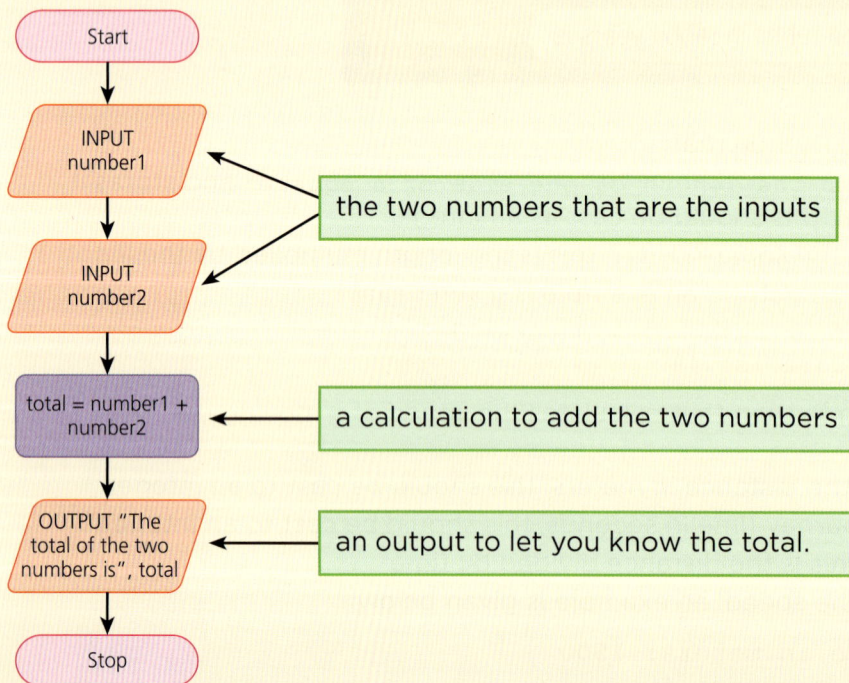

Start

INPUT number1 ← the two numbers that are the inputs

INPUT number2 ←

total = number1 + number2 ← a calculation to add the two numbers

OUTPUT "The total of the two numbers is", total ← an output to let you know the total.

Stop

Once you have planned a solution using a flowchart, you can then create the solution in Python. This makes it easier to solve as you have already broken down the problem and worked out the order; you need only get the **syntax** correct.

This shows the flowchart above written in Python:

```
number1 = int(input("Enter your first number: "))
number2 = int(input("Enter your second number: "))
total = number1 + number2
print("The total of the two numbers is:",total)
```

KEYWORDS

algorithm: a sequence of steps or instructions to solve a problem

flowchart: a diagram showing the sequence of actions in a computer program; a graphical representation to show the steps to solve a problem

syntax: the structure of the code used in a programming language

Practise

1 Predict the outcome of the flowchart on page 26 if the following values are entered:
   - number1 = 15, number2 = 20
   - number1 = 9, number2 = 17
   - number1 = 45, number2 = 36

2 Were your predictions correct?
   - Open the file **BasicAddition.py** provided by your teacher.
   - Enter the values above into your program. Are the answers the same as your predictions?

3 Using the correct symbols, create an algorithm using a flowchart that does the following:
   - Asks the user to input two numbers
   - Adds the two numbers together and then divides by 2 to find the mean average
   - Outputs the average.
   Try coding your flowchart in a new Python program.

4 Evaluate your flowchart and Python program. Ask a partner to check your flowchart with the following values. Do they get the correct output?
   - number1 = 7, number2 = 9; average should be 8
   - number1 = 15, number2 = 20; average should be 17.5

5 Discuss any problems with a partner and make corrections to your flowchart and/or Python code.

BIDMAS in Python

Learn

BIDMAS is an acronym to help you remember the order of operations when completing mathematical calculations.

When performing a mathematical calculation, a program will carry out the calculation in the following order:

- **B**rackets
- **I**ndices
- **D**ivision
- **M**ultiplication
- **A**ddition
- **S**ubtraction

> Indices are used to show numbers that are multiplied by themselves. For example, 2^3 is $2 \times 2 \times 2$, which equals 8.

Addition and subtraction are equal, so if both appear in a calculation they will be worked out from left to right.

Consider the following calculations:

Calculation	Outcome	Reason
3 + 4 * 5	23	4 * 5 will be calculated first before adding the 3
2 * 7 + 3 * 5	29	2 * 7 will be calculated first, then 3 * 5, then the two are added together
6 + 3 * 9 / 11	8.45 to 2 decimal places	9 / 11 will be calculated first, then multiplied by 3, then 6 is added to it
20 * (10 – 6) / 5	16	10 – 6 will be calculated first, then divided by 5 and then multiplied by 20

Applying BIDMAS is important when creating computer programs as otherwise you may receive the incorrect result.

Practise

Open IDLE and use Python in **interactive mode**.

- Copy and complete the table below and enter the different calculations into Python as they are written in the left-hand column. For each calculation, record the answer that is given.
- Now change the calculation using BIDMAS until you get the answer in the desired answer column. The first one has been done for you as an example.

Calculation	Answer	Desired answer	Calculation to get desired answer
5 * 8 + 6	46	70	5 * (8 + 6)
35 – 10 + 15		10	
9 + 3 * 5		60	
9 * 8 – 20 / 5		10.4	
60 * 40 – 3 * 4		8880	
18 * 6 – 2 / 8		9	

KEYWORD

BIDMAS: an acronym to help you remember the order of operations when completing mathematical calculations; a program will carry out the calculation in the following order: brackets, indices, division, multiplication, addition, subtraction

Error detection and correction

Learn

You have now created a number of different programs in Python and you will have encountered different errors where programs do not work or do not work as they should. Part of programming is being able to identify and **debug** (remove) the errors in your code.

Test plans

One way to check for errors is to apply a test plan. This is used to check whether a program is working correctly. The plan contains a number of tests that show what is expected to happen (the expected outcome).

Once you have created a program, you can apply a test plan to see whether the finished program does what you expect. An example of what a test plan could look like for a program that should add two numbers together is shown below:

Test number	Data entered	Expected outcome	Actual outcome	Pass/fail
1	num1 = 20 num2 = 15	total = 35	total = 300 fail	Fail
2	num1 = 19 num2 = 34	total = 53	total = 646 fail	Fail

> The program is not working as expected. Can you work out the error in the arithmetic operator used in the code?

There are a wide range of errors you may have come across, for example:

Missing brackets

A common problem is not including brackets in the correct place or not using them at all.

Incorrect code	Issue	Correct code
`print("Hello World"`	Missing a close bracket at the end of the line	`print("Hello World")`
`num1 = int(input("Enter a number:")`	Missing a close bracket at the end of the line; the code currently has two open brackets but only one close bracket	`num1 = int(input("Enter a number:"))`

Missing quotation marks

Adding quotation marks in an incorrect place or forgetting to include them can result in the program not running or not displaying the correct information.

Incorrect code	Issue	Correct code
`name = input(Enter a name")`	There is a missing quotation mark before `Enter`, after the open bracket	`name = input("Enter a name")`
`print("The name you entered was,name)`	There is a missing quotation mark after `was`, before the comma	`print("The name you entered was",name)`
`print("The name you entered was,name")`	There are no missing quotation marks. However, on line 2 the quotation marks are in the wrong place: when run, the program would say `"The name you entered was,name"` rather than the name that was entered – the quotation marks need to go after `was` and before the comma	`print("The name you entered was",name)`

Variable naming mismatches

Ensuring that the variable names you use throughout the program are the same is important; otherwise the program is likely to give an error as it cannot find a variable that you have specified.

Incorrect code	Issue	Correct code

`name = input("Enter a name")`
 	
`print("The name you entered was",names)`
	The variable used in line 2 `names` is not the same as the variable name when defined in line 1; they both need to match (both need to be called `name`)	`name = input("Enter a name")`
		
		`print("The name you entered was",name)`

`number1 = 15`
 	
`number2 = 20`
 	
`total = number + number2`
	The calculation on line 3 uses a variable called `number`; there is no variable in the program called number – this should be `number1`	`number1 = 15`
		
		`number2 = 20`
		
		`total = number1 + number2`

Variables not cast to the correct data type

Not casting variables to the correct type may mean you get the wrong answer to your calculations or you get an error message.

Code	Issue	Correct code

`num1 = input("Enter the first number:")`
 	
`num2 = input("Enter the second number:")`
 	
`total = num1+num2`
 	
`print("The total is",total)`
	Neither of the inputs is cast to an integer; this means when the calculation tries to add them together it will just join both numbers, e.g. If num1 = 50 and num2 = 100 it would say 50100, rather than 150 – both inputs need to be cast to an integer	`num1 = int(input("Enter the first number:"))`
		
		`num2 = int(input("Enter the second number:"))`
		
		`total = num1+num2`
		
		`print("The total is",total)`

What happens:

```
Enter the first number: 50
Enter the second number: 100
The total is 50100
```

KEYWORD

debug/debugging: the process of identifying and removing errors from a computer program

Practice

1 Open the file **ProductCost.py** provided by your teacher.

```
price = input("Enter the product price:)
quantity = input("Enter the product quantity: ")
cost = price + quantity
print("The total cost is: "+ total)
```

There are a number of errors in the code that prevent the program working.
The program should:
- ask the user to enter a price and a quantity
- calculate the cost (price multiplied by quantity)
- display the overall cost.

Work through the code line by line to identify and debug the errors.

Open the file **Product Cost Test Plan.docx** provided by your teacher. Apply the test plan to the file **ProductCost.py** to ensure that your amended program works correctly.

2 You now have the opportunity to sabotage a program! In pairs, one person should open **NumberTrick.py** and the other **RestaurantBill.py** provided by your teacher. The programs you have been given are fully working.

Your task is to create five errors.

Once you have sabotaged the program, swap programs with your partner and see whether they can identify and debug the program.

This is what the two programs should do when fully working:

Program 1

This program should complete a number trick where the result is always the number 3. It should:
- ask the user to input a number
- double the number entered
- then add six to it
- then halve it
- then subtract the number the user started with
- and finally display the result.

Program 2

This program should calculate the amount each person should pay for a bill at a restaurant. It should:
- ask the user to input the total bill
- ask the user to input the number of people eating
- calculate the tip: 15% of the total bill
- calculate the total bill including the tip
- work out the amount each person has to pay (the total including the tip divided by the number of people)
- display the amount each person has to pay.

Open the file **Sabotage Test Plan.docx** provided by your teacher. Apply the relevant test plan to the program you have just fixed to see whether it works correctly.

Making choices IF THEN ELSE in flowcharts

Learn

Using selection in a flowchart

Sometimes decisions have to be made in a program. This is usually because the program has reached a point where there is more than one option or choice. For instance, in a calculation game, if the user inputs two numbers which are added together and the total is over 50, it would display 'Great score'; if the total is under 50 it would display 'Better luck next time'. There are a number of possible pathways for the program to follow depending on how the player answers the questions.

Selection occurs when a question is asked. It is important in programming because the programmer can offer the user choices about the way in which they move through the program. Selection is achieved using IF statements. You may already have some experience of using IF statements in a block-based programming language such as Scratch.

For example:

Condition check: Checks if the number1 variable is greater than the number2 variable

If TRUE: if the condition is true it will display the number1 variable

If FALSE: if the condition is false it will display the number2 variable

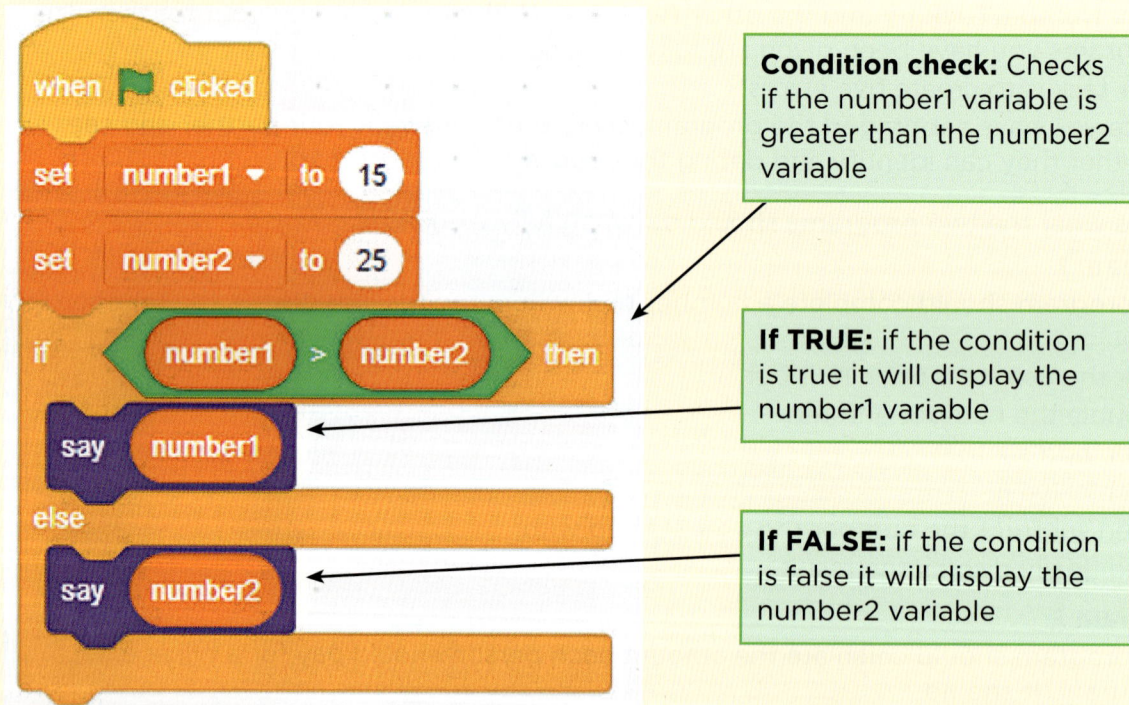

In the example above, the 'IF...THEN...ELSE' block (selection) is being used. This example checks whether the `number1` variable is greater than the `number2` variable. This is known as the **condition** (what is being checked). If the condition is **True**, it will display the `number1` variable and if it is **False** it will display the `number2` variable.

KEYWORDS

selection: a programming construct with more than one possible pathway; a condition is tested (using a question or criterion) before deciding which pathway to follow (the output)

condition: something that is checked to determine whether it is true or false

As a flowchart, the Scratch program would look like this:

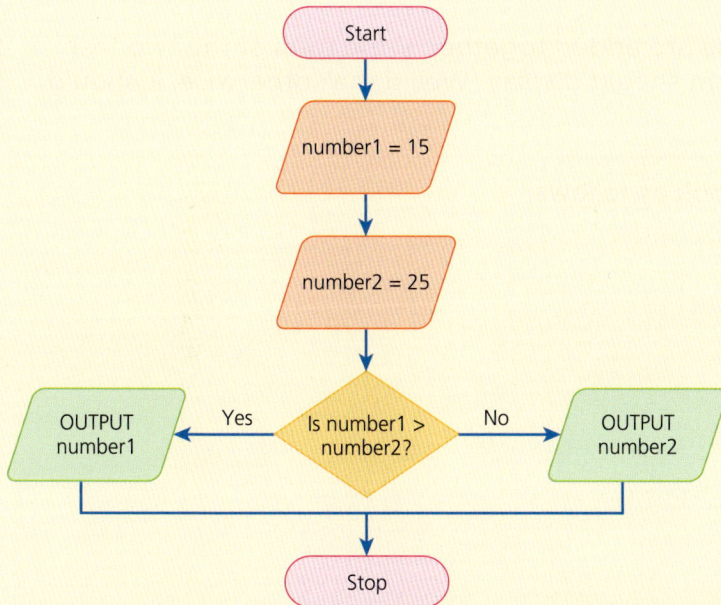

When using selection in any programming language, you need to use **comparison operators** to compare values. Comparing different values gives programs the ability to determine whether something is true or false and then decide which path to take next. The different operators that can be used when comparing values are:

Operator	What it means
==	equal to
<	less than
>	greater than
<=	less than or equal to
>=	greater than or equal to
!=	not equal to

This is what the same program would look like in Python:

```python
number1 = 15
number2 = 25
if number1 > number2:
    print(number1)
else:
    print(number2)
```

Can you see the similarities between Scratch and Python code?

Previously, you looked at what different flowchart symbols do. There is an additional symbol you now need to make use of: the decision symbol.

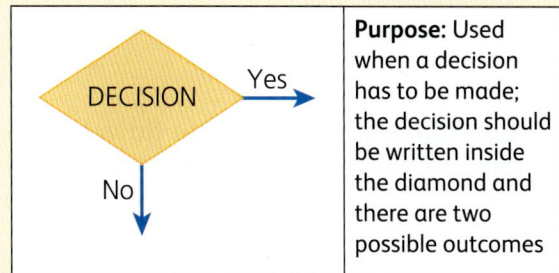

Purpose: Used when a decision has to be made; the decision should be written inside the diamond and there are two possible outcomes

KEYWORD

comparison operators: symbols used to compare values, e.g. >= meaning greater than or equal to

Consider the following scenario:

> A user enters two test scores; these are added together. If the total of the two test scores is over 100, then the program should display 'Well done'; otherwise, it should display 'Better luck next time'.

A flowchart for this scenario would look as follows:

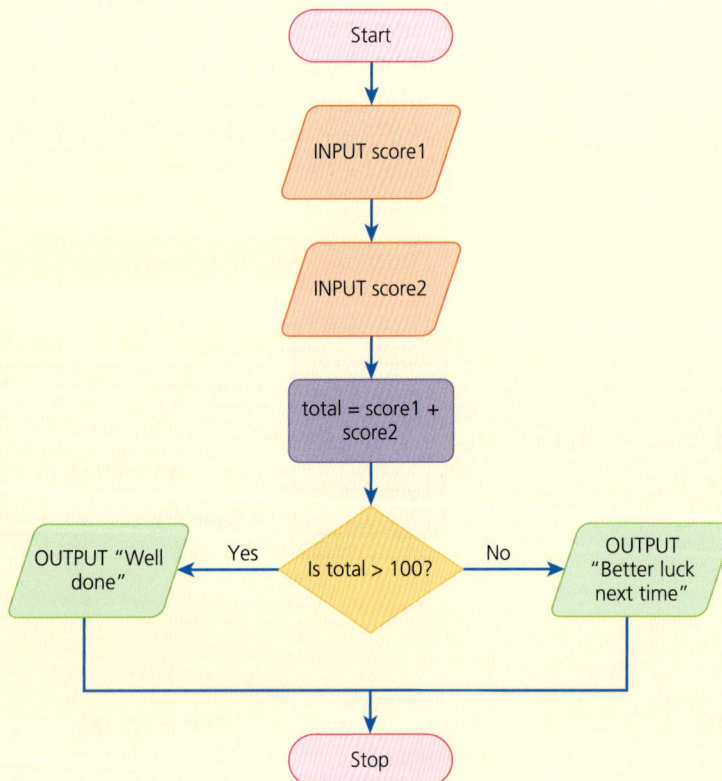

It is sometimes easier to create flowcharts to solve a problem by breaking down the problem into separate parts. Below is the scenario with the key parts highlighted. The flowchart has been colour coded so that you can see how it translates:

> A user **enters two test scores**; these are **added together**. If the **total of the two test scores is over 100**, then the program should display **'Well done'**; otherwise, it should display **'Better luck next time'**.

Here is an example to show what the solution would look like in Python, with the different areas highlighted so that you can see how it translates:

```python
score1 = int(input("Enter the first score: "))
score2 = int(input("Enter the second score: "))
total = score1+ score2
if total > 100:
    print("Well done")
else:
    print("Better luck next time")
```

Practise

1 Look at this Scratch example. When a number is squared (multiplied by itself), it is considered to be a 'Big Number' if it is greater than 100. Create a flowchart for this program.

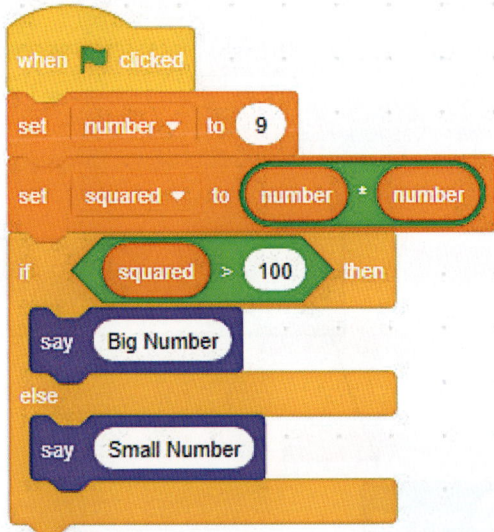

```
when 🚩 clicked

set   number ▾   to  9

set   squared ▾  to  ( number  * number )

if    ( squared > 100 )  then

    say   Big Number

else

    say   Small Number
```

Once you have created your flowchart, swap it with a partner's. Evaluate it carefully and check that it works correctly.

2 The alphabet used in English-speaking countries has 26 letters in it. Create a flowchart that asks for the number of letters in the English alphabet to be entered. If the number entered is 26 then it should display 'correct'; if it is not it should display 'incorrect'.

Once you have created your flowchart, ask a partner to evaluate it. Check your partner's flowchart to make sure that it works correctly.

3 Create a flowchart that satisfies the following criteria:
   - The user is asked to enter two numbers.
   - The flowchart checks to see whether the first number is greater than the second number.
   - If it is, then it should output the sum of the two numbers.
   - If it is not, it should output the difference between the two numbers.

Once you have created this flowchart, ask a partner to evaluate it. Check your partner's flowchart to make sure it works correctly.

Go further

Sub-routines

Sub-routines allow you to create mini programs inside your program that can be completed when requested. This avoids a program becoming too complicated. Another benefit is that you can use sub-routines multiple times in a program where you want to reuse the same code.

This is the start of a Scratch calculator program without sub-routines:

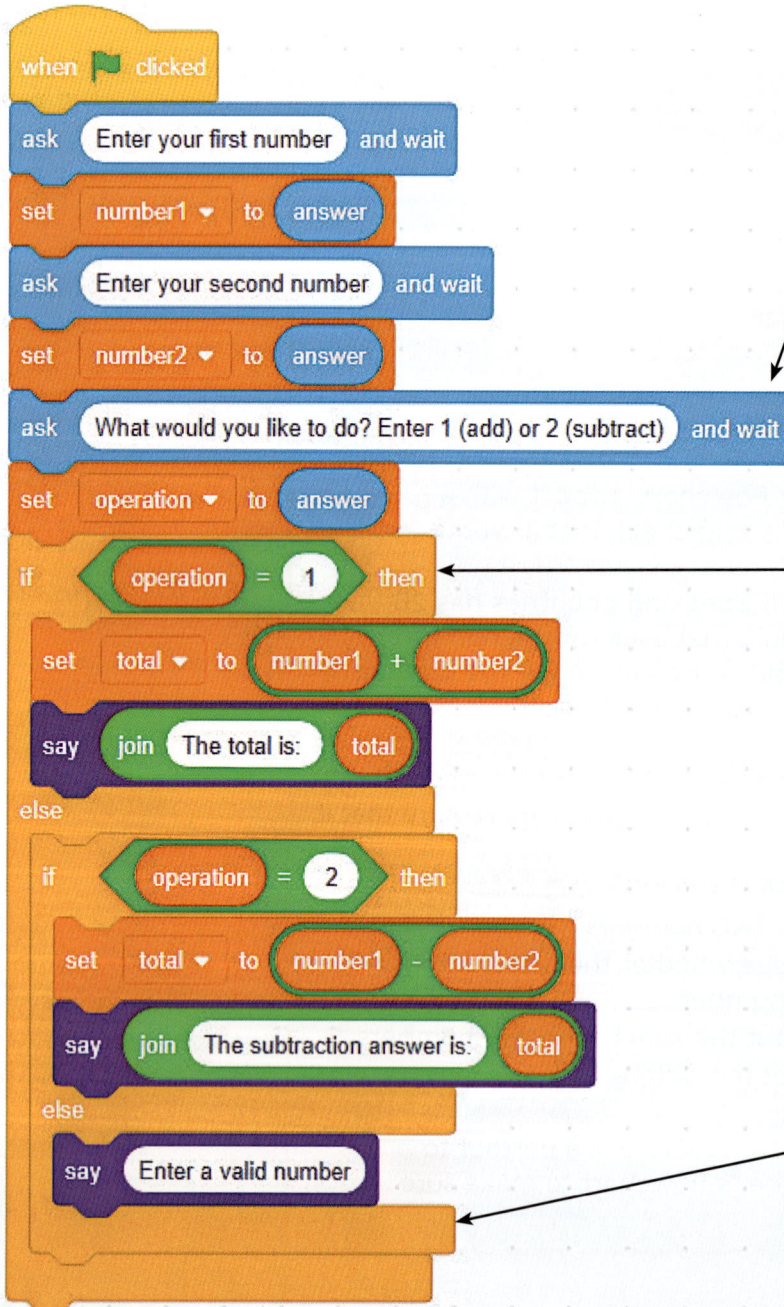

```
when [flag] clicked
ask (Enter your first number) and wait
set [number1 ▼] to (answer)
ask (Enter your second number) and wait
set [number2 ▼] to (answer)
ask (What would you like to do? Enter 1 (add) or 2 (subtract)) and wait
set [operation ▼] to (answer)
if <(operation) = (1)> then
    set [total ▼] to ((number1) + (number2))
    say (join (The total is:) (total))
else
    if <(operation) = (2)> then
        set [total ▼] to ((number1) - (number2))
        say (join (The subtraction answer is:) (total))
    else
        say (Enter a valid number)
```

It will ask the user to enter option 1 or 2.

Depending on the response, it will either add or subtract the numbers, or, if the user enters something else, it will ask them to enter a valid number. In this example, a valid number is either the number 1 or 2.

This program, if you continued to extend it, would get incredibly confusing to follow Therefore you can make use of sub-routines to make it easier to follow.

Here is the same program using sub-routines:

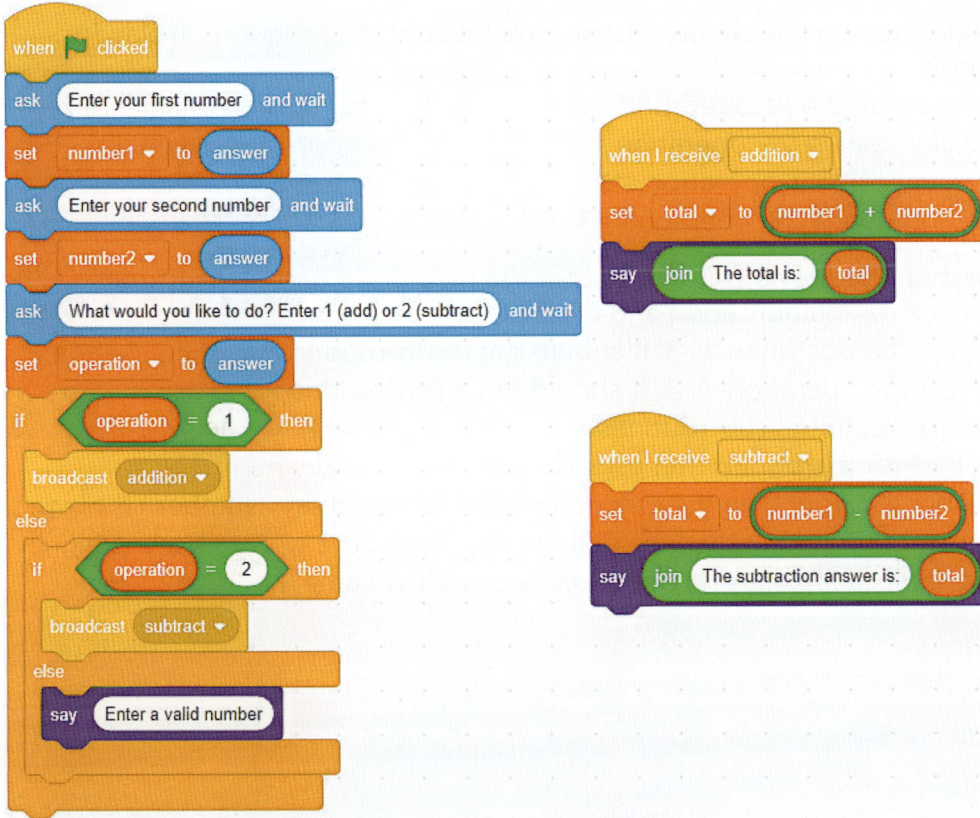

Each calculation is now in a separate sub-program. There is also a block that says **broadcast** followed by the name of the sub-routine; this makes the original program easier to follow and means you can reuse these sub-programs at any time.

Sub-routines in flowcharts

You can represent these sub-routines in flowcharts as well. They use the following symbol:

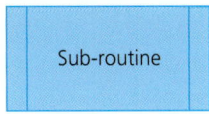

Here is a flowchart that uses sub-routines for the Scratch program above:

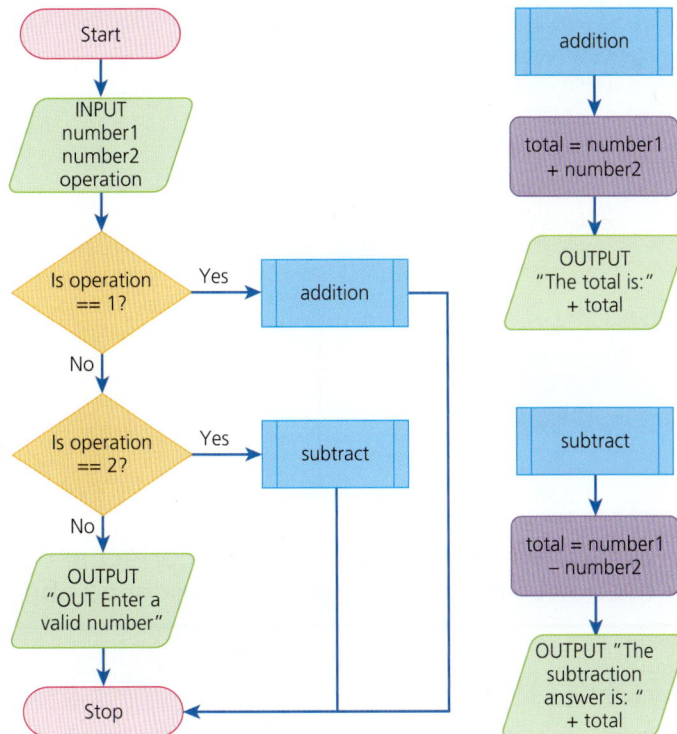

In the example above, the program will run a sub-routine, depending on the option chosen. The sub-routine is then a separate small program.

1 Following the algorithm on the previous page, what would the program display for these calculations?
   - number1 = 25, number2 = 19, operation = 2
   - number1 = 52, number2 = 23, operation = 1
   - number1 = 6, number2 = 9, operation = 3
   - number1 = 15, number2 = 78, operation = 1

> The variables in this program are `number1`, `number2` and `operation`.

2 Edit the flowchart on the previous page, so that the main flowchart also includes decisions that check for multiplication and division:
   - If the user enters the operation as 3, it should run a sub-routine for multiplication.
   - If the user enters the operation as 4, it should run a sub-routine for division.
   - You also need to create the sub-routines.

3 Below is a flowchart for a program that asks the user to enter two numbers:
   - If the first number is bigger than the second number, it should say 'Number 1 is bigger'.
   - If the second number is bigger than the first number it should say 'Number 2 is bigger'.
   - If they are the same, it should say 'Both numbers are the same'.

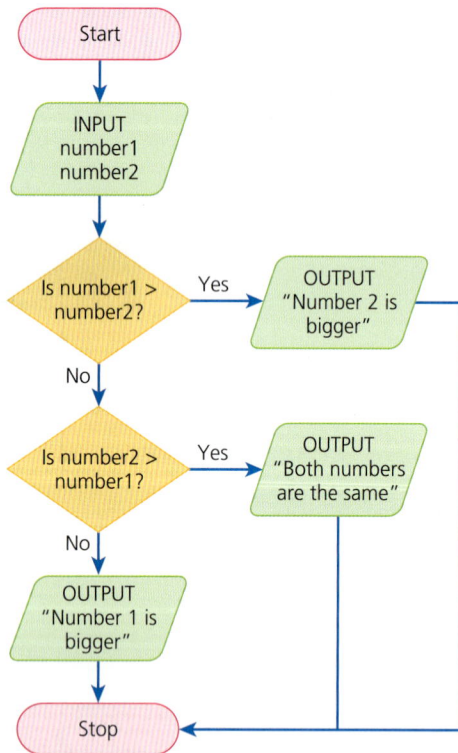

Unfortunately the flowchart is not correct and does not do what it should do. Correct the flowchart so that it works as described above.

KEYWORD

sub-routine: a mini program inside a program that can be completed or repeated when requested

Challenge yourself

Combine all of your Python skills to create a working program for a different scenario:

Create a program in Python that contains a series of questions.
- At the end of the program it should output all of the different answers in a single sentence.
- In addition, any of the answers that contained numbers should be added together and displayed at the end as the 'star' number.

The program needs to ask the following questions:
- What is your name?
- What is your favourite colour?
- How many days are there in a week?
- How many seconds are there in an hour?
- What is your favourite hobby?
- How many days are there in a year (not a leap year)?

Here is an example of what your finished program, might look like when run:

```
Welcome to the random questions game.
What is your name? Zainab
What is your favourite colour? blue
How many days are there in a week? 7
How many seconds are there in an hour? 3600
What is your favourite hobby? shopping
How many days are there in a year? 365
Hello Zainab it has been nice to meet you, thank you for telling me your favourite
colour is blue and your favourite hobby is shopping
The star number that has been generated based on your answers was 3972
```

1 Below shows part of the flowchart for this task. Edit the flowchart so that it shows the entire process.

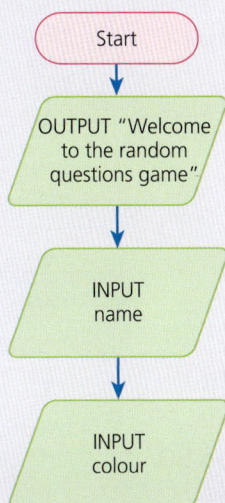

```
     ( Start )
         |
         v
  OUTPUT "Welcome
   to the random
  questions game"
         |
         v
      INPUT
      name
         |
         v
      INPUT
      colour
```

2 Open the file **ChallengeYourself.py** provided by your teacher. Complete the program in Python using the information provided above to create a fully working solution.

Final project

Look back to page 9 to remind yourself of the Scenario at the start of this unit. You are now going to complete a number of tasks to create and edit flowcharts and programs in Python that calculate answers to a range of calculations.

The separate programs should perform each of the following calculations:
- Addition
- Subtraction
- Multiplication
- Division
- Area of a square
- Area of a triangle
- Perimeter of a rectangle
- Average of three numbers

Each program should allow the user to enter the required values and then calculate an answer.

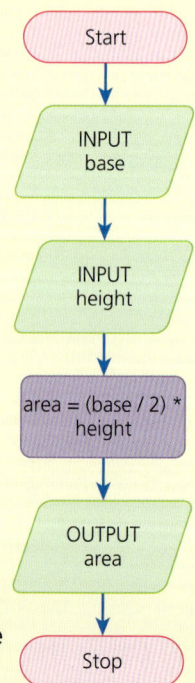

Complete the following tasks:

1 Addition:
  - Create a flowchart that:
    - asks the user to enter two numbers
    - calculates the total by adding the two numbers together
    - outputs the answer.
  - Write the code for your flowchart in Python.
  - Save the file as **FinalProjectAddition.py** and test it.

2 Subtraction, multiplication and division:
  - Open the file **FinalProjectSubtract.py** provided by your teacher. Add comments using **#** to identify the data type for each variable and explain why you have chosen that data type.
  - Edit the code so that it now multiplies the numbers instead of subtracting. Use the correct arithmetic operator to calculate the answer.
  - Save this file and test it.
  - Edit the code and create another variable called **divide** that stores **num1** divided by **num2**. Add another print statement to output the answer.
  - Save the file and test that it works.

3 Area of a square:
  - Open the file **FinalProjectSquareArea.py** provided by your teacher. Identify the error. Debug the code so that the program:
    - asks the user to enter the length of one side of the square
    - calculates the area by multiplying the length by the length
    - outputs the answer.
  - Save the file and test it.

4 Area of a triangle:
  - Look at this flowchart. The current flowchart:
    - asks the user to enter the base and the height of the triangle
    - calculates the area; this is half the base multiplied by the height
    - outputs the answer.
  - Edit the flowchart so it checks to see whether the area is greater than 50. If it is, it should say 'big triangle'; if it isn't, it should say 'small triangle'.
  - Open the file **FinalProjectTriangleArea.py**. There is an error. Identify the error and debug it so that the program does what is described above.
  - Save the file and test it.

Start

INPUT base

INPUT height

area = (base / 2) * height

OUTPUT area

Stop

5 Perimeter of a rectangle:
  - Create a program in Python that calculates the perimeter of a rectangle. The program should:
    - ask the user to enter the length and width of the rectangle
    - calculate the perimeter; this is two multiplied by the length plus width
    - output the answer.
  - Write the code for your program.
  - Save the file and test it by applying the test plan below:

Test number	Test data	Expected outcome	Actual outcome	Pass/fail
1	width = 8.5 length = 11	perimeter: 39		
2	width = 4.9 length = 9.2	perimeter: 28.2		
3	width = 3.4 length = 6.1	perimeter: 19		

6 Average of three numbers:
  - This shows the Scratch solution to calculate the average of three numbers:

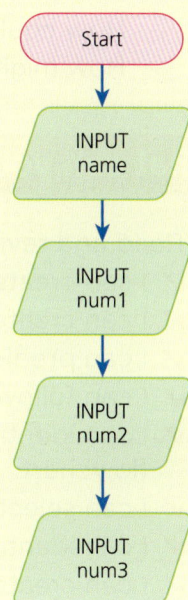

  - Create this program in Python to perform the same task.
  - The flowchart on the right shows part of this program. Complete this flowchart using a sub-routine to calculate the average.

Evaluation

1 Swap solutions with a partner and test each other's solutions. Give feedback on the following:

- Does it cover all the requirements? If not, which programs or flowcharts do not work correctly?
- Are the output messages easy to understand?
- Do the programs and/or flowcharts calculate the correct answer? Apply the following test plan to help you:

Test number	Program	Test data	Expected outcome	Actual outcome	Pass/fail
1	Addition	number1 = 10 number2 = 15	Answer: 25		
2	Division	number1 = 81 number2 = 9	Answer: 9		
3	Area of a square	length = 12	Area: 144		
4	Area of a triangle	base = 4 height = 7.5	Area: 15 Small triangle		
5	Perimeter of a rectangle	width = 11.2 length = 7.8	Perimeter: 38		
6	Average of 3 numbers	name = Ahmed number1 = 15 number2 =25 number3 =50	Thanks Ahmed, the average of the numbers was 30.		

2 Take a look back at your program's code. Reflect on what could be improved; things you may want to think about include the following:

- What other types of calculations may be useful?
- How could you add selection using flowcharts into your solutions?
- How might you be able to combine all of the separate programs into a single solution?

What can you do?

Read and review what you can do.

✔ I can create algorithms using flowchart symbols.
✔ I can create flowcharts that use selection statements.
✔ I can predict the outcome of flowcharts that use selection.
✔ I can follow, understand, edit and correct algorithms that use sub-routines.
✔ I can identify the constructs sequence and selection when solving problems using a flowchart.
✔ I can select and use appropriate comparison operators when creating flowcharts.
✔ I can identify and explain when to use different data types in a Python program.
✔ I can create programs in Python that use input and output.

✔ I can create programs in Python that use the data types string, integer and real.
✔ I can use variables in Python programs to store data.
✔ I can create a program that uses different arithmetic operators in Python.
✔ I can apply a test plan to ensure that a program works correctly.
✔ I can explain how errors can occur in Python.
✔ I can identify and correct errors in a Python program.

Get started!

A **smart device** uses **sensors** to gather data and uses this data to determine the correct output for the device (such as what should happen). For example, a heating system in a house can use a smart device to gather data about the temperature in the room. If the sensor in the **thermostat** detects that the temperature is too low, the heating will come on. When the sensor detects that the required temperature is reached, the heating will switch off.

Many computers today use sensors to **automate** what the device can do. The program has decisions to make, and the sensors are used to help make those decisions. You may have used computing devices with sensors, for example a smart phone or smart watch with a built-in **pedometer**. The movement is detected by the sensor and data is gathered within the device to count steps or measure distance.

Have you ever wondered how a **smart device** works and how it is **integrated** into a **physical computing device**? Discuss with a partner:

- What smart devices have you used?
- What sensors are used in a smart device?
- How would you plan a program for a smart device?

In this unit, you will explore how to create a smart device using sensors to decide the flow of the program. You will start by looking at MakeCode, a block-based programming language, and then use a text-based software, called MicroPython, to create your own program that will run on a BBC micro:bit (a physical computing device).

KEYWORDS

smart device: a device that utilises sensors and is connected to other devices

sensor: a device that is able to gather data from its surroundings to respond to or record

thermostat: a device that has a built-in sensor to detect changes in temperature

integrated: built into

automate: to reduce human interaction and leave the running of the device to sensors that determine the output

pedometer: a device that estimates the distance travelled on foot by recording the number of steps taken

physical computing device: a small microprocessor that that can be programmed using block or text-based programming languages

Learning outcomes

In this unit, you will learn to:

- explain how simulators are used to model real-life systems
- describe the difference between applications software and systems software
- follow, understand, edit and correct an algorithm represented as a flowchart
- follow the flow of a flowchart with selection
- create a flowchart that uses selection
- identify the difference between a string and an integer
- create a text-based program using MicroPython, which has an input and an output
- create and correct programs for micro:bit that use more than one input and output
- use a test plan
- discuss why a flowchart is important as a project plan
- evaluate a flowchart and program.

Warm up

In pairs, discuss and list any devices with sensors you encounter throughout your day. Some may be smart devices. What is special about that device? How are the sensors used? For example:

> A smart device has a program to define how it should work. Smart devices gather data from their surroundings with sensors.

The lights in a bathroom come on automatically when you enter the room and off when you leave. A motion sensor in the device detects movement in the room and switches on the light.

In this unit, you will see how sensors are used and how **selection** in a program can use the sensor data to determine the program output.

DID YOU KNOW?

The BBC micro:bit is a pocket-sized computer that introduces you to how software and hardware work together. It has an LED light display, buttons, sensors and many input/output features that, when programmed, let it interact with you and your world. You may have already used a micro:bit with a block-based programming language (such as MakeCode).

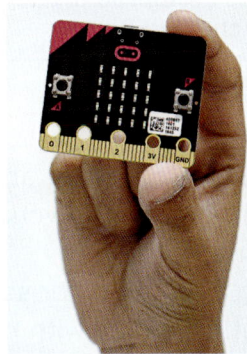

KEYWORDS

selection: a programming construct with more than one possible pathway; a condition is tested (using a question or criterion) before deciding which pathway to follow (the output)

software: aspects of a computing device that you *cannot* touch; the programs that run on a device

hardware: aspects of a computing device that you *can* touch; the physical components of a device

SCENARIO

The computing department at school has asked you to develop a **prototype** for a smart device that will use a sensor to detect whether someone is near a computer. This will help them to monitor the computers in the room and act as a theft-detection system to signal to others when someone is near or is taking the device.

The micro:bit has many built-in sensors that can be used to develop a prototype for a smart device. The new program should:

- use one of the sensors from the micro:bit: the light, touch or **accelerometer** sensors
- use the data to decide the next instruction to execute in the program

- be presented as a **flowchart** to show the flow of the program if the outcome to the question set is true or false
- use more than one input and more than one output.

You will first need to break down the problem to create a flowchart for your smart device, demonstrating the use of selection and **comparison operators**. You will need to test your flowchart with a range of possible inputs and document your outcomes by applying a **test plan**.

KEYWORDS

prototype: a sample, model or first release of a product, such as a program or device, built to test a concept or process

accelerometer: a sensor to detect movement

flowchart: a diagram showing the sequence of actions in a computer program; a graphical representation to show the steps to solve a problem

comparison operators: symbols used to compare values, e.g. > = meaning greater than or equal to

test plan: a structured approach to testing whether your solution works as expected; a document that describes the areas of a program to be tested – includes details of the tests to be applied to each area of the program, including test data and expected results

---

Do you remember?

Before starting this unit, you should be able to:
- ✔ create a simple algorithm using flowchart symbols
- ✔ identify flowchart symbols
- ✔ identify programming constructs for sequence and selection
- ✔ use a physical computing device with block-based programming programs such as MakeCode
- ✔ identify the difference between an input and an output
- ✔ identify how a variable is used in a program to store data temporarily.

Before starting this unit you will need to access MakeCode and MicroPython on a computer through online software.

To access MakeCode:
1 Open your chosen web browser software.
2 Go to **https://makecode.microbit.org**

To access MicroPython:
1 Open your chosen web browser software.
2 Go to **https://python.microbit.org**

You will also need the following physical computing devices:
1 micro:bit
2 USB cable
3 optional battery pack for micro:bit.

All about software

Learn

The easiest way to remember the difference between hardware and software is that you can touch hardware and you cannot touch software. Hardware is the physical parts of a **computing device**, and the software is the programs that we run on our computing device.

Software running on the computer ← → Computer parts we can touch are hardware

A computing device is made up of both hardware and software and cannot complete its tasks without either. You use software on devices every day, for example when you open a **web browser** on your device (such as a computer or phone) to search the world wide web (WWW), you are using software. The web browser is a piece of software that you install on your device to allow you to access the world wide web.

There are two different types of software:

- Systems software
- Applications software.

Systems software

Systems software is used to ensure that the computing device can function (work) as expected. The main example of systems software is the **operating system** (OS) and it is essential to the **functionality** of your device. There are different operating systems you can install on a computing device, including Windows, Linux, Mac OSX, Android and iOS.

> The operating system starts as soon as you turn a computing device on and is the link between the device's hardware and the software applications.

The central **processing unit (CPU)** can only carry out **binary** instructions (0s and 1s). This is because a computer is made up of switches, and these switches are only ever on (which is represented as a 1) or off (which is represented as a 0). Therefore, all software and any **input** into a computing device, for example a key being **pressed** on the keyboard, needs to be converted into binary so that the CPU can process and **execute** the instructions.

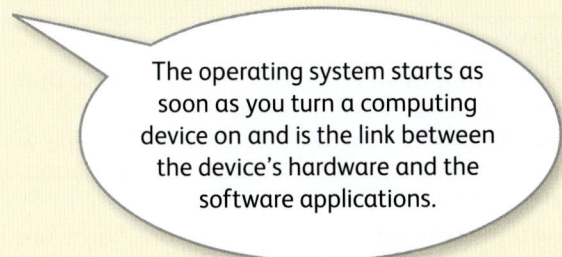

A → 01000001

A is pressed on the keyboard. This is the input.

The letter is represented in binary number to be executed by the computer.

Applications software

Applications software on a computing device helps you complete specific tasks. Examples of this are a web browser for searching the world wide web; word-processing software to help write letters; email software; Scratch for creating block-based programs; Python for creating text-based programs, and much more.

Some software on a computing device can be used for multiple purposes, like word-processing software that you use to create a wide range of documents. This is referred to as a **general-purpose application**.

There are also software applications created for specific purposes. An example of this is a flight **simulator**, which has specific software used to train pilots.

In medicine, surgeons use simulators to practise performing operations before completing one on a real person. It allows users to develop their skills before moving into a real-world situation. This helps keep people safe while someone is learning how to complete the task, whether that is flying or operating. The micro:bit has a simulator built into the MakeCode application that allows the program to be tested and developed before creating the first prototype on the physical device.

KEYWORDS

computing device: any device that follows the input, process, output model

web browser: a software application that allows users to locate, access and display information on the world wide web

systems software: software that runs hardware and software, i.e. the operating system

operating system: the systems software that manages hardware, software and resources on a device

functionality: the range of operations that can be run on a computing device

process: the function within a computing device where an instruction in a program is carried out, such as a calculation or display

input: a physical input into a computing device, e.g. keyboard, mouse, microphone, button

binary: a number system that uses combinations of two digits (0 and 1) to represent all numbers; used to represent data in computer systems

central processing unit (CPU): the processor in a computing device that executes all instructions

execute: another word for running a program

applications software: applications for general or specific tasks

general-purpose application: software that can be used for more than one purpose

simulator: software to simulate a real-world application

Investigate how simulators are used in different industries:

1 Choose an industry that uses simulators, for example medical, military, transport, agricultural or gaming.
2 Research:
   – what the simulator does and how it helps the industry
   – the systems software (operating system) used
   – the applications software used.
3 Present your research to a small group. Compare the different types of systems software and applications software used in the examples of your group.

Introducing the micro:bit

Learn

The micro:bit is a **physical computing device** with a range of **inputs** and **outputs** that can be programmed through block-based and text-based programming languages, such as MakeCode or MicroPython.

Here are some of the inputs and outputs on a micro:bit:

Input	Output
A Button	Display
B Button	Buzzer
Light sensor	
Temperature sensor	
Compass	
Accelerometer	
Touch sensor	
Microphone	

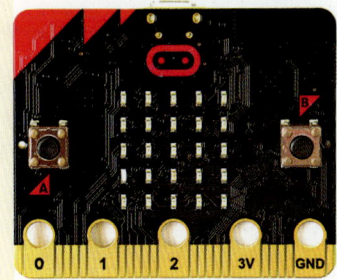

micro:bit physical device

The micro:bit has a purpose-built online programming environment. This is called MakeCode and is a software application. MakeCode has a built-in simulator that allows the programmer to test their programs and develop their programming skills before using the physical device (the actual micro:bit).

The software's **interface** has the simulator on the left-hand side. This is able to execute any programming that is created on the right-hand side.

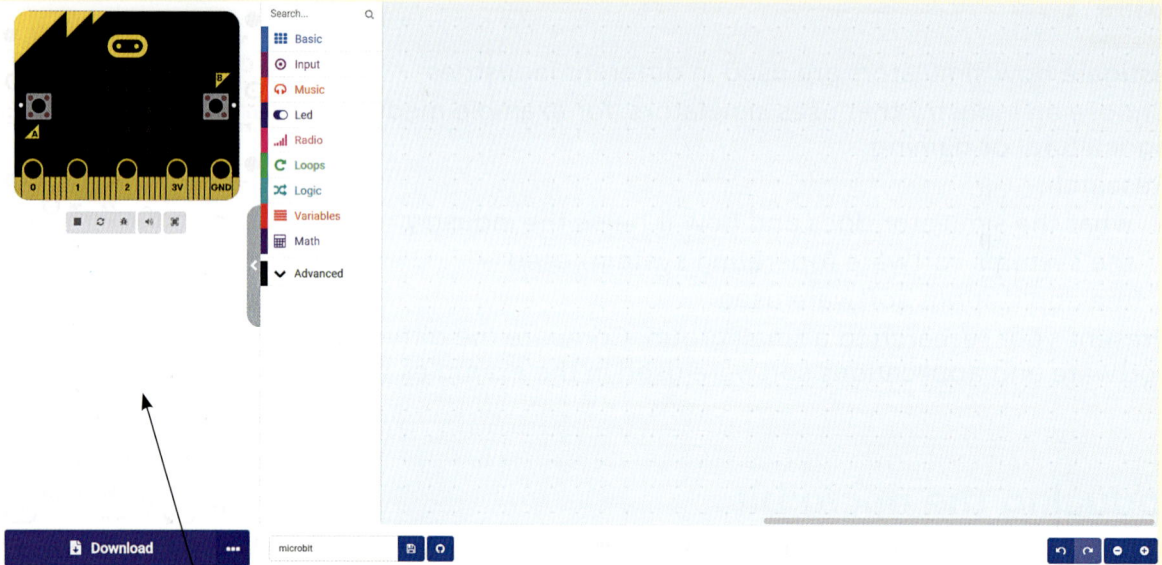

software application with simulator

Here's a reminder about how to create a flowchart. In this example, the program needs to display the word **"Hello"** and then a happy face if the A button is pressed.

Selection is used within this flowchart as a question needs to be asked.

Following the flowchart below, this question is asked within the decision shape: **If** the A button is being pressed **then** the word 'Hello!' will scroll across the micro:bit display, followed by a happy face being displayed.

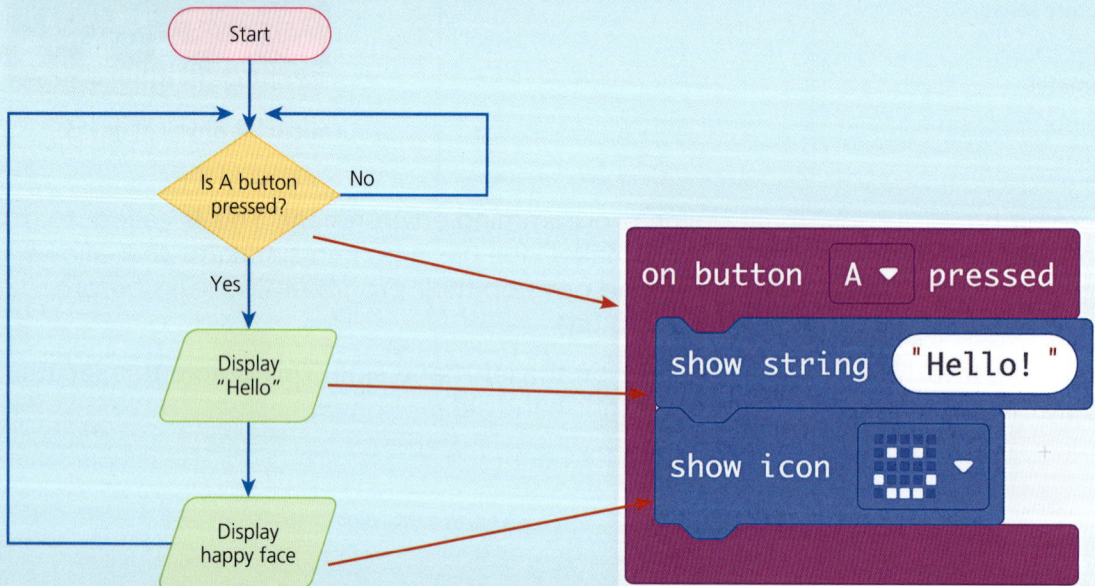

If the answer to the question **Is the A button pressed?** is *yes* (true), then the program will continue to run the code above.

If the answer is *no* (false), then the program will do nothing and wait till the answer is *yes*.

Using the built-in simulator, the user can now click the A button and see the program work as expected, scrolling the word 'Hello!' on the LED display and then displaying a happy face.

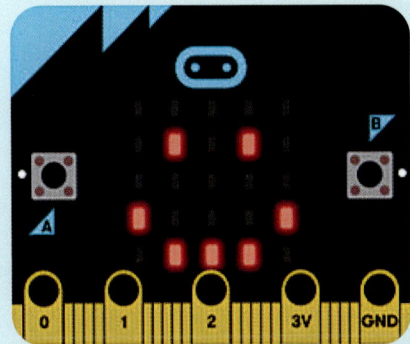

An **algorithm** is used to show what the program will do. This can then be represented as a flowchart. It is important to create a flowchart before coding the program so you can check whether the flow of the instructions is correct.

Remember: use these shapes to create a flowchart:

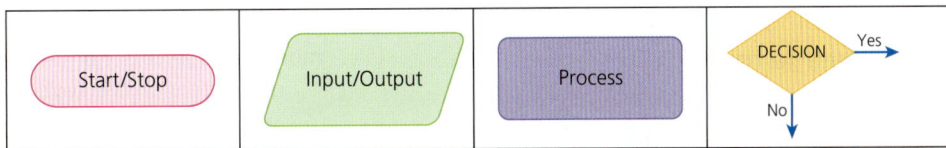

Start/Stop	Input/Output	Process	DECISION

KEYWORDS

physical computing device: a small microprocessor that can be programmed using block or text-based programming languages

input: a physical input into a computing device, e.g. keyboard, mouse, microphone, button

output: a visible or audible outcome on a device through, for example, the display, monitor, speakers, headphones

interface: a visual way of interacting with the software

algorithm: a sequence of steps or instructions to solve a problem

selection: a programming construct with more than one possible pathway; a condition is tested (using a question or criterion) before deciding which pathway to follow (the output)

Practise

1 Plan a program to test the micro:bit simulator using a flowchart. The program needs to display an output of your name followed by an image of your choice. Draw a flowchart to plan the program. Use the flowchart in the Learn box above to help you.

> To open a file in MakeCode, follow these steps:
>
> *Open* https://makecode.microbit.org
>
> *Select* Import.
>
> *Select* Import File.
>
> *Select* Choose File *and locate the file you require to view in MakeCode.*

2 Open the file called **MicrobitSequenceOutput.hex** provided by your teacher. Edit the code so that it follows your flowchart. Do this by:
   - adding the `show string` block into the `on button A pressed` block
   - editing the text to be displayed to your name
   - adding the `show icon` block after the `show string` block
   - editing the image to be displayed.

> Remember: a string data type is made up of letters, numbers or any characters on the keyboard.

3 Run the program using the simulator to make sure the outcome is as you expect.

> When you create a new program using the blocks, the colour on the simulator turns grey while the program is loaded to the simulator. Once the simulator is ready, the colour will return and you can test your program using the input on the simulator.

Using Python with the micro:bit

Learn

You can program using Python in the micro:bit applications software. From the software's interface, look at the top of the page (in the middle) and select the dropdown next to the word `JavaScript`. Then select `Python`.

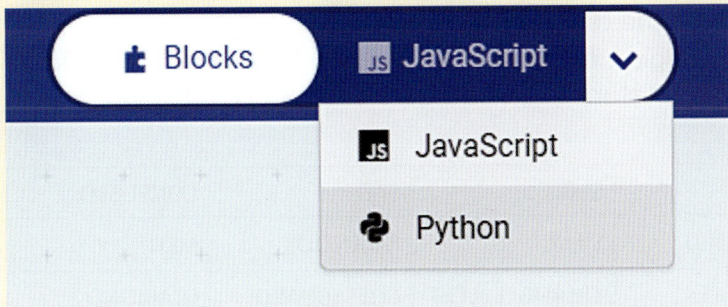

You will now see the Python code for the same program.

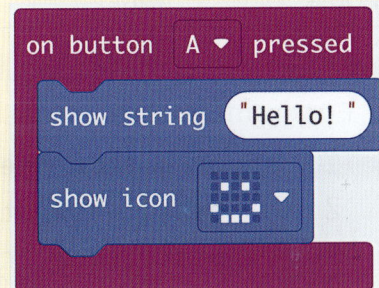

```
1  def on_button_pressed_a():
2      basic.show_string("Hello!")
3      basic.show_icon(IconNames.HAPPY)
4  input.on_button_pressed(Button.A, on_button_pressed_a)
```

The micro:bit uses **MicroPython** as the Python programming language. MicroPython is a version of Python that has been developed specifically for the micro:bit. It can only be used with the micro:bit.

The rules of a programming language are called the **syntax**. Like any programming language, the syntax of MicroPython is specific. The code must be written correctly for it to be able to run as expected.

KEYWORDS

MicroPython: the version of Python used with the micro:bit

syntax: the structure of the code used in a programming language

Practise

1 Open the file **MicrobitHodderSwitchSequence.hex** provided by your teacher.
   - Change the code view from MakeCode into Python.
   - Edit the program code to display a different image and text by following these steps:
     - Change the text: Locate the word `Hello!` inside the brackets, change it to your name and remember to keep the quotation marks " " around it. The quotation marks help tell the program that the text is to be kept as text.
     - Locate the word `HAPPY` and change it to one of the options from the table below. Notice that they are all in capital letters and should be entered like this into the program.

HEART	HEART_SMALL	HAPPY	SMILE	SAD	CONFUSED
ANGRY	ASLEEP	SURPRISED	SILLY	FABULOUS	MEH
YES	NO	TRIANGLE	TRIANGLE_LEFT	CHESSBOARD	DIAMOND
DIAMOND_SMALL	SQUARE	SQUARE_SMALL	RABBIT	COW	PITCHFORK
HOUSE	TARGET	TSHIRT	ROLLERSKATE	DUCK	SWORD
TORTOISE	BUTTERFLY	STICK_FIGURE	GIRAFFE	UMBRELLA	SNAKE

For example:

```
1  def on_button_pressed_a():
2      basic.show_string("Zaid")
3      basic.show_icon(IconNames.DUCK)
4  input.on_button_pressed(Button.A, on_button_pressed_a)
```

   - The micro:bit simulator will change slightly as you edit the code. Click the play button to run the code in the centre of the simulator, followed by the A button.
   - Run the program. Does it work? Try adding different names and images to see the different sequence outputs.

2 Open the file **MicrobitButtonOutputStart.hex** provided by your teacher. This is the code from page 53 but shown in MicroPython.
   - Change the input by adjusting the code so that there is an **A** button input and a **B** button input.
   - Run the code to test it.

3 Look at the flowcharts below. Use these to edit the code from the file above to allow the **A** and the **B** button to be used in this way:
   - If the **A** button is pressed, then the word `Hello` and a happy face are displayed on the simulator.

- If the **B** button is pressed, then the word Goodbye and a sad face are displayed on the simulator.
- Remember to use the correct syntax of UPPER or lower-case letters.

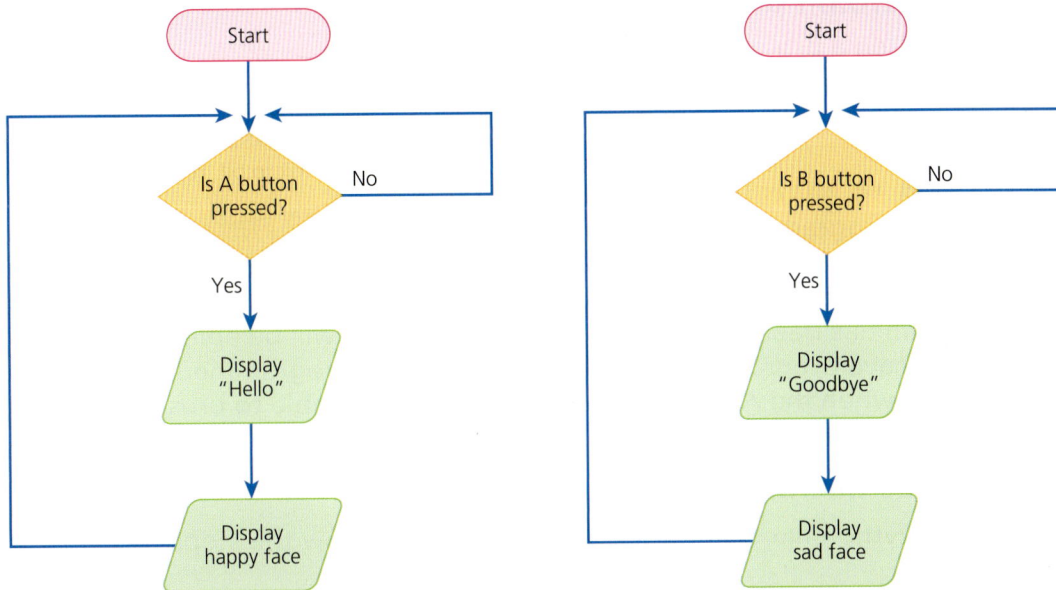

- Run and check the code. Correct it if necessary.

The micro:bit Python environment

Learn

In the previous themes, you explored how to use and edit code in MicroPython in the micro:bit applications software, MakeCode. This allowed you to work with block-based and text-based programming.

MakeCode can display the output of the program on the built-in simulator. Although you can download the program from MakeCode to use on the micro:bit (the physical device), it is a version of MicroPython that works best with the simulator and MakeCode.

To use MicroPython fully with the micro:bit (the physical device), you need to code in the micro:bit Python environment online. This is accessed through any web browser (see below for how to do this).

Connect micro:bit to the environment

In the micro:bit Python programming environment, you can still use a simulator and download the code onto the micro:bit to see it working. To download the program, you need first to connect the micro:bit to the environment.

Follow these steps to connect the micro:bit to the environment:
- Open **https://python.microbit.org** from any web browser.
- Use the USB cable to connect the micro:bit to the computer.

- Click on the `Send to micro:bit` button and select the micro:bit from the pop up.
- The program will be sent to the micro:bit. When you open the micro:bit Python programming environment, it will have a program already visible as an example.

Download the micro:bit program to the micro:bit

When you have written a program in MicroPython, follow these steps to download the program to the micro:bit to test whether the program code runs as expected:

> The program you have created is downloaded straight to the micro:bit, ready to use.

- Click on the `Send to micro:bit` button.
- Downloading the program is called **sending the program** on the micro:bit. When you click the `Send to micro:bit` button, it will display a message on the computer screen to say it is working and when it is complete. Once the program has been downloaded successfully, you will be able to use the micro:bit as you have programmed it. For example, if you programmed for a happy face to be shown when the A button is pressed, you will be able to press the A button on the micro:bit and see this output.

Open and save the micro:bit program

- To open a MicroPython file, select the `Open` button and follow the steps below to open a MicroPython file.

> When you select `Open` you have the option to load a given MicroPython file in either **.hex** or **.py** format.
>
> **.hex** format works only on the micro:bit and it is the format that is downloaded to the micro:bit when you send and run your program on the micro:bit. It can be opened only in applications software that can work with the micro:bit.
>
> **.py** format is a Python file format and can be opened in any Python applications software.

The example below shows how to display text and an image by creating the MicroPython program and sending it onto the micro:bit.

The program code looks like this:

```
from microbit import *

display.scroll('Hello')
display.show(Image.HEART)
```

As you have seen in the previous themes, to display an image on the micro:bit simulator (such as a happy face) that part of the syntax expects capital letters in the code. This is an example of one of the rules of the syntax. Other examples include the use of commas, brackets and specific command words in the code.

All programs using the micro:bit must start by importing the micro:bit **library**. This library is like a list of all the programming commands you can use. Without this at the start of every program you write, the program would not know what to do with the code written. The code that is at the start of every program is **from microbit import ***. The star (*) means 'import everything to do with the micro:bit'.

To create a program in the micro:bit Python online environment, the syntax is slightly different. Notice that the syntax still uses capitals for the image to be displayed and the code to display the image now starts with `display`.

KEYWORDS

sending the program: downloading the MicroPython program file to the micro:bit to run

library: a list of all programming commands that are available under the library name

Practise

1. Connect the micro:bit to the computer using the USB cable.
2. Select `Connect` on the applications software to connect the micro:bit.
3. Open the file **FirstMicroPythonProgram.py** provided by your teacher, using the `Load/Save` button.
4. Send the program to the micro:bit to view the output sequence.
5. Edit the text to be displayed and send the program again to the micro:bit to view the updated program output.
6. Edit the image to be displayed and send the program again to the micro:bit to view the updated program output.

Remember to check the syntax of UPPER and lower-case letters.

Correcting errors using a flowchart

Learn

A flowchart allows you to follow the flow of the program one instruction at a time. It is important to understand the plan for the program before you write the program code. A flowchart allows you to plan and understand what the program should do.

Look again at this flowchart from an earlier theme. What is going to happen in this program?

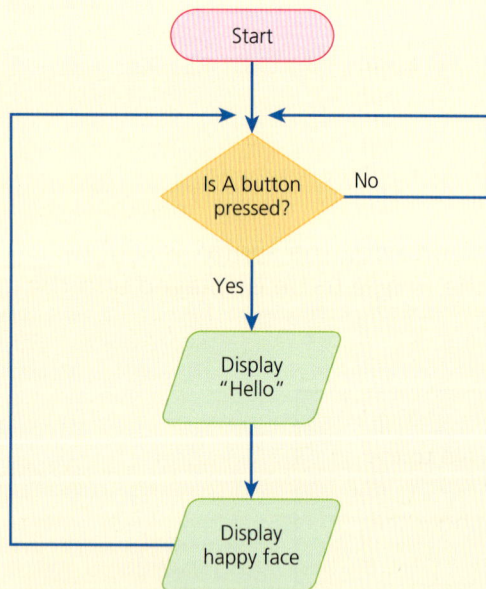

The decision flowchart shape shows the use **of selection** within the program. **IF** the A button is pressed, **THEN** the program continues.

To help minimise errors, you need to understand what the program is expected to do and follow the flowchart to help with this understanding. It is easy for errors to be introduced in a text-based program as the syntax has to be written in a specific way. You have already seen the importance of writing the image in UPPER-case letters. If this is not done, the program will not run.

When coding in MicroPython you can use a flowchart to identify errors systematically and fix them. This is called **debugging**.

The code below is meant to follow the flowchart below, but the program is not working as it is expected to do.

```
1   from microbit import *
2
3   while True:
4       if button_b.is_pressed():
5           disply.show(Image.sad)
6           display.scroll(Hello)
```

By following each step of the program on the flowchart, you can identify the errors in the code. The lines of the code, as seen in the example below, show where they are represented in the flowchart:

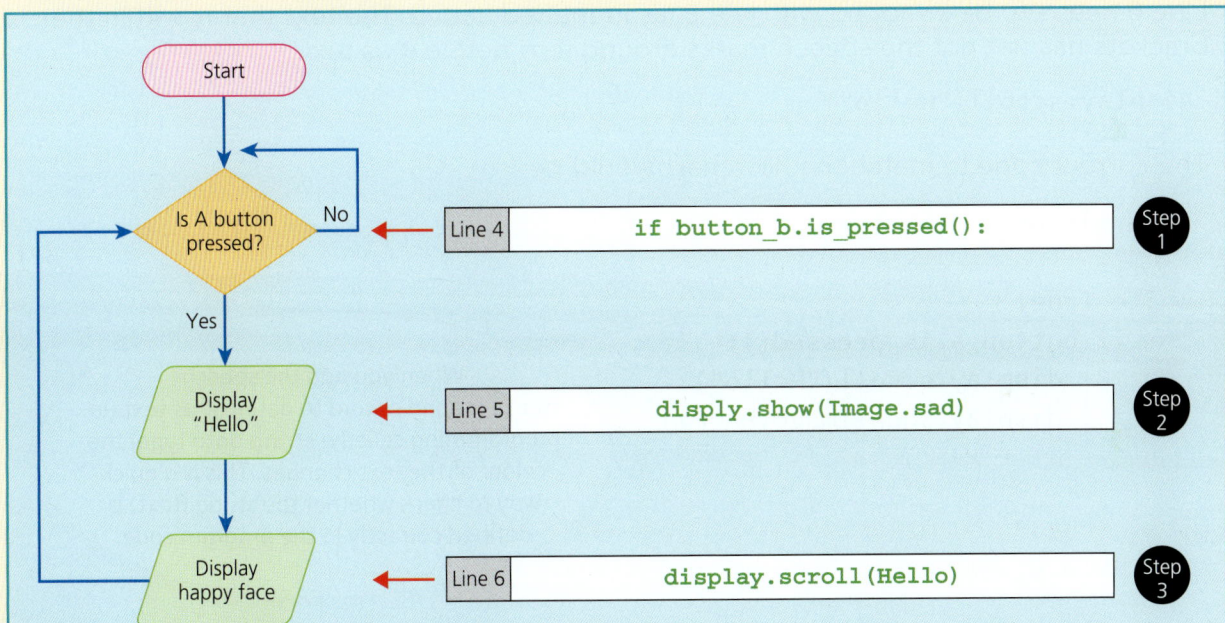

Step 1

Line 4: The line of code shows the selection statement `if button _ b.is _ pressed():` but the flowchart wants the program to run if the **A** button is pressed. The program code is running for the wrong button and needs **B** to be changed to **A** on line 4.

```
if button_a.is_pressed():
```

Step 2

Line 5: The line of code shows `disply.show(Image.sad)` but the flowchart shows that the next instruction in the sequence is to display the text `"Hello"`. This line of code is in the wrong position and should be in the last position of the program sequence.

- When moved, you can also see that the word `disply` is spelt incorrectly. This needs to be amended to `display`.
- The image to be displayed is a happy face and the code says `sad` instead. This needs to be changed and – remembering the syntax of an image to be displayed – it should be written in capital letters.

```
display.show(Image.HAPPY)
```

Step 3

Line 6 needs to be swapped with line 5, as identified above. The text that is within the brackets has not got the speech marks around it to define it as text.

```
display.scroll("Hello")
```

The correct code to match the flowchart would be:

```
from microbit import *

while True:
    if button_a.is_pressed():
        display.scroll("Hello")
        display.show(Image.HAPPY)
```

When you add the speech marks around a word to define it as text (in programming called a string data type) the colour of the text changes. This is a quick way to check whether the string (text) is defined correctly in the program code.

KEYWORDS

debug/debugging: the process of identifying and removing errors from a computer program

string: data that is made up of letters, numbers or any characters on the keyboard

Practise

1 Look at the following flowchart and follow the flow of the program:

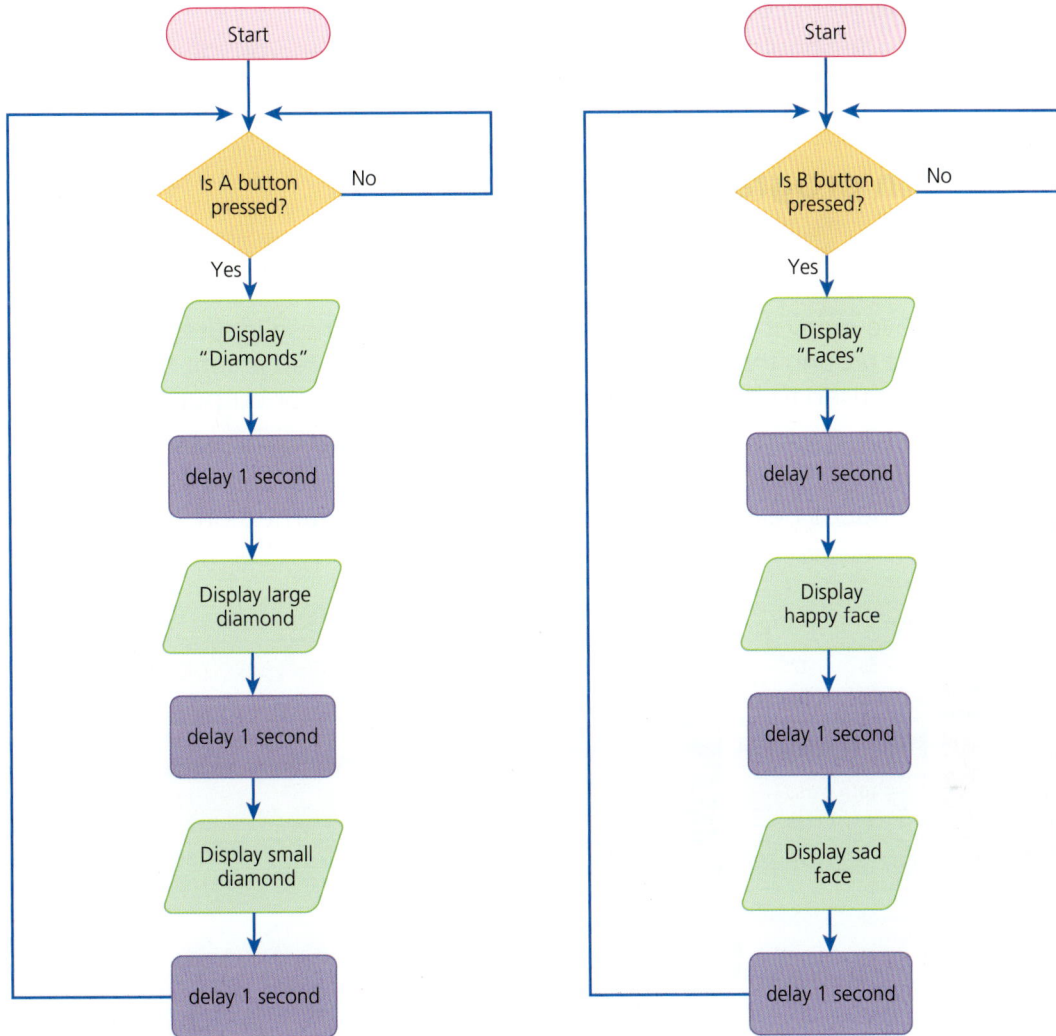

```
Start                                    Start

Is A button    No                        Is B button    No
pressed?                                 pressed?
  Yes                                       Yes

Display                                  Display
"Diamonds"                               "Faces"

delay 1 second                           delay 1 second

Display large                            Display
diamond                                  happy face

delay 1 second                           delay 1 second

Display small                            Display sad
diamond                                  face

delay 1 second                           delay 1 second
```

Discuss with a partner:
- What happens when the A button is pressed?
- What happens when the B button is pressed?

2 Look at the following MicroPython program code:

```python
if button_a.is_pressed():
    display.show(Image.DIAMOND)
    display.scroll("Hello")
    display.show(Image.DIAMOND_SMALL)
    sleep(1000)
if button_a.is_pressed():
    display.show(Image.SAD)
    display.show(Image.SAD)
    display.scroll(Faces)
    sleep(1000)
```

The **Sleep(1000)** means to pause for 1 second and is important to use in between the two images to allow both to display on the micro:bit one after the other.

- Create flowcharts to match the MicroPython program code.
- Compare the original flowcharts above with your flowcharts (created from the MicroPython program code).
- The program code should follow the flowcharts above. Can you identify any errors in the program code by comparing the flowcharts?

Using sensors in programming

Learn

Programming can have many inputs. Sensors, which are one of these inputs, gather data from the environment around the physical device. The data gathered is sent to a computing device where it can be used to determine the next instruction and/or output to execute.

Sensors are used in many household devices, for example a temperature sensor is built into the central-heating system's thermostat. If the temperature within the environment around the sensor reduces below a set number, the heating is turned on.

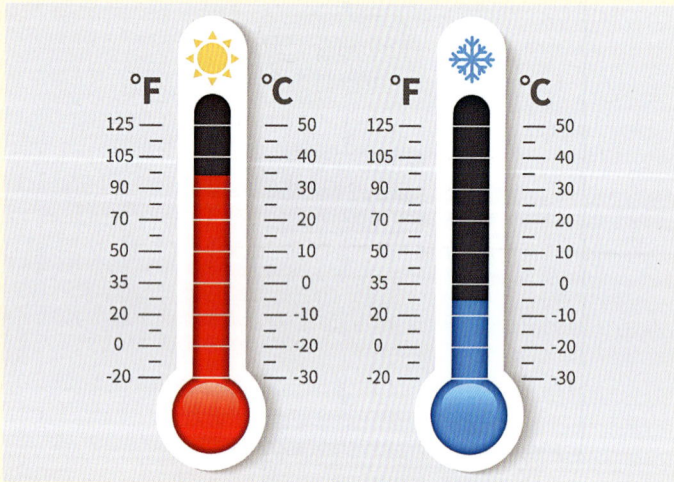

Here is an example of a flowchart for the heating system:

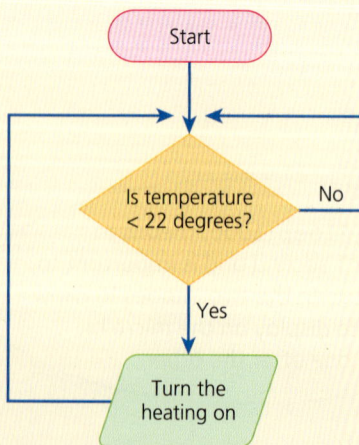

The question being asked within the decision flowchart symbol is **if** the temperature reduces below 22 degrees.

The temperature sensor is constantly gathering data – it is constantly asking the same question – until the answer is *yes*, and **then** the heating is turned on.

There are many examples of sensors being used in computing devices. When a valuable item is kept in an area, a range of preventative measures can be put in place to secure it from burglars. Sensors can be used to help detect any attempt to remove the valuable item.

Sensors that can be used to set off a burglar alarm could detect:

- touch
- temperature
- sound
- movement
- light changes.

The micro:bit version 2 has a selection of sensors built into it that can be used to program the physical device to use the sensor data to activate a specific output.

1 Touch sensor on the logo on the front of the micro:bit
```
if pin_logo.is_touched()
```
2 Temperature sensor built into the processor
```
temperature()
```
3 Sound sensor built into the microphone
```
if microphone.current_event() == SoundEvent.LOUD:
```
4 Movement sensor built in using an accelerometer
```
if accelerometer.was_gesture('shake'):
```
5 Light sensor built into the LED display
```
if display.read_light_level() > 100:
```

Imagine that you want to protect the micro:bit from being taken. You can use the touch sensor that is located on the logo at the top of the micro:bit.

The flowchart below shows the algorithm for this program. Explain to a partner what will happen when the logo is touched on the micro:bit.

> The logo for micro:bit is located at the top centre of the micro:bit. It has a touch sensor on this area of the micro:bit.

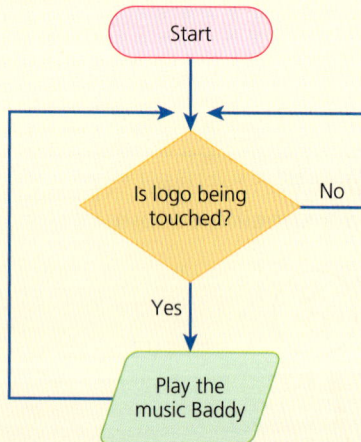

```
              Start
                │
    ┌───────────┼───────────┐
    │           ▼           │
    │      ╱─────────╲      │
    │     ╱  Is logo  ╲  No │
    │     ╲  being    ╱─────┘
    │      ╲ touched? ╱
    │       ╲───────╱
    │           │
    │          Yes
    │           │
    │           ▼
    │      ╱─────────╱
    └─────╱ Play the ╱
          ╱ music Baddy ╱
         ╱─────────╱
```

Here is the code for the flowchart. Can you spot the error in the code? What symbols need to be added to the flowchart to match this code?

```
if pin_logo.is_touched():
    display.show(Image.SURPRISED)
    music.play(music.BADDY)
```

The input to this program is the touch sensor built into the logo, located top centre of the micro:bit. The output is the music played when the touch sensor is touched.

Practise

1 Look at the flowchart and follow the flow.
  In pairs, discuss what will happen if the light level is:
  – 67
  – 130

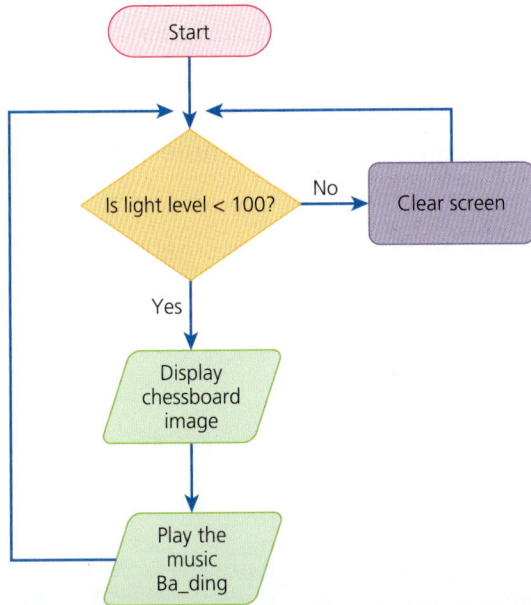

Start

Is light level < 100? → No → Clear screen

Yes

Display chessboard image

Play the music Ba_ding

Remember: to represent **greater than** in a program you use the symbol **>**

To represent **less than** in a program you use the symbol **<**

The light level is continuously being checked by the light sensor.

2 Look at the MicroPython program code below. To use the micro:bit light sensor in a program, the code is `if display.read _ light _ level()`
  Compare the program code to the flowchart above and identify the error.

```
if display.read_light_level() > 100:
    display.show(Image.CHESSBOARD)
    music.play(music.BA_DING)
else:
    display.clear()
```

3 Open the file **MicroPythonDebugActivity2.py** provided by your teacher.
  – Find and fix the error.
  – Send the program (download the program) to the micro:bit.
  – Run the program. The light sensor is located within the micro:bit display. Cover the display to reduce the light level.

When you open the MicroPython program code, there is additional code to allow the program to run. Your program needs to be added *below* `while True:` and *indented* so that the micro:bit continually checks the data gathered from the light sensor. This works in the same way as the forever block in MakeCode.

Note that another library is imported at the start of the program to allow the music output to be added to the program.

Flowcharts for algorithm planning

Learn

You have seen in previous themes that flowcharts are a tool to plan an algorithm. It is important to plan the program before you write the code to ensure that you are clear about what you are creating and any elements that need to be included.

If you are using **selection** in the program, like the light level, you will be asking a question about the level detected through the sensor. The question uses **IF** statements and this is used to determine what happens next in the program flow. For example:

IF the light level is below 100 **THEN** the light will be turned on.

The symbols that represent the **comparison operators** you use when creating the flowchart need to be considered carefully to ensure that the correct ones are used in the program.

Here's a reminder of the **comparison operators** used in a flowchart:

<	less than
>	greater than
<=	less than or equal to
>=	greater than or equal to
!=	not equal to
==	equal to

For example:

Flowchart symbol	If light level >= 128	If light level < 128	If light level == 128
IF statement	If the light level is greater than or equal to 128	If the light level is less than 128	If the light level is equal to 128

The use of these comparison operators allows the sensor data (the light level) to be compared to the **IF** statement question. The program will consistently compare the sensor data (the light level) to the **IF** statement question and, depending on the answer, determine the next instruction in the program.

The output in some programs is defined when the answer to the **IF** statement is *yes*. There can also be an output defined when the answer to the **IF** statement is *no*; this is referred to as **ELSE**.

For example:

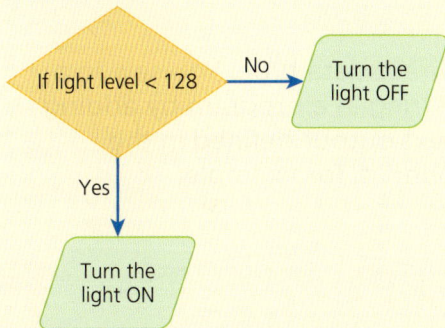

> The light level detected through the sensor is being compared to the IF statement question: **IF the light level is less than 128?** If the answer is *yes*, the light is turned on. **ELSE,** if the answer is *no*, the light is turned off.

Changing the comparison operator can change the program. If the comparison operator was changed to greater than (>), then the lights would come on when the light level detected was above 128, when a light is not needed. It is important to check the comparison operators that you want to use in a program.

KEYWORDS

comparison operators: symbols used to compare values, e.g. <= meaning greater than or equal to

selection: a programming construct with more than one possible pathway; a condition is tested (using a question or criterion) before deciding which pathway to follow (the output)

Practise

1   Create a flowchart for the following program using selection **IF** statements:
    A program that will turn the lights on and close the curtains **if** the light level is < 20, **else** the lights will be off and the curtains open.

2   Look at the flowchart example and describe to a partner how the sensor is being used in the **IF** statement.
    Predict what the output would be if the light level detected was:
    –   10
    –   50
    –   51
    –   45

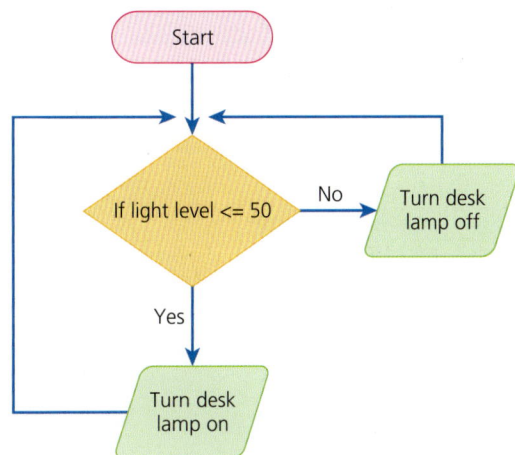

Algorithmic solutions and data types

Learn

When using data in a program, it should be set as the correct data type. You saw in a previous program (on page 60) that text is defined as a string in a program by adding quotation marks around it. Remember that a string is a text output defined in the program code with single or double quotation marks around it, for example:

`"Hello, World"` or `'Hello, World'`

```
display.scroll("Hello, World")
```

The data gathered by a sensor is a number. To be able to use the data gathered by the sensor in an **IF** statement question, the program code needs to know that it is a number. To do this, it has to be defined as a number data type called an **integer**: a whole number.

> You can use single or double quotation marks around the text to define it as a string. Any series of characters can be added as a string, including numbers and text.
>
> This is the same as the **print statement** that you used in Python in Unit 7.1. You can use either single or double quotation marks, for example:
>
> `print('Hello, World')`

In MicroPython with the micro:bit, the data gathered by the micro:bit sensor is automatically set as an integer so that it can be used in the **IF** statement question.

Following the flow of the flowchart can help to check whether the output is correct. Predicting what the output would be, and then testing this on the flowchart, can help you find and fix errors before you write the code.

KEYWORDS

print statement: a Python statement used to output text or values onto the screen

integer: whole number

Practise

1 What would the data type be for the following:
   - 12
   - "Pass123"
   - 'light'
   - 3456?

2 Look at the flowchart below and describe to a partner what the program will do.

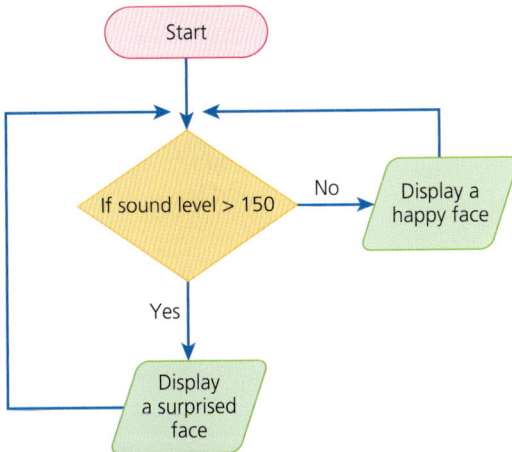

```
                    ┌─────────┐
                    │  Start  │
                    └─────────┘
                         │
        ┌────────────────┼──────────────┐
        │                ▼              │
        │          ◇─────────────◇  No  ┌──────────────┐
        │          │ If sound    │─────▶│ Display a    │
        │          │ level > 150 │      │ happy face   │
        │          ◇─────────────◇      └──────────────┘
        │                │
        │               Yes
        │                ▼
        │          ┌──────────────┐
        └──────────│ Display      │
                   │ a surprised  │
                   │ face         │
                   └──────────────┘
```

   - What data type will the data from the sound sensor be stored as?
   - What would the output be if the sound level detected was:
      - 160
      - 86
      - 200
      - 51?

3 Open the file **SoundSensorProgram.py** provided by your teacher.
   - Follow the flowchart above and the program flow to find and fix the error.
   - Send the program (download the program) to the micro:bit to test.

> **DID YOU KNOW?**
> Programmers use a wide range of methods to help debug a program. One way is to work as a pair. This is called pair programming. Two programmers work together; one is the driver and uses the computer to type the code. The other is the navigator and watches the driver to look for errors and talk through the program.

Planning a smart solution

Learn

A smart home uses lots of sensors. The sensors could be used to control:

- lighting
- heating
- blinds
- household appliances such as a washing machine
- doors.

The sensors allow the device to be controlled from a **pre-set program** with selection or from a mobile device.

To create a flowchart for a section of a smart house with one input and one output, you need to consider what should happen to activate the output. What question do you want to ask that can be compared with what the sensor detects?

For example:

> The blinds in the house need to open and close automatically at appropriate times.
>
> **When do the blinds need to be open?**
>
> When there is daylight, the blinds need to be open.

A light sensor can be used to detect the light level. If the light level is over a set value, the blinds will open.

On the micro:bit the light level values range from 0 (no light) to 255 (very bright). Imagine that the halfway point is where the light level is changing from light to dark. You can therefore use 128 as the midpoint and the following flowchart symbol:

If lightLevel < 128

> The comparison operator is set to less than 128. This is the question that will continuously be asked to find an answer of *yes* (**true**) or *no* (**false**). The value is temporarily stored in the variable `lightLevel` each time the sensor gathers the data.

The next step is to consider the outputs if the outcome to the question is *yes* (**true**) or *no* (**false**). The blinds need to close when the light level is reduced. The question is **if the light level is less than 128**, so the blinds need to close when the outcome is *yes* (**true**):

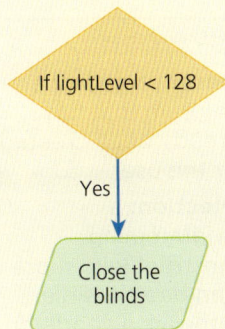

If lightLevel < 128

Yes

Close the blinds

> **If the light level is less than 128** then the answer is *yes* and the outcome is **true**, and the next instruction is to close the blinds.

You now need to consider the next instruction if the answer is *no* and the outcome is **false**, where the light level is *not* below 128. The light level is greater than 128 and therefore the blinds are open.

This section of a flowchart shows the selection stage. A **selection** is made when asking the question and, depending on the answer to the question, the next instruction is selected.

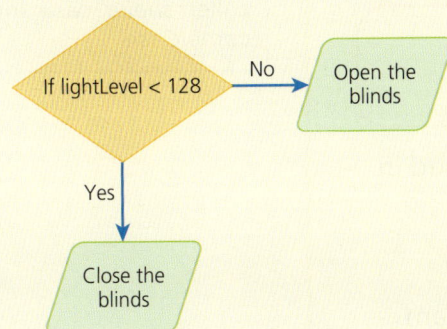

If lightLevel < 128

No → Open the blinds

Yes

Close the blinds

> If the light level is less than 128, then the blinds are closed. If the light level is greater than 128, then the blinds are open.

To develop this flowchart into an algorithm, the flow of the program needs to be considered fully. The start point to the program needs to be defined:

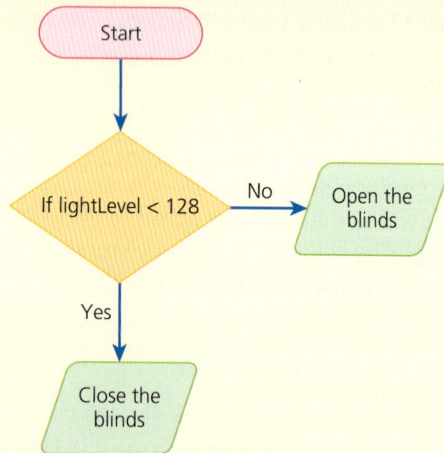

Start

If lightLevel < 128 — No → Open the blinds

Yes

Close the blinds

> The program starts and flows into the selection. The question is asked, and the next instruction is decided based on the answer. What happens next?

DID YOU KNOW?

A variable is given a name that has no spaces and can be written in two ways:
- When it is written as `light_level` it is using a naming convention called *snake_case*. This is where the words are written all in lowercase and spaces are replaced by underscore lines.
- When it is written as `lightLevel` it is using the naming convention called *camelCase*. This is where there are no spaces and lower-case letters are used but from the second word onwards the first letter is capitalised.

As a programmer, you decide how to write your variables and use the same naming convention throughout your program. A variable name should always describe what sort of data it is storing, so that it is easy to recognise and makes sense when it is used in your program.

KEYWORDS

preset program: a program that has already been created for the user

selection: a programming construct with more than one possible pathway; a condition is tested (using a question or criterion) before deciding which pathway to follow (the output)

naming convention: a specific way of writing a variable name; the two main ways are called *snake_case* and *camelCase*

Practise

1   Create a flowchart to plan the program for another part of your smart home, the garage doors:

> The garage doors need to open when the button is pressed on the key in the car.

   - Plan the **IF** statement question that needs to be asked in the selection.
   - What is the output if the outcome is **true**?
   - What is the output if the outcome is **false**?
   - Check the flowchart in pairs to make sure the program works as expected.

2   Discuss in pairs how the program will work to control the garage doors.

Effective testing

Learn

You have seen in previous themes that it is important to follow the flow of the flowchart to see what the output will be based on a specific input. This is how testing works. You decide on a range of inputs, predict what the output should be and then test what the output actually is.

The flowchart below has been created as part of a burglar alarm. The light level detected by the sensor is used to detect whether someone is near. If someone gets close to the sensor, then the light around it will be reduced by the presence of the person and can be used as the input.

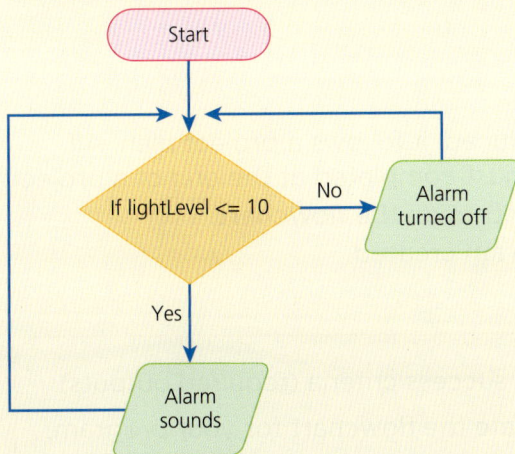

IF the light level is less than or equal to 10, **THEN** the alarm will be turned on; **ELSE** the alarm will be off.

As you explored in Unit 7.1, applying a test plan can help the testing process. It is important to test a range of inputs to check that the program works as expected.

Below is an example test plan for the flowchart above (with the first test complete).

Test number	Data entered	Expected outcome	Actual outcome	Pass/fail
1	Light level = 0	Alarm sounds	Alarm sounds	Pass
2	Light level = 150	Alarm off		
3	Light level = 10	Alarm sounds		
4	Light level = 9	Alarm sounds		
5	Light level = 80	Alarm off		

The tests are continued to check all the actual outcomes against expected outcomes. This is called **algorithm tracing**. The process of following the flow of a flowchart for a specific input tests that it works as expected.

KEYWORD

algorithm tracing: the process of following the flow of a flowchart using a specific input

1   Test the program for the flowchart in the Learn box above.
    - Open the file **TestingProgram.py** provided by your teacher.
    - Send the program (download the program) to the micro:bit.
    - Copy and complete the test table in the Learn section. Apply the tests on the micro:bit. Complete the actual outcome for each test.
2   Compare your results with a partner. If you find any errors, correct the code so that the outcome is as expected on the test plan

Evaluating a program

Learn

When a new program or product is designed or produced, it follows a project plan. All projects need to be tested and evaluated. This is not just completed at the end of a project:

- You are doing this when you are tracing the algorithm on the flowchart.
- You are doing this when you are testing the program created.

A project plan consists of the following stages:

> **Plan:** You **decompose** the program and outline the success criteria (required outputs).
>
> **Design:** You plan the steps in the program and create the flowchart for your program.
>
> **Create:** You create or edit the program code.
>
> **Test:** You apply a test plan, using specific inputs to check the outputs are as expected.
>
> **Evaluate:** You review the test plan and final program to check that it meets all the expectations of the final program.

An element to consider in the planning stage of the project plan is the **user**: Who is going to use the program? Will they be able to use the program and will they understand it? To help with this, testing can be carried out by a chosen user and by asking them specific questions about how they will use the program. The questions can be around the **usability** of the program or device.

A smart home requires a variety of possible solutions using a range of sensors. A programmer needs to consider all the users that will be using the devices in the home.

For example: Is the output suitable and easy to understand?

If the image to be displayed is a happy face, this is going to make the user feel at ease and good about the output.

If the image to be displayed is a sad face, this is going to make the user feel uneasy and bad about the output.

Colours, images and sounds can affect how the user feels (for example, whether the user likes using the program or device). Therefore, these elements should be considered carefully when designing, creating, testing and evaluating a new program.

KEYWORDS

decompose: break down into smaller parts

user: person who will use a program

usability: considering how a user will interact with a program

---

Practise

1 Explain to a partner the purpose of a project plan using the stages outlined in the Learn box above.

2 Considering the impact specific images and sounds will have on users will help you to plan a new program. It is important to explore all the image and sound options available, to help you decide which is best to use. The micro:bit comes with a wide range of pre-set images and sounds that can be used.

– Create a table with the headings *Positive images* and *Negative images*.

– Open the file **TestImages.py** provided by your teacher.

– Edit the image displayed to a new image of your choice. Use the image table below to help you.

```
display.show(Image.HAPPY)
```

HEART	HEART_SMALL	HAPPY	SMILE	SAD	CONFUSED
ANGRY	ASLEEP	SURPRISED	SILLY	FABULOUS	MEH
YES	NO	CLOCK12	CLOCK11	CLOCK10	CLOCK9
CLOCK8	CLOCK7	CLOCK6	CLOCK5	CLOCK4	CLOCK3
CLOCK2	CLOCK1	ARROW_N	ARROW_NE	ARROW_E	ARROW_SE
ARROW_S	ARROW_SW	ARROW_W	ARROW_NW	TRIANGLE	TRIANGLE_LEFT
CHESSBOARD	DIAMOND	DIAMOND_SMALL	SQUARE	SQUARE_SMALL	RABBIT
COW	MUSIC_CROTCHET	MUSIC_QUAVER	MUSIC_QUAVERS	PITCHFORK	SNAKE
PACMAN	TARGET	TSHIRT	ROLLERSKATE	DUCK	HOUSE
TORTOISE	BUTTERFLY	STICKFIGURE	UMBRELLA	SWORD	GIRAFFE

- Send the program (download the program) to the micro:bit to view the image.
- Would this image be positive or negative to a user? Insert the image names that have a positive effect under the *Positive* heading in your table.
- Test some other images. Insert the image names that have a negative effect under the *Negative* heading in your table.

3 Create a table with the headings *Positive sounds* and *Negative sounds*.
- Open the file **TestMusic.py** provided by your teacher.
- Edit the sound displayed to play a different sound of your choice. Use the table below to help you.

```
music.play(music.BIRTHDAY)
```

DADADADUM	ENTERTAINER	PRELUDE	ODE	NYAN
FUNK	BLUES	BIRTHDAY	WEDDING	FUNERAL
PYTHON	BADDY	CHASE	BA_DING	JUMP_UP
JUMP_DOWN	POWER_UP	POWER_DOWN	WAWAWAWAA	PUNCHLINE
RINGTONE				

- Send the program (download the program) to the micro:bit to hear the music.
- Would this music be positive or negative to a user?
- Test some other sounds. Insert the sound names that have a negative effect under the *Negative* heading in your table. Place the sound names that have a positive effect under the *Positive* heading.

Go further

In this unit, you have looked at how the different sensors on the micro:bit can be used in a program. The **accelerometer** has different **gestures** that can be used in a program's selection statement. A gesture is a specific movement.

The different gestures are:
- shake
- up
- down
- left
- right
- face up
- face down
- freefall.

You can use these to start an output **IF** the gesture is detected on the micro:bit accelerometer sensor. The program code for the IF statement using the gesture is:

```
if accelerometer.was_gesture('shake'):
```

To see this in a program, you need to add an output image to test whether the accelerometer sensor is detecting the gesture. The output can be any of the images available; here it is the *tick*, which is called **YES** in the program code:

```
if accelerometer.was_gesture('shake'):
    display.show(Image.YES)
```

Start

If shake is detected

Yes

Display
a tick

1 Open the file **GestureTests.py** provided by your teacher.
   - Edit the gesture in the code to one listed above.
   - Send the program to the micro:bit.
   - Test that the gesture works. If the gesture is working, the micro:bit will display a tick.
   - Discuss with a partner what the gesture is and how it works on the micro:bit.
2 Edit the code to try the other gestures. Copy and complete this table to help you to remember what each gesture does.

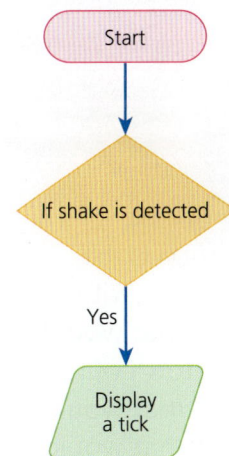

Gesture	How does it work?

KEYWORDS

accelerometer: a sensor to detect movement
gesture: a specific movement on the micro:bit

Challenge yourself

Apply what you have learned about sensors to this scenario:

A museum has asked for help to protect a priceless new crown that is on display. The crown needs to be protected against potential thieves.

1 Discuss with a partner:
  – What would you put in place to help protect the priceless crown from thieves?
  – How could you use sensors to protect the priceless crown?
  – What would the **IF** statement be for your protection method?
  – What would happen **if** the sensor detected the crown was stolen?
  – What **else** would happen when the sensor was *not* triggered?
  – How could you test your idea using the micro:bit?
2 Draw a flowchart to represent the **IF** statement you would need.
3 Try coding your flowchart for the micro:bit.
4 Test the program code and make changes as necessary.
5 Evaluate your idea to check that it meets the requirements of the scenario above.

Final project

The skills you have learned in this unit are all about the different sensors that can be used on the micro:bit and how the data gathered by the sensor can be used to set selection, if statements in a program.

Look back to page 45 to remind yourself of the Scenario at the start of this unit. You are now going to develop a prototype using the micro:bit. It will use a sensor to detect whether someone is near a computer to help staff monitor the computers in the room, and act as a theft-detection system to signal to others when someone is near or is taking the device.

> The software solution should:
> - use one of the sensors from the micro:bit: the light, touch or accelerometer sensor
> - use the data to decide the next instruction to execute in the program
> - be presented as a flowchart to show the flow of the program if the outcome to the question set is **true** or **false**
> - use more than one input and more than one output.

1   Discuss with a partner and write down your initial thoughts about:
    -   the benefits of using a simulator for this type of software-development project
    -   whether this program will be application software or system software
    -   what sensor could be used and what the IF statement could be.

2   Before creating anything, you need to consider the project plan. Take time to plan and write the answers to the following questions:
    -   What is it you are going to create?
    -   What does the project outline require the software to have in it? (See the box above.)
    -   What hardware and software will you need to develop the software?
    -   When does the project need to be completed?
    -   How will you know whether you have been successful?

3   Discuss with a partner how your software solution could work:
    -   Which sensor will you use to detect a potential theft?
    -   What output will you have in your solution to alert others to a potential theft of a computer?
    -   How could you use selection to use the sensor's data?
    -   Will the data generated by the sensor be a string or an integer?
    -   What will happen if the sensor is activated?
    -   What else will happen when the sensor is not detecting anything?

4   Once you have planned your software solution, create a flowchart to show how the sensor will be used and what the output will be.
    -   Discuss with a partner your flowchart and how it represents the solution.
    -   Look at the test table below. Select the rows linked with the sensor you are using and copy and complete the table by following the flow of the flowchart.

Test number	Data entered	Expected outcome	Pass/fail
1		Light detected	
2		Light not detected	
3		Touch detected	
4		Touch not detected	
5		Movement detected	
6		Movement not detected	

- Discuss with a partner the benefits of creating and testing a flowchart before starting to create a prototype.

5 Open the file **FinalProject2.py** provided by your teacher.
- Complete your software solution by adding more than one output in your solution to alert others to a potential theft of a computer through the use of a sensor.
- Connect the micro:bit.
- Send the program (download the program) to the micro:bit.
- Test your program works by completing the test table above linked to the sensor you are using.
- Debug by finding and fixing any errors, if required.

Evaluation

1 Swap programs with a partner and test your software solution. Comment on the following:
- Does it work as expected?
- Is the solution easy to use?
- Are the outputs correct for the **IF** statement?
- Would the software solution be successful as an alert to a potential theft of a school computer?
- Does the software solution follow the project plan?

2 Now open your own program and look at the code. Reflect on what could be improved. Things you might want to think about include the following:
- Could sound be added to the output following the image?
- Based on the evaluations, make a list of recommendations to improve your smart software solution.

What can you do?

Read and review what you can do.
- ✔ I can follow, explain and evaluate an algorithm using a flowchart.
- ✔ I can edit and correct errors in a flowchart.
- ✔ I can create an algorithm using flowchart symbols.
- ✔ I can explain and create a flowchart using the selection statements IF, THEN, ELSE.
- ✔ I can predict the outcome of a flowchart that uses selection.
- ✔ I can identify and explain when to use a string or an integer in a program for the micro:bit.
- ✔ I can create a MicroPython program using an input and an output on the micro:bit.
- ✔ I can evaluate a prototype of a software solution on the micro:bit.
- ✔ I can explain the purpose of a project plan to help define the project and what is required to complete a successful final software solution.
- ✔ I can apply a test table to test a flowchart and a program.
- ✔ I can evaluate, find and fix errors detected in a MicroPython program used to control an input and an output on the micro:bit.
- ✔ I can use MicroPython to create a program with multiple inputs and outputs for the micro:bit.
- ✔ I can identify where simulators are used to model real-life simulators and how they benefit learning.
- ✔ I can describe the difference between application software and system software.

Get started!

There are many different methods of connecting to networks and the internet, such as using wires or wireless transmission methods to send and receive data. Bluetooth, Wi-Fi and cellular data are always improving, so it's important to know the key differences.

Discuss the following with a partner:
- What was the last thing that you did online?
- How many devices that connect to the internet are in your home?
- What's the most unusual device that you know can connect to the internet?

In this unit, you will discover the technical differences between the different methods of connecting to the internet. You will explore how devices connect and how connecting to the internet gives you access to the world wide web. You will also develop your understanding of how the internet works and how our devices can access the global network of connected devices.

Learning outcomes

In this unit, you will learn to:
- explain different ways that devices can transmit data
- understand how DNS enables users to access websites on their devices and explain the steps DNS takes
- understand how IP addresses and web servers work
- explain what the structure of a URL looks like and identify the different parts
- explain what types of encryption can be used on websites
- find information on the security certificates of a website
- understand how errors can occur in data transmission and apply ways to check that a message has been sent correctly
- modify an algorithm in a flowchart based on a basic cipher
- encode and decode messages using a cipher
- understand how search engines categorise data
- explain how AI is used to improve search-engine results
- understand why a web browser is a type of application software.

Warm up

It's quite likely that, in the last 24 hours, you have used a device to connect to the internet.

Write a list of the devices that you have used over the last week to connect to the internet.

For each device, you should note:
- what type of device you used (PC, mobile phone, tablet, and so on)
- how you connected to the internet (plugged a cable in or wirelessly).

When you have developed your list, discuss your findings with your partner as you will be investigating a number of **connectivity** methods in this unit.

SCENARIO

A local technology company wants to develop a new website for young people to share information about the latest technologies. The tech company would like to add a 'news' page to the website and has asked for your help to develop this. To do this, you will need to understand, collect and explain how connectivity technologies work.

First, you need to learn how the connections are made between devices. Your challenge is to understand how the internet works, including aspects such as **artificial intelligence**, websites, **DNS**, security and connectivity. At the end of this unit, you will combine everything you have learned into a presentation, which the technology company could use on their news page.

KEYWORDS

connectivity: the method that devices use to connect to each other to form a network
artificial intelligence: an area of computing that focuses on creating intelligent computers that can mimic the way humans think and make decisions; a computer system able to perform tasks normally done using human intelligence, such as understanding speech
DNS (Domain Name System): a system used to translate a URL to an IP address

DID YOU KNOW?

Tim Berners-Lee invented the world wide web in 1989. The internet was originally created so that scientists could share information automatically between universities.

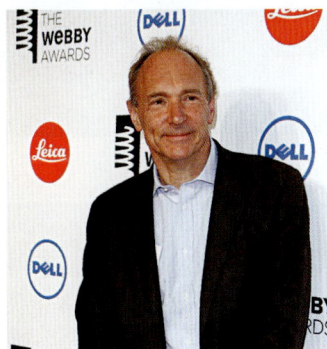

Do you remember?

Before starting this unit, you should:
- ✔ know that digital content is stored on servers
- ✔ understand how digital devices can transfer data wirelessly
- ✔ understand how bandwidth can affect a network
- ✔ know that networks can be overloaded, if too many devices are on the network
- ✔ understand that data needs to be transmitted securely
- ✔ be able to describe how user authentication (passwords, fingerprints and facial recognition) works.

Getting online

Learn

There are many ways of getting online, whether at home, school or outdoors. The most convenient way to connect is usually wirelessly, as this requires no wires and means that your devices can be **portable**. A range of devices are used to connect to networks, including mobile phones, tablets, laptops and PCs. Even some washing machines can now connect online!

Data can be transferred from one device to another wirelessly using radio waves. The most popular methods of wireless data transfer are **Wi-Fi**, **Bluetooth** and **cellular data**. For example, the image below shows how data is sent wirelessly between devices using cellular data. Each method of transmitting data wirelessly has some advantages and disadvantages. Some are more useful in certain situations than others.

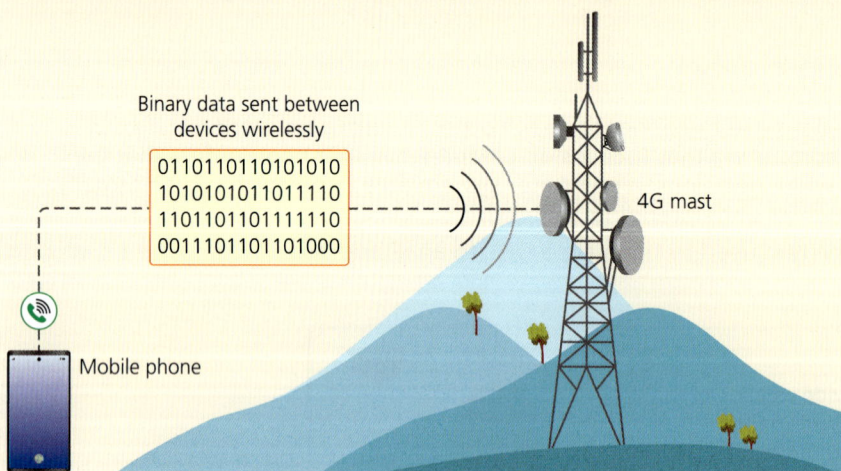

Binary data sent between devices wirelessly

```
0110110110101010
1010010011011110
1101101101111110
0011101101101000
```

4G mast

Mobile phone

KEYWORDS

portable: something that can easily be moved around

data: raw facts and figures; computers understand only binary data, which is 0s and 1s

Wi-Fi, Bluetooth, cellular data: methods for computing devices to communicate with one another using radio waves

1 In a small group, discuss the following questions:
   – When was the last time you used Wi-Fi? What device were you using? What were you doing on the device?
   – When was the last time you used Bluetooth? What device were you using? What were you doing on the device?
   – When was the last time you used cellular data? What device were you using? What were you doing on the device?
2 For each type of transmission (wireless data transfer), discuss:
   – what you think the advantages or disadvantages might be
   – what information about the type of transmission would be important to include on a technology news page.
3 Summarise the points from the discussions above, as these may help you later in this unit.

Transmission methods

For each wireless transmission method, it is important that the following characteristics are considered:

Bandwidth

Bandwidth is the amount of data that can be transmitted within a certain amount of time. This is important for actions like streaming video and is probably why you may have seen a video 'buffer' (spinning circle) when trying to stream content. Videos typically have large file sizes so lots of data needs to be transmitted. This means that videos need lots of bandwidth to play without buffering.

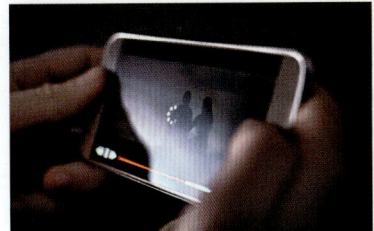

Transmission distance

Transmission distance is how far a signal can be sent using the transmission method. It is likely that you will have moved too far away from a **Wi-Fi access point** and have had the problem that your connection has dropped.

Security

When you consider which types of transmission are best for certain situations, it is crucial that security is considered. Some transmission methods can be **hacked** more easily than others!

Interference

Most transmission methods are affected by **interference**. It's important to understand which of the transmission methods are more likely to be affected by interference. Interference is often caused by other electronic devices near to a network, or by physical obstructions such as walls. For example, equipment such as microwaves can cause laptops to lose connection to a Wi-Fi network because the radio waves in a microwave can interfere with the signal.

The most important considerations for each of the transfer methods are the bandwidth and the transmission distance that it can send data. For example, if you wanted to transfer data between devices over a 500 metre distance, then Bluetooth would not be appropriate as it does not reach that far!

You measure the amount of data that can be transmitted in bits per second (bps), kilobits per second (Kbps = 1 thousand bits), megabits per second (Mbps = 1 million bits) or gigabits per second (Gbps = 1 billion bits).

There are always new versions of each of the transfer methods in development, so these speeds get faster and the distances get longer every year.

KEYWORDS

bandwidth: the amount of data that can be transmitted within a certain amount of time

transmission distance: how far data can be sent using the transmission method

Wi-Fi access point: a hardware device that allows devices to connect to a network using Wi-Fi

hacked: when somebody accesses a system when they are not supposed to; this is often illegal

interference: what happens when something interrupts the transmission of a signal; this could be a physical obstruction such as a wall, or other radio waves

Practise

For each of the scenarios below, identify the characteristic of the transmission method that has caused the issue. For example, if a mobile phone is in a tunnel and has no connection to the wireless access point, this would be caused by interference.

Scenario 1

Abid uses Wi-Fi to connect his laptop to the network to share some important files containing personal information (his name, address and medical details). Abid has set up his network without a password, so that anybody who joins the network can view his files.

Scenario 2

Alyssa uses cellular data to access the internet on her mobile phone while walking around a local town. Alyssa has entered a supermarket and her internet has stopped working.

Scenario 3

Adam has connected his Bluetooth headphones to his PC to listen to music. However, when he goes downstairs to the kitchen his headphones stop working.

Transmission characteristics

Learn

Take a deeper look at the characteristics of each wireless transmission method:

Wi-Fi

Characteristic	Information
Wired/wireless	Wireless
Bandwidth	Wi-Fi is currently capable of transmitting data at 9.6 Gbps.
Transmission distance	Wi-Fi can transmit data up to about 50 metres indoors, but this can be affected by interference. This means that devices can be moved around, but are only portable across one site (a home, school or office, for example).
Security	Security is poor. Anybody within range of the Wi-Fi network can see the network and connect to it using a password. Wi-Fi passwords can be hacked using brute-force attacks (a computer program trying lots of different combinations of letters and numbers until a password is cracked).
Interference	Wi-Fi signals can be affected by walls and electronic equipment such as microwaves and TVs.

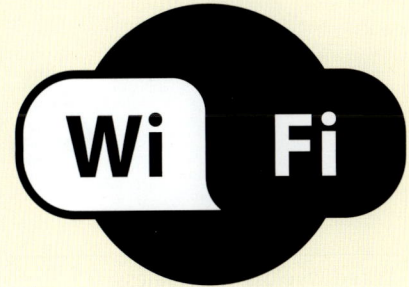

Bluetooth

Characteristic	Information
Wired/wireless	Wireless
Bandwidth	Bluetooth 5 is capable of transmitting data at 2 Mbps.
Transmission distance	Bluetooth 5 can transmit data 40 metres indoors, but this can be affected by interference. This means that devices are portable, but only across one site (a home, school or office, for example).
Security	Security is poor. Anybody within range of the Bluetooth transmission can see the device. There are a number of issues with Bluetooth security, including Bluesnarfing, which means that a hacker connects to a device without the user knowing.
Interference	Bluetooth devices work best when there is a clear line of sight between the devices (they can physically see each other). Wi-Fi networks, as well as walls and objects, can cause Bluetooth interference.

KEYWORDS

brute-force attack: a type of cyber-attack that a hacker can make on a computer – it attempts to guess a password by using a large bank of words and phrases; it keeps trying different combinations until it finds the correct password

Bluesnarfing: a method that hackers use to access the data on a device with Bluetooth

Cellular data

There are two modern transmission methods using cellular data: 4G and 5G.

Characteristic	4G information	5G information
Wired/wireless	Wireless	Wireless
Bandwidth	The average speed of 4G is between 8 and 10 Mbps.	The average speed of 5G is around 100 Mbps.
Transmission distance	16 kilometres	500 metres
Security	Security for both 4G and 5G is excellent, as cellular providers have advanced security features.	
Interference	4G and 5G signals can be affected by walls and electronic equipment such as microwaves and TVs. They can also be affected by the landscape: hills, valleys and weather.	

Practise

1 For each of the scenarios below, discuss with a partner which transmission type would be most appropriate. Remember to say why: for example, Wi-Fi would be an appropriate transmission type to send data to laptops and other devices on a home network. This is because most homes are no larger than 50 metres, which means that the signal will reach the devices without interference.

   - Wirelessly connecting a PC to a network in the home
   - Wirelessly connecting a keyboard and mouse to a PC
   - Connecting a mobile phone to a tablet computer to share photos
   - Connecting a mobile phone to the internet while out walking

2 Which transmission method is most likely to be used to view a news page by someone using a tablet computer or mobile phone?

DID YOU KNOW?

Before 3G, 4G and 5G became available, the highest cellular network speed was only 114 Kbps. At this speed, it would have taken over five days to download an HD film!

Accessing web pages: IP addresses

Learn

When you access content on the internet, you are actually accessing files that are stored on a **server**. This is the case for web pages, video and audio **streaming** and **messaging services**. The files are stored on servers in the same way that you would store files on your devices; the difference is that the files on servers can be accessed via the internet. Servers are often grouped together in one location, which is known as a *server farm*. There may be hundreds, or even thousands, of servers in a single server farm.

To publish files on the internet, **administrators** add files to the **hard disk drive** of the server. Users can then access the files through their **web browser** by typing in a **URL** (web address).

> Servers typically have lots of storage space and power to supply web pages, video, audio or messaging as quickly as possible to the user. They look slightly different from a PC, as they are stored in racks, so that many servers can be stacked on top of each other. Servers that store web pages are known as **web servers**, which allow users to access their files online.

IP addresses

Each device that is on a network has an **IP address** assigned to it. *IP* stands for 'Internet Protocol'. On a **home network**, this address will be given to each device on the network and it will be **unique**. An IP address is designed to identify a device on a network, so that devices can communicate with each other. Think of it as the 'address' of the device.

An IP address consists of four numbers, each separated by a full stop. Each number is between 0 and 255. An example of an IP address could be:

192.124.2.213

In the example below, a Wi-Fi robot vacuum cleaner is connected to the home network and has been given the IP address 192.168.1.42. If another device wanted to send a message to the vacuum cleaner, it would use the address 192.168.1.42 and not the name '360_CleanRobot_X9', in case there were two devices with the same name.

Device name	IP Address
Windows laptop	192.168.1.2
Android phone	192.168.1.3
Apple iPad	192.168.1.4
Kitchen lightbulb	192.168.1.5
Robot vacuum	192.168.1.6
Hallway smart plug	192.168.1.7
Living room TV	192.168.1.8

> In this example, all of the IP addresses start with **192.168.1.**, which is common on home networks.

IP addresses on the internet work in the same way. Each server has an IP address assigned to it, so that it can be identified uniquely on the network.

> **KEYWORDS**
>
> **server:** a hardware device that stores and manages files and services for a network
>
> **streaming:** watching or playing media over a computer network; playback can be started before all of the data has downloaded
>
> **messaging service:** software that allows users to send and receive text messages between devices
>
> **web server:** a server that provides access to web pages stored on them
>
> **administrator:** a person who is responsible for managing a network
>
> **hard disk drive:** a hardware device that is used to store digital data
>
> **web browser:** a software application that allows users to locate, access and display information on the world wide web
>
> **URL:** Uniform Resource Locator; the address of a web page
>
> **IP (Internet Protocol) address:** an address assigned to each device on a network that is unique to the network
>
> **home network:** a network of devices that can be found in a household
>
> **unique:** only one exists; there are no duplicates

Practise

1   Explain to a partner what a server is and what it does.

2   In pairs, look at the list of IP addresses of servers for large websites below.
    -   Now you know what IP addresses should look like, identify whether they are correct (valid) or incorrect (invalid).
    -   If you find any that have problems, explain why the IP address is not valid.
    -   Copy and complete the table to show your answers.

Server IP address	Valid or invalid?	Why?
69.171.224		
199.59.149.230		
255.255.255.255		
256.21.211		
207.9756		
74.125.65556.91		
65.55.72.541		
198.78.201.252		
212.58.241.7543		
98.137.149.56		
65.55.175.259		

3   Think about what the readers of the technology company news page might need to understand about IP addresses.

URLs

Learn

If you were asked to remember the IP address for 20 different websites, do you think you could do it? That's why we use URLs!

A URL, or Uniform Resource Locator, is used to locate a file on a web server on the internet. They are easier to remember than an IP address.

URL	Server IP address
https://www.google.com	172.217.169.78
https://micropython.org/	176.58.119.26
https://www.microsoft.com	104.215.148.63

A URL has to be written in a certain way.

The different parts of a URL direct devices to the correct server. The **domain name** (an easy-to-remember name) is the part that changes, depending on which web server you would like to visit using your web browser.

Domain levels

A top-level domain (or TLD) is the part at the end of the domain name. There are over 1000 TLDs available to buy, but the most common is **.com**

http://www.africanews.com

top-level domain name

Other popular TLDs are:

TLD	Use
.com	Commercial
.org	Organisation
.net	Network
.in	India
.au	Australia
.ng	Nigeria
.ph	Philippines
.eg	Egypt
.ae	United Arab Emirates
.id	Indonesia

KEYWORD

domain name: an easy-to-remember name for a website, e.g. www.hoddereducation.com

Practise

1. Create a table listing five domain names that you have visited in the previous few weeks. Identify the URL, domain name and TLD for each, for example:

URLs	Domain name	TLD
https://www.netflix.com	netflix.com	.com

2. Work with a partner and explain what a URL is to another pair. Make sure you include the following vocabulary in your explanation:
   - URL
   - Domain name
   - TLD.

Accessing web pages: DNS

Learn

> Remember: every website is stored on a web server that holds the files for the website and each web server is assigned an IP address.
>
> It would be extremely difficult to remember the IP addresses for all of the websites that you use, so URLs make them easier to remember.

How does a URL link to an IP address? **DNS**!

DNS (Domain Name System) is a system used to translate a URL to an IP address, so that you don't have to remember the IP addresses for web servers.

DNS allows you to type a URL (like **google.com**) into your web browser to retrieve the files from the web server with the matching IP address (such as 142.250.74.142.) A DNS server stores a large database of URLs and corresponding IP addresses. It looks like a list of IP addresses and URLs, similar to the example below:

google.com 209.85.231.104

microsoft.com 207.46.170.123

yahoo.com 72.30.2.43

micropython.org 176.58.119.26

wikipedia.com 208.80.152.2

dell.com 143.166.83.38

You can think of DNS as being similar to the contacts list in a mobile phone. If you want to call somebody, you look them up by their name, as it would be very difficult to remember all of the phone numbers!

What happens when you type a URL into your web browser?

1 A user types into their web browser the URL of the website they would like to visit, for example http://www.africanews.com
2 The URL (africanews.com) request gets sent to the DNS server to find the matching IP address.
3 The IP address of the web server where the website is kept (81.92.228.150) is sent back to the user's computer.

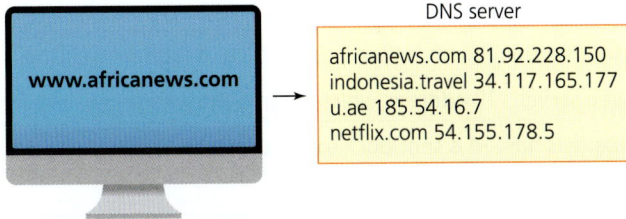

DNS server
africanews.com 81.92.228.150
indonesia.travel 34.117.165.177
u.ae 185.54.16.7
netflix.com 54.155.178.5

4 a If the DNS cannot find the IP address in its database, this search is then passed on to a **higher-level DNS** (another DNS that has access to an even larger list of domain names).
  b If the higher-level DNS still cannot find it, a **404 error** is returned. This means that the page was not found and the web server sends an error page to the web browser.
5 The web browser then sends a request to the web server's IP address that returns the web page.

81.92.228.150

DNS server
www.africanews.com
africanews.com 81.92.228.150
indonesia.travel 34.117.165.177
u.ae 185.54.16.7
netflix.com 54.155.178.5

→ 81.92.228.150

Web server

On average, DNS takes between 20 and 120 milliseconds to translate a URL to an IP address!

KEYWORDS

DNS (Domain Name System): a system used to translate a URL to an IP address

higher-level DNS: another DNS that is used for checking large lists of URLs and IP addresses

404 error: an error sent to a web browser if the DNS could not find the web server

Practise

1 Explain to a partner how DNS enables users to access websites. Use this vocabulary in your explanation:
   - URL
   - IP address
   - Web browser
   - DNS server
   - Request
   - Web page.

2 The following table shows the steps that DNS takes to translate a URL to an IP address, but they are in the wrong order.

   Rewrite the steps in the correct order.

| The URL gets sent to the DNS server to find the correct IP address. |
| If the higher-level DNS still cannot find it, a 404 error is returned. |
| If the DNS cannot find the IP address in its database, this search is then passed on to a higher-level DNS. |
| The web browser then sends a request to the web server's IP address, which returns the web page. |
| The IP address of the web server where the website is hosted is sent back to the user's computer. |
| A user types into their web browser the URL they would like to visit. |

3 Explain to a partner how a user would be able to view the Technology Company News Page. Use the vocabulary in the first task above.

Computational thinking – algorithms

Look at the flowchart below. It shows a basic version of how a DNS works to translate a single URL to an IP address.

- Follow the flowchart. Discuss with a partner what you think this program will do if **netflix.com** is entered.

- Create your own version of this flowchart that returns the correct URL for:
  - **yahoo.com**
  - 72.30.2.43

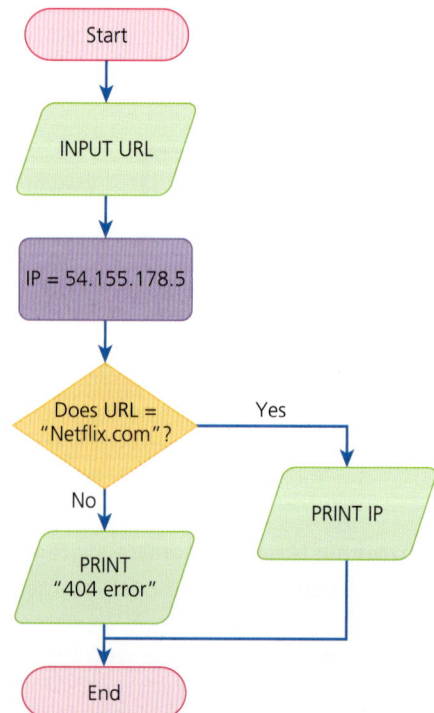

```
          Start
            │
         INPUT URL
            │
      IP = 54.155.178.5
            │
      Does URL =          Yes
      "Netflix.com"?  ──────────┐
            │                   │
           No                   │
            │                   │
         PRINT               PRINT IP
       "404 error"             │
            │                   │
            └─────────┬─────────┘
                     End
```

Padlocks and HTTPS

Learn

Web browsers are used to view web pages and content on the world wide web. When a user requests a webpage on the world wide web, the web browser retrieves the content (using DNS) and displays it in the **display window**.

> A web browser is applications software, as it performs the specific task of browsing the world wide web.

There are lots of different web browsers available and most of them are free, but they all have a similar layout and similar functions. All web browsers have **navigation buttons** alongside the **address bar** that allow a user to go back and refresh web pages.

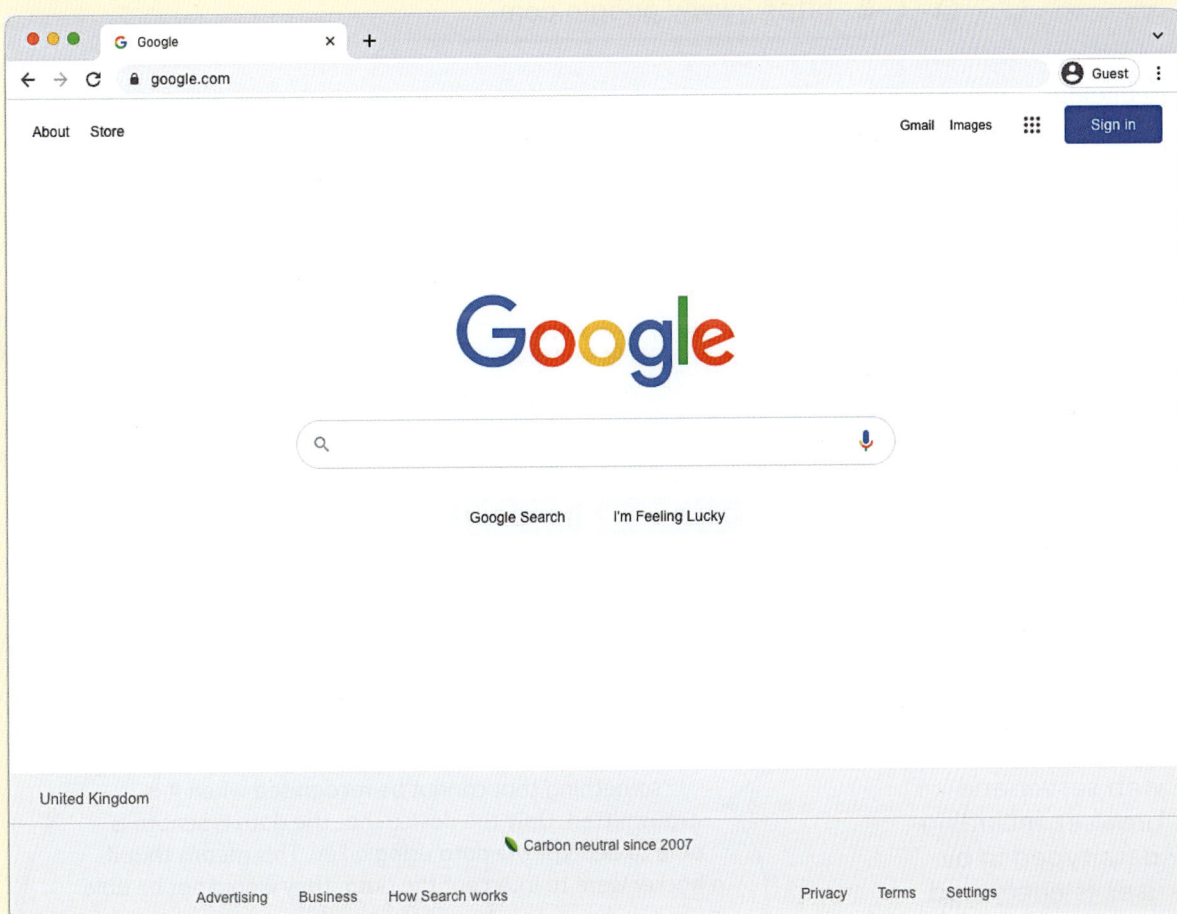

How secure are the web pages that you visit?

When using the internet, it is important to know whether a web page is secure. There are many web pages that are secure, but there are also millions of websites that do not require a high level of security.

Websites that take payment details online should use high-security **SSL (Secure Sockets Layer) certificates**, otherwise the data could be seen by hackers, whereas a website that simply displays information (for example, a list of cricket fixtures) would not need to use an SSL certificate.

It can be difficult to tell which websites are secure and which are insecure, but web browsers have some built-in tools that can help you decide whether to use them.

The address bar displays information about the security of a web page.

- Look at the **padlock icon** in the address bar. This shows that the page has an **SSL certificate**. This certificate proves that the owner of this website is genuine.
- The address bar also shows the **protocol** that data is sent by. In the following example, you can see that the URL begins with **https**, which is the secure way to send data between your computer and the webpage.

- By clicking on the padlock, further information about the website's security can be seen.

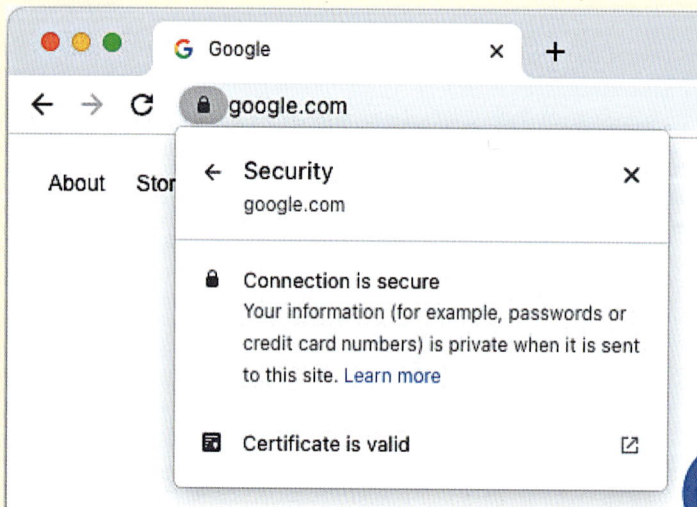

If a website has an SSL certificate, it means that anything sent between the web server and the browser, including any data typed in by the user, is encrypted (or scrambled) before it is sent and is then decrypted when it is received.

Encryption converts data into something that cannot be recognised when it is transmitted. Only the device that the data is sent to is able to decrypt the data using a key. This means that if a hacker were to intercept the data, they would not be able to understand it.

In the example of google.com, the website uses a type of encryption that would take modern computers 500 billion years to decrypt without the key.

KEYWORDS

display window: where the content is displayed when downloaded from a web server

navigation buttons: back, forwards and refresh buttons are included to help navigate pages; all browsers also have bookmark features for saving pages

address bar: allows the user to type in a URL to go to a chosen website, via DNS

SSL (Secure Sockets Layer): technology for keeping a connection between devices secure through encryption

SSL certificate: a digital certificate that confirms that a website is genuine and allows it to use an encrypted connection using SSL

padlock icon: shows in the address bar if the page is sent via HTTPS and is secure

protocol: set of rules for how data is sent between devices

encryption: a process that scrambles data so that it cannot be read by unauthorised users; only the device that the data is sent to is able to decrypt the data using a key

Practise

1   Explain to a partner how encryption is used to send data from one device to another.

    Give some examples in your day-to-day life where you think it would be important to keep data secure during transmission.

2   Look at these examples and explain to a partner which need to be secure and which do not:
    - A website that takes card payments for sports tickets
    - A website that shows a list of top sports players and the number of points they have received in their sport
    - A website that allows users to send pictures of their pets, including the owner's name and address.

3   Discuss with a partner whether a technology company's news page would need to be secure.

4   Explain to a partner exactly what to do to check a website's security.

Insecure websites

Learn

Some websites do not use HTTPS with an SSL certificate. This means that if you were to enter any information on this website, it would not be encrypted before it was sent, which means that **hackers** could read your data.

This is what the address bar looks like on an insecure website. When you click the triangle icon, a message will appear.

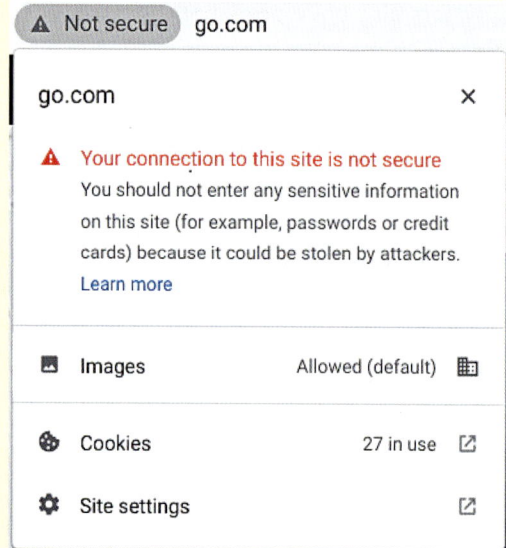

⚠ Not secure   go.com

go.com   ✕

⚠ **Your connection to this site is not secure**
You should not enter any sensitive information on this site (for example, passwords or credit cards) because it could be stolen by attackers.
Learn more

🖼 Images   Allowed (default) ▦

🍪 Cookies   27 in use ↗

⚙ Site settings   ↗

Checking the validity of a website

Just because a website uses SSL and HTTPS does not mean that it is entirely safe. If your computer had a **virus**, it could trick your web browser into thinking that a website is secure when it is not.

There are ways to **verify** the trusted certificate of a website, to check whether it is as secure as your web browser states:

● By clicking the padlock, the certificate can be viewed. Below you can see the certificate given to **micropython.org**. You can also see who gave MicroPython the certificate: in this case, R3.

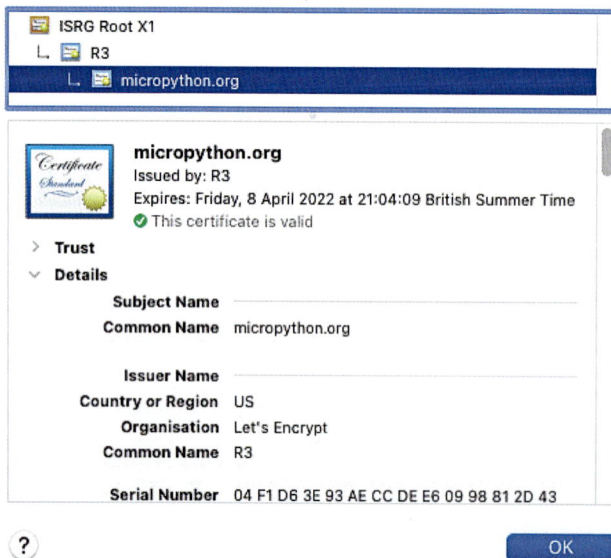

📄 ISRG Root X1
  └ 📄 R3
     └ 📄 micropython.org

micropython.org
Issued by: R3
Expires: Friday, 8 April 2022 at 21:04:09 British Summer Time
✓ This certificate is valid

❯ **Trust**
❯ **Details**
        Subject Name
  Common Name micropython.org

        Issuer Name
  Country or Region US
  Organisation Let's Encrypt
  Common Name R3

  Serial Number 04 F1 D6 3E 93 AE CC DE E6 09 98 81 2D 43

?   OK

● It is also possible to check who owns the domain name, to make sure that this company actually owns the website. The website **https://who.is** can be used to find the owner of a website, and usually provides an address and contact details for the owner of a domain name.

KEYWORDS

hackers: people who may try to access data that they are not allowed to access

virus: software designed to cause damage to computer systems

verify: to check that something is correct

Practise

1   Identify whether the websites in the table below are secure or insecure.
    –   If it is secure, find the SSL certificate issuer (the organisation who gave the website its SSL certificate).
    –   Copy and complete the table to show your results.

> To find the SSL certificate issuer, you should click on the padlock, then click the `'certificate is valid'` option to see the certificate details. This will reveal who issued the SSL certificate.

Domain	Secure or insecure?	SSL certificate issuer
neverssl.com		
bbc.co.uk		
info.cern.ch		
nasa.gov		

2   Visit three websites that you use often to find out whether they are using an SSL certificate. Add these to the table.
3   Visit **https://who.is** and find out as much information as you can about the domain names listed below. This could include the owner, location or email address.
    –   **neverssl.com**
    –   **bbc.co.uk**
    –   **amazon.com**
    –   **nasa.gov**
4   Discuss with your partner why you think the websites you found with an SSL certificate have one. Do they send personal data?
    What about the websites that do not have an SSL certificate? Why is this?

Keeping it all secure

Learn

Security is important when transmitting messages and using networks. Messages that are transmitted between devices on a network can be intercepted, risking sensitive information being stolen or misused. If devices were to send messages without protecting them in any way, then the **plaintext** messages sent between devices could be read and understood by anybody able to capture the message.

Encryption allows devices to send messages to each other securely. These messages can still be intercepted, but if the message is encrypted, the message could not be understood. Encryption encodes or scrambles data into a format that cannot be understood and that can only be decrypted using the correct key.

> If a bank wanted to send you details to log into your account, would they send a message in plaintext? Explain your answer to a partner.

Computer 1
Message:
Your password is: aXa1239

Your password is:
aXa1239

Computer 2
Message:
Your password is: aXa1239

Unencrypted data transmission

Computer 1
Message:
Your password is: aXa1239

Your password is:
JHAF&^£-FDJG£

Computer 2
Message:
Your password is: aXa1239

Encrypted data transmission

Encryption algorithms

To encrypt data, an **algorithm** is used and agreed with the device receiving the data, so that the device can decode the message.

The Caesar cipher

The Caesar cipher is a famous technique that can be used to encrypt messages. This cipher works by shifting the alphabet along by a specified number of places. The first row (containing the alphabet) is plaintext. The second row shows the **cipher text**. For example, a Caesar cipher with a shift of two would look like this:

plaintext	A	B	C	D	E	F	G	H	I	J	K	L	M	N	O	P	Q	R	S	T	U	V	W	X	Y	Z
cipher text	Y	Z	A	B	C	D	E	F	G	H	I	J	K	L	M	N	O	P	Q	R	S	T	U	V	W	X

Simple substitution cipher

A simple substitution cipher works in a similar way to the Caesar shift. This time, letters are shifted at random, and to decode it, a user or device would need to know the full character list.

plaintext	A	B	C	D	E	F	G	H	I	J	K	L	M	N	O	P	Q	R	S	T	U	V	W	X	Y	Z
cipher text	C	K	U	J	B	Q	T	P	Y	H	I	O	A	X	R	Z	F	W	M	N	E	S	G	L	V	D

For example:

The message in plaintext is: **HELLO**

Encrypted using a simple substitution cipher it is: **PBOOR**

> SSL is a form of encryption that is incredibly powerful and cannot be decoded if the data is intercepted.

KEYWORDS

plaintext: a message before encryption or after decryption; a message that can be read easily

encryption: a process that scrambles data so that it cannot be understood by unauthorised users; only the device that the data is sent to is able to decrypt the data using a key

algorithm: a sequence of steps or instructions to solve a problem

cipher text: a message once it has been encrypted

Practise

1 **a** Using the given Caesar cipher with a shift of two, write down the encrypted message for the plaintext message "COMPUTER".

A	B	C	D	E	F	G	H	I	J	K	L	M	N	O	P	Q	R	S	T	U	V	W	X	Y	Z
Y	Z	A	B	C	D	E	F	G	H	I	J	K	L	M	N	O	P	Q	R	S	T	U	V	W	X

b Now encrypt the word 'CIPHER' using the Caesar cipher table above.

2 Using the given simple substitution cipher, write down the decrypted message for the cipher message "UYZPBW".

A	B	C	D	E	F	G	H	I	J	K	L	M	N	O	P	Q	R	S	T	U	V	W	X	Y	Z
C	K	U	J	B	Q	T	P	Y	H	I	O	A	X	R	Z	F	W	M	N	E	S	G	L	V	D

3 Copy and complete this grid to create a Caesar cipher with a shift of six.

A	B	C	D	E	F	G	H	I	J	K	L	M	N	O	P	Q	R	S	T	U	V	W	X	Y	Z

- Create an encrypted message (a word of your choice).
- Swap this message with a partner.
- Decode each other's messages.

4 Why is encryption used during data transmission? Explain to a partner how encryption works. Include this vocabulary in your explanation:
- Network
- Security
- Plaintext
- Scramble.

5 Discuss why is it important that users understand how encryption works.
- How can users check whether websites they use are encrypted?
- How would you explain to somebody who has not created a cipher before how to encrypt and decrypt a message?

Sending messages

Learn

On networks, data is frequently sent between devices. When devices send data between each other, they use IP addresses to identify where to send the information.

Computers communicate with each other using **binary** code, but sometimes these binary messages can be **corrupted** or interfered with, causing errors.

> Look back to page 47 for a reminder about binary code.

There are a number of reasons why errors can occur:
- **power surges**
- broken or damaged cables
- **electrical interference**
- hacking.

These issues can cause binary **bits** to flip between 1 and 0, causing errors in the data being sent.

Imagine that one computer (Computer 1) is transmitting a single **byte** of data to another computer (Computer 2). The computer that is receiving the data has a faulty cable.

Computer 1 wants to send the byte 01000101 but, due to the faulty cable, Computer 2 receives it as 00000101.

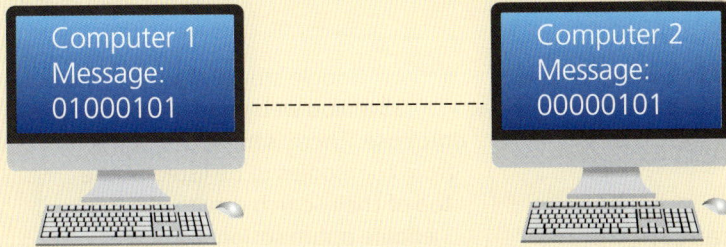

In this example, the broken cable has caused the second digit of the byte to be flipped from a 1 to a 0, resulting in an error on Computer 2.

KEYWORDS

binary: a number system that uses combinations of two digits (0 and 1) to represent all numbers; used to represent data in computer systems

corrupted: binary code can be lost or scrambled if an error occurs

power surge: computer hardware can be damaged by a temporary increase in power, often caused by lightning

electrical interference: when lots of electrical devices are operating in a small area, the electrical and radio waves can cause other devices to work incorrectly

bit: short for 'binary digit'; a single bit of data, either a 0 or a 1

byte: a group of 8 bits of data, often used to represent a single character in a computer, e.g. 01010011

Practise

In a small group, produce a mind map containing a section for each of the two bullet points below:
- why errors occur in data transmission
- what an error looks like.

Intelligent search engines

Learn

Search engines on the internet store large **databases** of websites and their content. Users type queries into the search engine's website and a list of webpages from the database that match the search criteria are returned.

Search engines are becoming more accurate from the use of **machine learning** and **artificial intelligence**.
- Search engines use keywords to find content. They do not require users to write in full sentences and most searches are for one, two or three words.
- Search engines are a quick and easy way for users to find information online. The example below shows a user searching for game consoles.
- Search engines will pick out the keywords from a query, so if the user typed 'Show me the latest game consoles' the search engine would focus on the words 'game consoles'.

Search engines have started to use artificial intelligence to improve their search results, to make them more appropriate for what the user is looking for. For example, every time somebody searches for 'helicopters', search engines remember which page the user actually wanted. They then move this page further up the search listings, to make it easier for other users to find it quickly.

Some search engines track your location so that relevant information is displayed. For example, if a user in Cairo searches for 'bicycle repair shops', it would show results in the Cairo area.

Google stores over 35 trillion web pages in its database. There is huge competition from companies to be listed at the top of their search results. Search-engine optimisation is a career path that many interested in the internet and searching take.

KEYWORDS

search engine: a website designed to search for content on other websites

database: a computer application that is used to organise data that can then be stored, processed and accessed electronically

machine learning: computer systems that are able to learn and adapt by analysing patterns in data

artificial Intelligence: an area of computing that focuses on creating intelligent computers that can mimic the way humans think and make decisions; a computer system able to perform tasks normally done using human intelligence, such as understanding speech

---

Practise

1 Open the file **Think like a search engine.docx** provided by your teacher.
   - Match the appropriate search phrases to the keywords.
   - Match the keywords that you have identified for each phrase to an appropriate website. You should copy and paste the link from the address bar of your web browser into the 'Website returned' column of the table, for example:

Search phrase	Keywords	Website returned
'A picture of a helicopter landing on an island'	helicopter landing island	https://www.researchgate.net/figure/The-helicopter-landing-spot-on-Nuulua-Island-used-for-dropping-the-monitoring-team-and_fig2_258927849
'Pictures of fast red cars driving'		
'A website with lots of information about the coolest gadgets'		
'Find me the top new songs that I can play'		
'What is the most popular film this year that I could watch?'		

2 Think about the way in which search engines select the keywords from the search phrase. With a partner, discuss these questions:
   - Why is it important to have an awareness of keywords when typing a search phrase?
   - Did you find any examples that required more keywords to find the information you needed? Why?

AI and reverse image searches

Learn

Search engines are programmed to focus on the topic of the search query, picking keywords from long search queries and ignoring anything that is not necessary. But what if users want to search for something without typing in keywords?

Search engines have programmed their artificial intelligence to provide new ways to search. It is now possible to search for pictures using an image. To do this, search engines use **image-recognition** technology. This method of searching is called a *reverse image search* and uses artificial intelligence to 'view' the image and decide what the image is of.

How reverse image searches work

From the web browser, select 'search by image'. After pasting or uploading the file of an image into the browser, a selection of similar images and links to relevant web pages will appear.

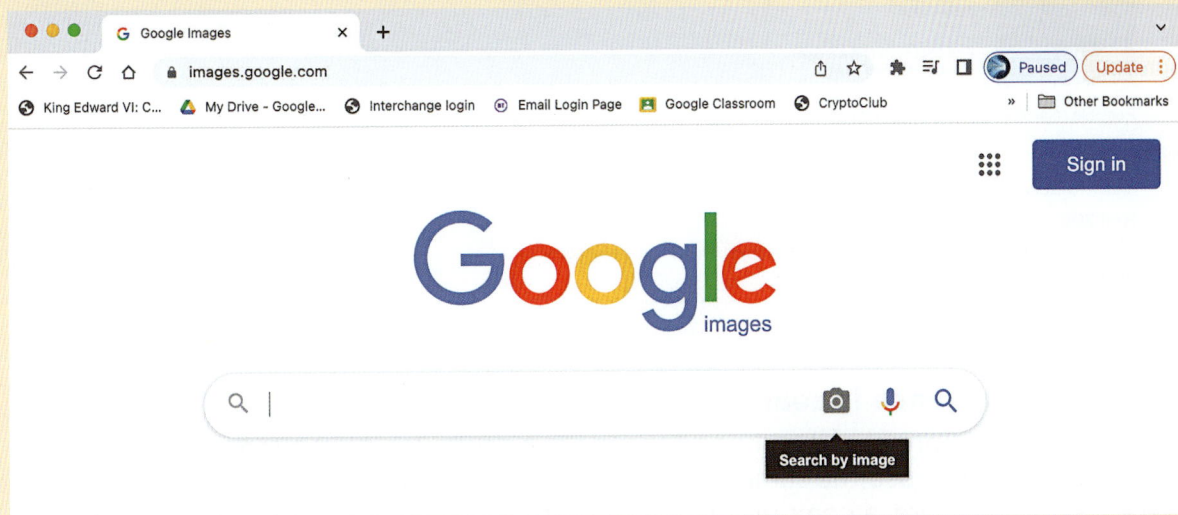

When a user uses a **digitised image** to search, the image gets compared with billions of other images in the database. The computer looks at distinctive points, colours, lines and textures and compares what it 'sees' against billions of other images in its database. When similar images are found in the database, these are returned to the user.

In the example below, an image of a helicopter was uploaded. The reverse image search identified that the image was a helicopter and even managed to identify the exact make and model, a 'Bell 206'.

There are an estimated 5.6 billion searches using the Google search engine per day, which means Google has vast amounts of data for its AI systems to learn from. In the case of the helicopter, Google has automatically catalogued images similar to the helicopter image that was provided for the reverse image search. Gradually, search engines get more and more accurate, learning from previous searches. In this case, Google would learn only to return images of helicopters, as that is what the user is looking for.

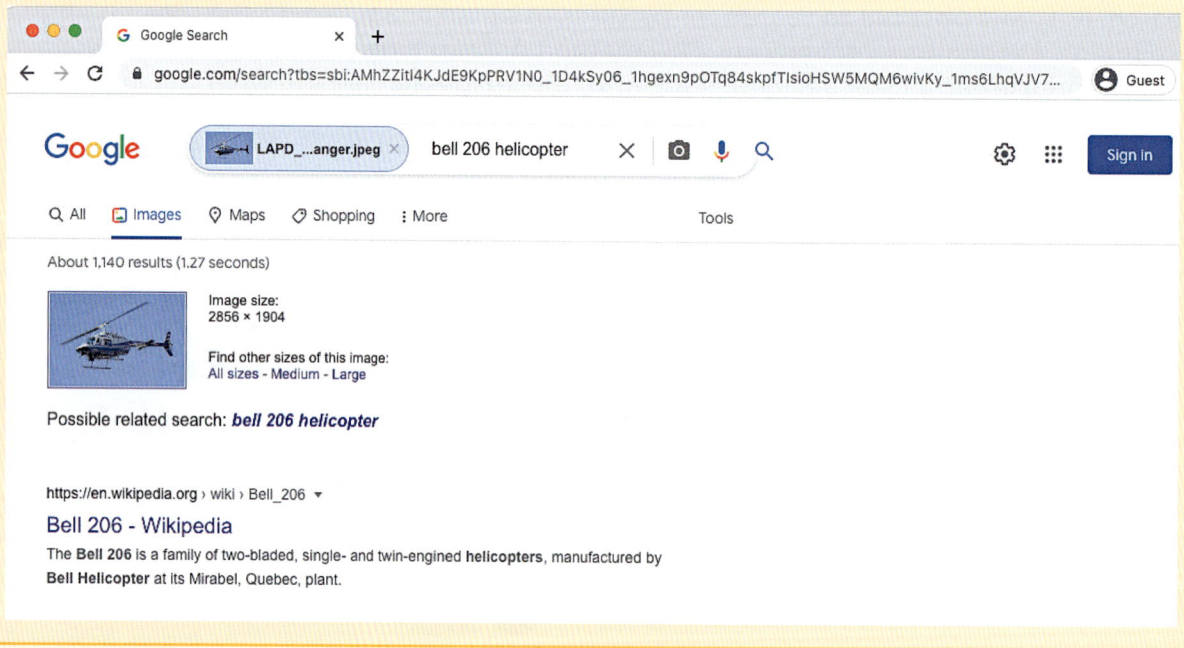

Artificial intelligence in searches

AI technology is improving rapidly, and the more people use AI, the more accurate it gets. Search engines use the same machine-learning technology as shown in the example on the next page. Here, a computer has learned to match images drawn by the user with images that have been drawn previously by other users.

You were asked to draw giraffe

You drew this, and the neural net recognized it.

It also thought your drawing looked like these:

Correct match	2ND closest match	3RD closest match
giraffe	shovel	flamingo

In the example above, the website challenges the user to draw a picture (a giraffe) and the AI in the program tries to work out what it thinks the user's picture looks similar to. As the user was drawing a giraffe, the machine learning and **neural networks** (a type of machine learning designed to mimic the way the human brain works) were looking back at all of the other users who drew a giraffe to try to find examples where the other users were drawing a similar item.

Search engines are making use of image recognition to improve the results they can offer to users in their searches, but also to offer new ways to search.

KEYWORDS

image recognition: computers identifying similarities in lines, colours, textures and shapes of an image in an attempt to identify objects

digitised image: a computer representation of an image, often in file formats such as JPEG, GIF, PNG or TIFF

neural network: a type of machine learning designed to mimic the way the human brain works

---

DID YOU KNOW?

Machine-learning technology has allowed new types of apps to be made, for example an app that allows users to take a photo of something, which then identifies the object from the picture.

Practise

1 Open the file **Reverse Image Search World Tour.docx** provided by your teacher.
   - Find the location of as many images as you can.
   - For each image, perform a reverse image search and complete a row in a table like the one below, for example:

Image name	Image	Location
Image 1		Colosseum, Rome, Italy

2 Explain to your partner how AI has improved the way that search engines work.

Go further

This flowchart shows a basic example of the Caesar cipher algorithm, used for encryption of messages.

1 Look at the algorithm, used to encrypt and decrypt messages sent.
   - In pairs, copy the flowchart and annotate it to show what each part of the algorithm does.
   - Explain to your partner in less than one minute how this algorithm works, from start to finish.
   - If plaintext = 'CHALLENGE' and shift = 2, what would be the output on the flowchart?
2 Create your own flowchart algorithm for the Caesar cipher.
   - Your flowchart should allow a user to input their name in plaintext.
   - Any inputs will be shifted by five to the right.
   - When completed, your algorithm should output the word 'ENCRYPTED', followed by the cipher text.

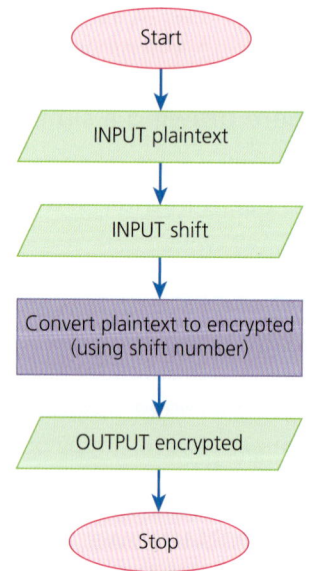

Start
↓
INPUT plaintext
↓
INPUT shift
↓
Convert plaintext to encrypted (using shift number)
↓
OUTPUT encrypted
↓
Stop

Challenge yourself

Your challenge is to investigate the IP addresses of the devices that you use. For this task, you should gather any devices together that you have easy access to. This could include laptops, PCs, mobile phones and tablets.

If you are in class and you do not have access to more than one device, you should swap computers with someone else in your group and find the IP address of their computer. You should amend the table below if required.

1   Copy the table below and add a row for any other devices that you have access to. Leave the IP address column blank.

Device	IP address
Mobile phone	
PC	
Laptop	
Tablet	

Finding the IP address of devices

There are a number of ways to find the IP address for your devices. The appropriate method will depend on what **operating system** your device uses.

Mobile phones and tablets

The IP address of these devices can usually be found by visiting `Settings > Network Settings > Wi-Fi Networks > Click your Wi-Fi network`.

Mac computer

Go to `Settings > Network` then click on the `Currently Connected` network.

Windows

To find your IP address on Windows, move your mouse pointer over the network icon in the task bar at the bottom right of the screen and click `properties`.

2   Find the IP address of each of your devices and complete the table.

Final project

Look back at page 83 to remind yourself of the Scenario at the start of this unit. Your task is to create a presentation to collate information about how certain technologies work. The information in your presentation will be used on the news page for the technology website.

1 Open the file **Final Project.pptx** provided by your teacher. Use this file to create your presentation, following the criteria from the technology company below.

The requirements of your presentation are:

Slide 1

a Explain how somebody could use Bluetooth, Wi-Fi and cellular data (4G and 5G) to connect their mobile device to the internet to access a web page.

b Describe when it may be better to use 5G than 4G and explain why.

Slides 2–3

a Explain what IP addresses are, how they work and what they are used for.

b Explain the structure of a URL and why we use URLs to locate web pages.

Slides 4–5

a Explain two ways that show a web page is secure and how to find information on the security certificates of a website.

b Explain how data can be transmitted securely using encryption, what this is and why it is important.

c Outline the reasons why errors can occur in data transmission.

Slides 6–8

a Explain how a search engine categorises data (selects keywords from a search query).

b Explain how AI is used in search-engine results.

c List the steps that a computer takes when using AI to match images.

d Outline another way in which AI is used, apart from search engines.

---

2 Check that your presentation has covered all the requirements outlined above. Make sure that it explains the technologies clearly. You could add diagrams or images to the slides.

Evaluation

1 Swap presentations with a partner and read each other's content. Add comments on each slide as follows:
   - Does it cover all of the requirements?
   - Is the content easy to understand?
   - How could the presentation be improved?
2 Open your presentation and read the comments left by your partner.
3 Make a list of recommendations to improve the information on the presentation. Apply some of the recommendations to your presentation.

What can you do?

Read and review what you can do.
✔ I can explain how IP addresses work and are used.
✔ I can explain what the structure of a URL looks like and how it is used.
✔ I can explain how DNS enables users to access websites on their devices.
✔ I know the different ways in which devices transmit data and can explain the difference between the networks.
✔ I can explain how errors occur in data transmission and apply ways to check that a message is sent correctly.
✔ I can explain the use of encryption to keep data safe during transmission.
✔ I can encode and decode messages using a cipher.
✔ I can explain how to check if a website is secure.
✔ I can find information on the security certificates of a website.
✔ I can explain how AI is used to improve the output of search-engine results.
✔ I can explain the uses of AI in internet searching and other applications such as image recognition technologies.
✔ I understand that a web browser is a type of application software.

Have you or your family ever needed to analyse a large amount of information or data to help you make a decision or solve a problem?

Discuss the following with a partner:
- What was the situation where you had a large amount of data to **analyse** to help you solve a problem?
- Give some examples of the data you needed to analyse.
- When you collected all of the data, did you carry out any calculations or extra processing to help you make your decision?

It can be difficult to make decisions using a large amount of data. Computer applications can be used to create a **model** of the problem you are trying to solve. Doing this helps you to understand the data. Once you understand the data, you can easily use it to make decisions.

In this unit, you will use Microsoft Access (a database application) and Microsoft Excel (a spreadsheet application) to select and use data to help make decisions.

KEYWORDS

analyse: examine something in detail to ensure you fully understand it

model: a computer application that replicates a real-life environment, where data is changed to see what happens; simple models can be built in spreadsheet software

Learning outcomes

In this unit, you will learn to:
- explain what is meant by a data model
- identify a range of real-life scenarios where data models and simulations are used
- describe how spreadsheet and database applications can be used to model real-life scenarios
- evaluate the layout of a data capture form to decide if it is an effective model and easy to use
- write rules for applying conditional formatting in a spreadsheet and in database applications to highlight important data
- explain why a primary key is needed in a database table
- identify an appropriate field to use as the primary key in an existing database table
- amend the structure of a database to include a primary key
- use criteria such as > or < to search a pre-existing database for useful information
- describe how data is used to model scenarios in a range of industries.

Warm up

In pairs, discuss the **data** you would need to collect to organise a student end-of-year party. Imagine that you have a **fixed budget**.

Think about the data you would need to collect. Create a mind map to describe the data by adding questions about the details you will need to collect:

- **Venue:** How much does it cost to hire the venue? What date is the party? What time is the party? When should the party finish?
- **Guests:**
- **Food and drink:**
- **Entertainment:**

Note your ideas on the mind map.

Discuss the following questions with a partner. Add your ideas for each question to the mind map:

- What other things do you need to consider when you are organising a party?
- What calculations are needed to make sure you stay within budget?
- What software application could you use to help you analyse your costs?
- What software application could you use to help you keep track of invitations and who will attend?

SCENARIO

Your school wishes to host a gaming competition to help raise funds to purchase new portable digital devices for students in your school; the target is $5000.00. As part of the fundraiser, the school is also planning on hosting a **meet and greet** with a gaming celebrity as well as selling **merchandise** in advance of the day.

The main organiser has started to create a database to hold the usernames and some personal details of all of the competitors so that they can match gamers to the correct competition levels.

The event is going to take place in four weeks and the organiser has asked for your help.

Your challenge is to help the organiser plan the event. You will need to help them complete the **database** they need to use to collect and store competitors' details and show them how to use the database to organise competitors for different competitions.

They also need your help using a **spreadsheet** to keep track of profits and losses in the sales of competition merchandise.

KEYWORDS

data: raw facts and figures

fixed budget: a fixed amount of money available to complete a task

meet and greet: an event where members of the public are able to meet famous individuals

merchandise: items that can be bought at events

database: a computer application that is used to organise data that can then be stored, processed and accessed electronically

spreadsheet: a computer application that uses rows and columns to organise data and carry out calculations using that data

DID YOU KNOW?

Database applications are more common than you realise. For example, each time you use an internet streaming service (for example, to watch a film or play an online game) you are accessing a large database that generates lists of games, TV shows and films for you to watch or play.

Do you remember?

Before starting this unit, you should be able to:

✔ design a spreadsheet and a database to collect, organise and process data correctly

✔ identify the data required in a problem to solve a data-processing task

✔ design and create a single table database for storing data in an appropriate format

✔ select appropriate data attributes for each of the fields in a database application

✔ design a form for collecting data that is to be stored in a database

✔ use the search facility to retrieve data from a database

✔ design a spreadsheet that can be used to store data and carry out calculations on the data using mathematical symbols and some functions such as SUM and AVERAGE

✔ use cell ranges in a spreadsheet formula

✔ give examples of where data is collected and used to solve problems in different applications.

Before starting this unit, you will need to install the following software on your own personal device (or use a similar database and spreadsheet software application):

● Microsoft Access
● Microsoft Excel

Data models, simulations and real-life scenarios

Learn

Computer models are representations of real-life situations created using software or specially designed programs. In a computer model, data is used to represent the real-life situation. Rules that link the data are coded using **formulae** and programming instructions.

Models keep track of the **factors** that represent a real-life scenario. For example, when trying to decide whether you can buy something in a shop, one of the factors to consider is how much money you have. Simple models can be created using applications such as spreadsheets. The factors inside the model are represented using spreadsheet labels and data. The links between the factors are represented using formulae. For example, we could create a model to show the costs of organising a birthday party:

	A	B	C	D	E
1			**Birthday Party Costs**		
2					
3	**Party Budget**		$100.00		
4					
5	**Item**	**Quantity**	**Price Each**	**Cost**	
6	Pizza for 10	2	$12.00	$24.00	
7	Cupcakes for 10	2	$13.00	$26.00	
8	Bottle water for 10	2	$5.00	$10.00	
9	Party Balloons (Pack 40)	1	$5.00	$5.00	
10	Party Hats (Pack 20)	1	$5.00	$5.00	
11	Party Cups (Pack 20)	1	$4.00	$4.00	
12	Party Napkins (Pack 20)	1	$3.00	$3.00	
13	Birthday Banner	3	$3.00	$9.00	
14					
15					
16			**Total cost**	$86.00	
17			**Still to spend**	$14.00	
18					

Can you list the factors used in this birthday-party model? What formulae are used to link the factors in this model? Think carefully about how the cost of individual items, total cost and still to spend would be calculated.

Do you remember how to create formulae that use SUM and AVERAGE to calculate the SUM (total) and AVERAGE of a list of numbers automatically in a spreadsheet application?

The spreadsheet below uses the average function to calculate each student's Average score in Tests 1, 2 and 3.

How could this be changed to calculate their total score in Tests 1, 2 and 3?

F2 | =AVERAGE(C2:E2)

	A	B	C	D	E	F	G
1	Firstname	Surname	Test 1	Test 2	Test 3	Average	
2	J	Allen	56	76	39	57	
3	J	Kumar	55	72	46	58	
4	P	Huang	62	67	44	58	
5	R	Ali	63	78	51	64	
6							

Databases can also be used to model real-life situations. In a database model, a table is used to model important data about a situation. The data relating to the model is organised under **field headings**. For example, in the image below, which shows part of a database used to represent a group of students who are entering a computer-gaming competition, these are username, password, email, and so on.

Registration Data				
Username	Password	Email	Age	Date Joined
student001	9PHKJHYT7	student001@school.com	11	09/09/2021
student002	3EDGFBNA6	student002@school.com	12	15/09/2021
student003	9LKNAJGK6	student003@school.com	13	10/09/2021
student004	4DFAECHY7	student004@school.com	11	07/09/2021
student005	2APFGBET6	student005@school.com	11	03/09/2021
student006	5MAOEJHD4	student006@school.com	11	17/09/2021
student007	4ALKEBFU8	student007@school.com	12	08/09/2021
student008	9JHYTABG6	student008@school.com	13	09/09/2021
student009	3EDASJHB8	student009@school.com	11	15/09/2021
student010	2QDRCHYT7	student010@school.com	12	25/09/2021
student011	4SSJYTFV6	student011@school.com	12	29/09/2021
student012	8ASLKIJH7	student012@school.com	13	25/09/2021
student013	5CDENHYF8	student013@school.com	11	03/09/2021
student014	9JHWGYTV5	student014@school.com	12	09/09/2021
student015	7GHTYAKH7	student015@school.com	13	24/09/2021

> Discuss in a small group any additional factors (data items) you think should be represented in this data model. Think carefully about what the data model might be used for; this will help determine what data is required in the data model.

Databases and spreadsheet applications can be used to create complex models of real-life situations. Databases and spreadsheets use words, numbers and formulae to represent a real-life scenario, such as the students participating in a gaming convention. **Simulations** are more complex models than those created using databases and spreadsheets. Simulations will often use complex **graphics** to help represent the real-life situation they are modelling. Simulations allow the user to see a visual representation of a scenario, for example a gaming simulation that the user can interact with.

Here's a reminder about the different ways in which models and **simulators** can be used:

Medicine and healthcare

Medical staff collect a wide range of data about patients (for example, data about a patient's age, symptoms, current medication). This can be used with specialised databases to help diagnose patients' illnesses. Using digital models in this way means doctors can collect and analyse a huge amount of data quickly to help decide what treatment a patient might need.

Training

An example is training a pilot. Trainee pilots are placed in simulators that look and feel like a real aeroplane. They can interact with the aeroplane controls to complete tasks such as take-off and landing in different weather conditions. This helps to ensure that the trainee pilots and their instructors are safe and there is no danger to life or to an expensive aeroplane.

Scientific experiments

Scientists use data models to help them make predictions, such as how changing temperature might affect a nuclear reaction.

Weather and climate

Modelling is used to assess the impact of climate change or changes in weather patterns. Weather-forecasting models use complex formulae to help predict how weather patterns will change over time. Data is collected from all over the world and from space and fed back into the models to help make predictions.

Business

Businesses can use data collected over a long period of time to identify patterns in sales of items at different times of the year. Using this data, the businesses are then able to make predictions about how stock levels will change at certain times of the year. This helps them make sure that they have the correct number of items in stock to meet demand. For example, in summer months most stores will know that they need to increase their stock of bottled water and sun-protection cream.

Data models and simulations are used to represent real-life situations such as flying an aeroplane. Data models use data to represent the scenario while simulations use a large amount of data and complex graphics. All of the data used to create data models or in simulations is stored in a database. Simulations tend to be very complex and can have many advantages and disadvantages:

Pros of simulations	Cons of simulations
Using a simulation for training can help avoid loss of life	Expensive to produce
Lots of different situations can be modelled	Too many factors for all outcomes to be considered
Cheaper than using the real equipment	

KEYWORDS

computer models: computerised representations of real-life situations created using software or specialised software applications

formulae: mathematical calculations expressed with letters

factors: the key data items represented in a data model

field heading: a word or phrase used to describe the contents of a field in a database

simulation: a computer model that can predict the outcome of a real-world system or scenario

graphics: the use of images to illustrate a real-world situation

simulator: software to simulate a real-world application

Practise

1 Create an **infographic** to show how databases and spreadsheets can be used to represent real-life situations and how they might be used to help with training, decision-making or even designing products.
   - Copy the infographic outline on the next page.
   - Expand your infographic to include three examples of applications where databases can be used to help with training, decision-making, designing products or in some other way.
   - Add more detail to your infographic to include examples of where spreadsheets could be used to analyse data to help with training, decision-making or designing products.

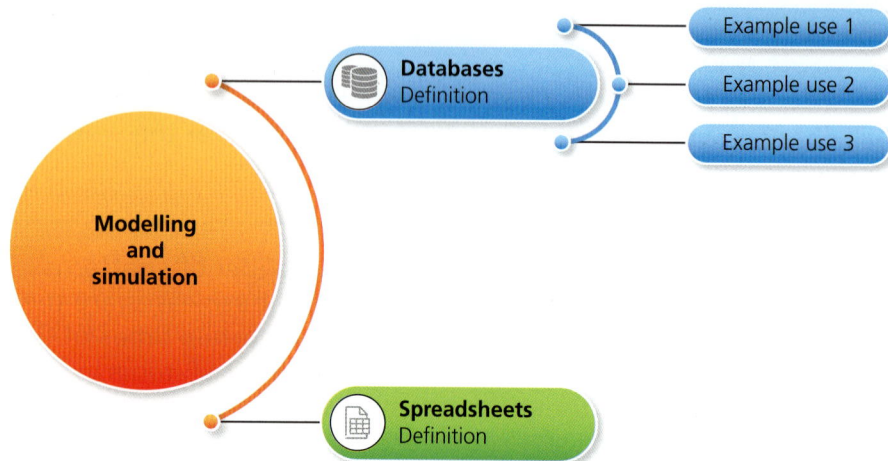

2   Carry out some research into the use of simulations and how they are used in real-life situations.

-   Discuss your findings with a partner and then expand your infographic. Add a new strand that has the title 'Simulations'. The new section of your infographic should be shaded a different colour from the other two.

-   Expand your infographic to include three examples of applications you know of where simulations can be used to help with training, decision-making, designing products or in some other way.

3   In a small group, discuss some of the ways in which businesses and other organisations could use data modelling to help make decisions in the following scenarios:

-   modelling supermarket queues
-   modelling the design of a new car for car-safety tests
-   simulating the impact that reducing pollution has on climate change
-   modelling traffic flow on a busy road with new traffic-control systems.

-   Create an infographic to show how data modelling and/or a simulation can be used in one scenario.

-   Use your infographic to illustrate the advantages and disadvantages of data modelling or a simulation in that scenario.

4   Discuss the following questions with a partner:

-   How could the gaming competition organisers use a database to model the competition entry?

-   Can you think of any other ways they could make use of a database?

-   How might the gaming competition organisers use a spreadsheet application to model the sales of merchandise at the event?

5   If the gaming competition organisers decided to include a simulation game in the competition, do you think this would make the competition more appealing? Why?

KEYWORD

infographic: a chart or a diagram that represents information in a visual way

Spreadsheets: Using Microsoft Excel

Learn

MS Excel is one example of a spreadsheet application. Spreadsheets such as MS Excel can contain worksheets that are divided into rows and columns. The rows and columns in a spreadsheet are identified using numbers and letters.

Spreadsheets are used mainly for applications that require a lot of calculations to be carried out quickly.

Spreadsheet models start out as a table of words and numbers. They become more complex data models when you add **formulae** to link the data in the model. This can help the user see patterns in the data.

Worksheets in a spreadsheet are divided into boxes called **cells**. Each cell can contain text, numbers or a formula. Formulae can then be used to enable the user to carry out calculations involving other data items in the spreadsheet.

The letters and numbers along the top and side of the spreadsheet are used to identify each cell. For example, cell D3 is coloured bright blue in the spreadsheet shown below. When the column letters and row numbers are used to identify a cell this is known as a **cell reference**.

> A formula can be added to a spreadsheet cell by clicking on the cell and typing the formula into the **formula bar**.

> In a spreadsheet, it is also possible to select more than one cell in a group. In the yellow shaded area of this spreadsheet, cells F5 to F8 have been selected.

A formula can be entered into an area of the spreadsheet called the formula bar. All formulae in a spreadsheet must start with an = sign. After the = sign, the formula can contain combinations of numbers, cell references and mathematical symbols. Formulae can be used to perform calculations on individual cells or a **cell range**. Formulae can also include some **built-in functions**, which are designed to provide the user with a quick way of carrying out common processing tasks.

Some of the most common spreadsheet functions include the **SUM** and **AVERAGE** functions.

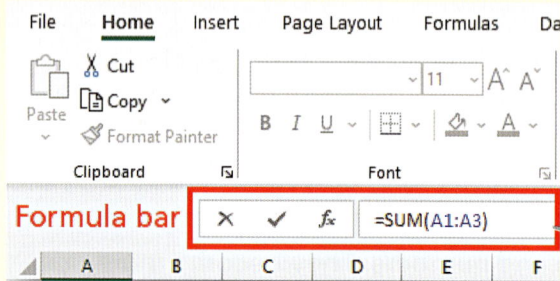

Formula bar — ✗ ✓ *fx* =SUM(A1:A3)

Discuss with a partner:

How would you amend this formula if you wanted to calculate the total of cells B1 to C11? Can you think of another way of performing this calculation?

How would you amend this formula if you wanted to calculate the average of the data stored in cells A1 to A10?

The formula shown above will automatically calculate the SUM (total) of the data stored in cells A1:A3.

In the spreadsheet below, a formula has been used to calculate a student's average score in three tests.

The formula shown in this example calculates the average value of the data in all of the cells between cells C2 and E2. Note how the formula starts with = and contains the cell range C2:E2.

F2 — ✗ ✓ *fx* =AVERAGE(C2:E2)

	A	B	C	D	E	F
1	Firstname	Surname	Test 1	Test 2	Test 3	Average
2	J	Allen	56	76	39	57
3	J	Kumar	55	72	46	58
4	P	Huang	62	67	44	58
5	R	Adeyemi	63	78	51	64
6						

Formulae allow spreadsheets to carry out calculations using values in other spreadsheet cells. A formula will tell the computer what mathematical operation (+, −, /, *) needs to be applied to the cells included in the formula. Some formulae, such as the ones shown above, use special functions to carry out more complex calculations.

You will notice that some of the text (the spreadsheet **labels**) in this spreadsheet is styled differently from the data stored in the spreadsheet. Styling labels in a different format makes the spreadsheet easier to understand. It helps separate the data from the labels.

MS Excel provides a wide range of tools that can be used to change the appearance of text in the spreadsheet. Most of the tools available are the same as those used in word-processing applications. To change the presentation of the contents of a cell, you highlight the cell and click on the correct tool. For example, to format the cells A1 to F1 so that the text is darker than the rest of the spreadsheet, you click on cell A1, keep your finger on the mouse button, highlight all of the other cells from A1 to F1, then click on B. The 'B' button will format the text so that it is displayed in bold format.

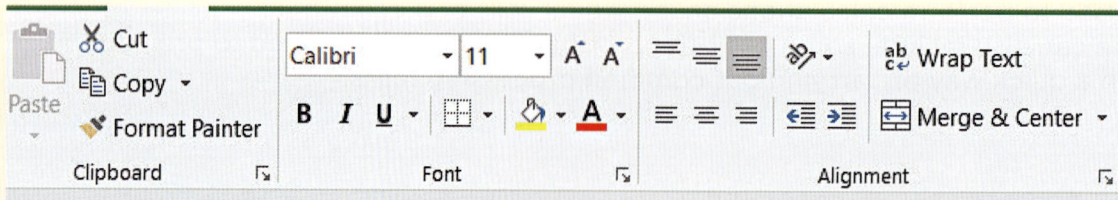

KEYWORDS

formula: a combination of numbers, mathematical symbols, cell references and functions used to process data in a spreadsheet

cell: an area where a row and column intersect and data can be entered

cell reference: a combination of letters and numbers used to identify individual cells in a spreadsheet

formula bar: an area in the spreadsheet window where a formula can be entered

cell range: a group of cells in a spreadsheet, identified by naming the first and last cells in the group, e.g. A1:A5

built-in functions: carry out a set of tasks or operations using data specified by the user; the function will output a result for the user

labels: headings used in a spreadsheet application to aid the understanding of data

Practise

1   Open the file **Introducing Spreadsheets.xlsx** provided by your teacher.

–   Change the format of cells A1:F1 and A2:A5 so that they are formatted in bold.

–   Copy to cell F2 the formula = `AVERAGE(C2:E2)`, which calculates the average for the first student.

–   Use the same method to add a formula that calculates the average score for the remaining students.

–   Can you think of any other ways of calculating the average score for a student in this spreadsheet? Think about how you might add together the students' three scores and then divide the result by 3. Discuss with a partner how you might add this formula to the spreadsheet instead of using the AVERAGE function.

> It is important that you follow the rules for the formula exactly and do not leave out any brackets or symbols. If your formula does not work exactly as you expect it to, check carefully what you have entered against the example shown.

2   The teacher wishes to record the students' total scores in column F instead of the average score. Discuss with a partner how you could use the SUM function to calculate the total scores in this column, instead of AVERAGE.

Change the label text in cell F1 to read **Total** and add an appropriate formula for each student to enable you to calculate their total score.

3   Spreadsheets are often used for modelling and decision-making, especially in scenarios where numeric data and calculations are involved. Now open the file **School Trip.xlsx** provided by your teacher. This spreadsheet is being used by a teacher to keep track of payments made by students each month for an upcoming school trip.

◢	A	B	C	D	E	F	G	H	I	J	K	L	M	N	O	P	Q
1	StudentID	Jan	Feb	March	April	May	Jun	Jul	Aug	Sept	Oct	Total Paid	Balance		Trip Cost	550	
2	1	20	30	150	25	50	25										
3	2	50	45	75	20	15	30										
4	3	20	30	150	75	20	15										
5	4	20	30	20	20	30	50										
6	5	45	50	50	20	30	50										
7	6	100	20	30	45	20	100										
8	7	25	50	50	50	20	30										
9	8	45	20	30	45	45	30										
10	9	20	30	60	45	50	20										
11	10	40	50	25	25	20	30										
12																	

- With a partner, discuss what calculations are needed in columns L and M.
- Highlight cells B2 to M11 and format those cells to represent currency data. To select a different format for the data in a spreadsheet cell, highlight the cells, then right-click and select `Format Cells ...` Then select `Currency`.
  Select the correct currency, for example $.
- With a partner, discuss the spreadsheet structure. Are there any additional cells that should be formatted in currency format?

> What about **Trip Cost**? Think carefully about what the value in this cell might be used for.

- Amend the contents of cell L2 to include a formula that will calculate the total of all of the payments made by Student 1 in this example.
- When you are happy with the formula entered into cell L1, you need to copy this formula into cells L2 to L11 so that you can calculate the **Total Paid** for the remaining students.

> We have looked at SUM and AVERAGE formulas so far. Which one is most appropriate for this task?

  - Click on cell L1 and hover the mouse over the bottom-right hand corner of the cell. A small plus sign will appear: this is called a **fill handle**. Keep your finger on the mouse button and drag down to highlight cells L2 to L11. The formula will automatically copy into the remaining cells. You are able to copy the formula in this way because we have used **relative cell referencing** in this formula.

> Remember to include the cells for every month in your formula, even though the students have not made a payment for the remaining months yet!

4 Now calculate the balance remaining for each student. Think about how you could use the value in cell P1 to help calculate the balance remaining for each student:

L	M
Total Paid	Balance
300	✗

Balance = Trip Cost - Total Paid

- Can you add a formula to cell M1 to perform this calculation?

> =P1−L2

- Check that the Balance calculated for Student 1 is correct.
- Now fill this formula down to calculate the balance for the remaining students.

L	M	N	O	P
Total Paid	Balance		Trip Cost	550
300	250			
235	-235			
310	-310			
170	-170			
245	-245			
315	-315			
225	-225			
215	-215			
225	-225			
190	-190			

> The balance calculated for these students is incorrect, e.g. 550 – 235 = 315, not –235.

- The results are no longer correct. Examine the formula to work out what has gone wrong.
  - Using $ in a cell reference in this way tells the spreadsheet not to update the cell reference when the formula is copied. This is known as an **absolute cell reference**.
- Save your spreadsheet.

> Click on cell M3 and look at the formula carefully The formula now reads =P2–L3
>
> Sometimes relative cell referencing is not useful when you are trying to copy formulae. In this example, you want the formula always to point to cell P1 to read the correct cost of the trip.
>
> Update your formula in cell M2 to read =P1–L2
>
> Copy the updated formula into the cells for the remaining students. The correct balance should now appear for each student.

KEYWORDS

fill handle: a square that appears in a spreadsheet cell to let the user know that the contents can be copied and filled into the cells the user drags the fill handle into; when you hover over it the plus sign appears, which is what you click on and drag to replicate the contents

relative cell referencing: a cell reference that will be updated as part of a formula if the formula is copied and pasted into another cell

absolute cell referencing: a cell reference that will not be updated as part of a formula if the formula is copied and pasted into another cell

Modelling tools: Conditional formatting

Learn

Spreadsheet applications allow users to format data using **conditional formatting**. This can be useful if you want to highlight important data.

You could do this in a number of ways. For example, in our school trip model we could set the cells in column M to green if the balance for a student is 0.

> **KEYWORD**
>
> **conditional formatting:** formatting a data item that meets a specific rule

Practise

In the school trip example from the last theme, the teacher might wish to see quickly who has paid all $550.00 towards their school trip. Open your saved copy of the file **School Trip.xlsx**.

- Highlight cells M2 to M11.
- Select `Conditional Formatting` from the Home Tab, then select `Highlight Cell Rules` and set the cell rule to be equal to 0, and select the `Green Fill` formatting option.

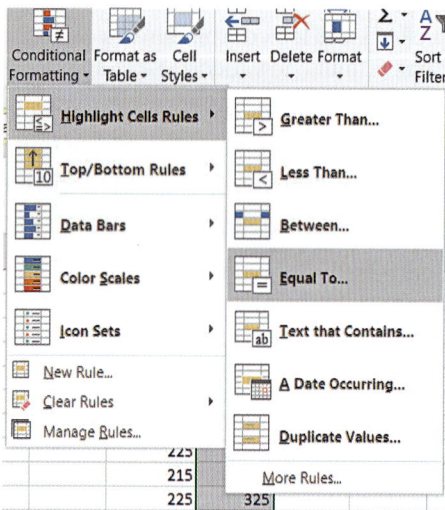

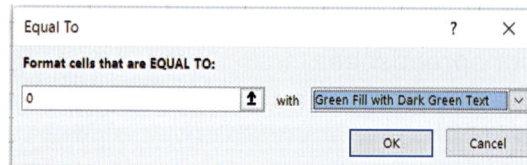

- Nothing should happen just yet. Add the following payments for Student 1 in the months July to August.

50	50	100	100

- Add additional payments for the remaining students for the months of July to October, so that some have not yet paid the full balance of the trip.

> Do this by increasing payments already recorded for some students.

- Test your spreadsheet and conditional formatting now that some students have paid the entire balance of their trip.
- Now change the overall cost of the trip to $600. How does this affect the data highlighted in the spreadsheet?

Databases: Using Microsoft Access

Learn

MS Access is an example of a database application that can be used to store data that represents a real-life scenario.

In MS Access, data is stored in a table structure. The data in the table is organised under special headings called **field headings** and each data item must be assigned a specific **data type**. Each field in the database can be assigned a data type. A data type is used to describe the kind of data the field can store.

Some of the main data types used in MS Access include:

Data type	Use
Text	Used to store data that is a mixture of text and numbers. Normally used to store data that is not used as part of a calculation.
Number	Stores data that may be used as part of a calculation. Different number types are available, e.g. **integer** or decimal number.
Date/Time	Different date and time formats can be selected so that a field can be used to record a date such as 12 October 2021, or a time, e.g. 10:04 pm.
Currency	Money values can be stored using this data type, and different currency formats such as dollar can be selected.
Autonumber	Can be used to assign a number to each record in a database. The computer creates a new sequential number for each record added to the data table. Once a number has been assigned to a record, it cannot be used again, even if that record is deleted.
Yes/No	Data entered into a field can have only one of two values, such as **YES/NO** or **TRUE/FALSE**.

> MS Access automatically sets aside 255 characters for each field that has been set as a text data type. Database developers can set the field size for text fields to make sure memory is not wasted. For example, when you create a text field to store 'Surname' in a database, MS Access will automatically assign this a field size of 255 characters. Most people's surnames would not need 255 characters so when you are making a field to store surnames in a database you could set the field size for the Surname field to 30 characters instead of 255.

In large databases it is important that you are able to identify each record individually in a database table.

The database table shown below was used to store details of the members of a group of students going on a trip. In the database, there are two students with the same first name. When teachers are using the database to look up student details they would use their name to locate each individual student record. In this case, they need to make sure that they have selected the record for the correct student.

Surname	First Name	Stage	Class	DOB
Bhat	Aran	7	7T3	12/01/2010
Alarcos	Julia	7	7T2	09/04/2010
Arias	Gustav	7	7T5	01/06/2010
Gomez	Arianna	7	7T5	03/04/2010
Bhat	Aran	7	7T3	07/12/2010
Bekal	Genevieve	7	7T2	18/06/2010

To help uniquely identify one student from the other, an additional field called a **primary key** is added. The primary key will contain a unique value for each record. This helps make sure that the correct record is selected each time data needs to be accessed.

Many database developers use the autonumber data type when creating a primary key. This means that a new number is automatically assigned to that field each time a new record is added. You will see in the Practise box below how to set appropriate data types for fields in a MS Access table.

Adding a primary key field to the school trip table would mean the table would now have an extra column containing the primary key field, 'StudentID'.

StudentID	Surname	First name	Year	Class	DOB
1	Bhat	Aran	7	7T3	12/01/2010
2	Alarcos	Julia	7	7T2	09/04/2010
3	Arias	Gustav	7	7T5	01/06/2010
4	Gomez	Arianna	7	7T5	03/04/2010
5	Bhat	Aran	7	7T3	07/12/2010
6	Bekal	Genevieve	7	7T2	18/06/2010

Students with the same name could now be distinguished from each other using their StudentID.

KEYWORDS

field heading: a word or phrase used to describe the contents of a field in a database

data type: the different ways in which data can be stored, e.g. integer, string, decimal number

integer: whole number

primary key: a value that is unique for every record in a database

Practise

1 Practise using MS Access with the small school trip database from the Learn box above.
- Open the file **SchoolTrip.accdb** provided by your teacher.
- Double-click on the table in the database, called `Student Table`.

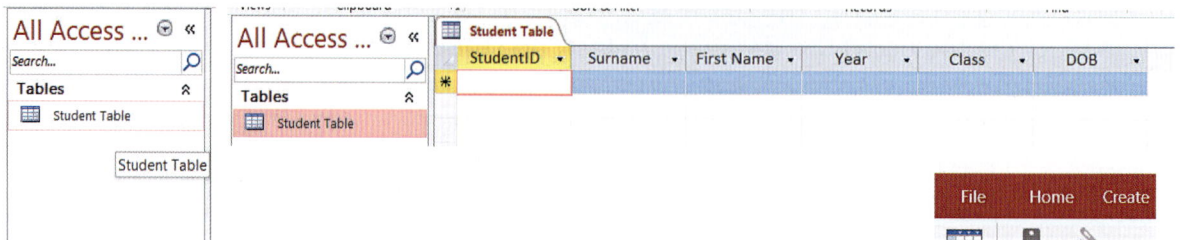

- This will open a blank database table. Click on the **design view** icon. You will see that data types for each field have been set as `short text`. This means that each field can be used to record up to 255 letters, numbers or other keyboard characters.

- In this database, we will use StudentID as a primary key. MS Access provides a special data type that will automatically assign a number to each record in a database. Each time a new record is added this number is automatically increased by 1.
- Click on the field heading 'StudentID' and select the autonumber data type for this field to ensure that this happens with StudentID.
- Click on the 'StudentID' field again. This time you are going to set this field to be the primary key field for the database.
- Do this by clicking on the Primary key icon. **Surname**, **Firstname**, **Year** and **Class** can all remain as 'short text' data types. However, **DOB** should be formatted using the 'date/time' data type.

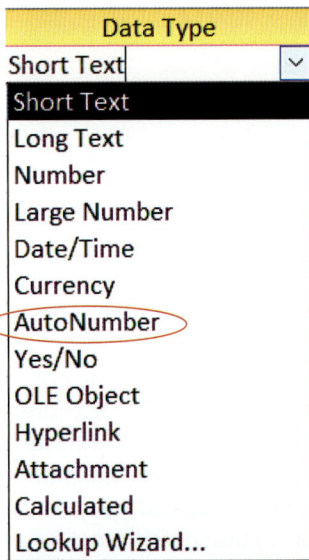

Primary Key

Data Type
Short Text
Short Text
Long Text
Number
Large Number
Date/Time
Currency
AutoNumber
Yes/No
OLE Object
Hyperlink
Attachment
Calculated
Lookup Wizard...

> Can you work out how to edit the data type for the DOB field in the database in design view? If so, select an appropriate data type for this field.

2 You have now successfully edited your first MS Access database table! To add data to the database table you must now exit design view and instead enter **data sheet view**.
- Add the details for each of the students attending the school trip using the table of information provided in the Learn box. Do this by clicking on each cell in turn and adding the students' details under each field heading.
- Save your database by clicking on **File** and then **Save**.

> Note how the StudentID field now appears in the database. Discuss with a partner why you think it is displayed with the word **New)** already under the field heading.

KEYWORDS

design view: a method of viewing content in MS Access where the layout of the database can be changed

data sheet view: a method of viewing content in MS Access that allows the user to edit data

Database models: Setting up your data model

Learn

The database table in the gaming competition Scenario will hold details about competitors. Before the data can be stored, it is important to think about the type of data each field needs to store. In the school trip database (in the previous theme), you updated the database to ensure each field had the appropriate data types (shown below). Each field heading represents one factor in this data model:

Field name	Data type
StudentID	Autonumber
Surname	Short text
Firstname	Short text
Stage	Short text
DOB	Date/Time

You are able to leave Stage (for example Stage 7) as a short text data type as you do not plan to use this field later in any calculations.

Database developers, just like programmers, have to think carefully about the data type they assign to each piece of data stored in a database. This is because the data type selected will affect the type of processing you can carry out on the data item. For example, if you identify a field as being a text data item, you would not be able to carry out calculations using that data item.

Practise

1   Examine the car database example shown below and discuss with a partner the questions that follow. Write down your answers.

Registration	Make	Model	Colour	Mileage	Price
395 BYN	Nissan	Sunny	Red	34,000	$7000
765 GGT	Kia	Ceed	Blue	45,000	$4500
765 MNE	Toyota	Corolla	White	12,000	$8995
223 PWL	Kia	Rio	Black	67,000	$6598
990 UJN	Opel	Corsa	White	78,658	$4656

- Which field would be best used as a primary key and why?
- What data type would you select for each field?
- What would be an appropriate field length for each field?
- What do you think should be the maximum number of characters required for each field?

2 Consider the most appropriate data types for the gaming competition database table called 'Registration Data'.

Username	Password	Email	Age	Date Joined	Gamer Level	Parental Permission
student001	9PHKJHYT7	student001@school.com	11	09/09/2021	Beginner	✓
student002	3EDGFBNA6	student002@school.com	12	15/09/2021	Intermediate	✓
student003	9LKNAJGK6	student003@school.com	13	10/09/2021	Expert	✓
student004	4DFAECHY7	student004@school.com	11	07/09/2021	Expert	✓
student005	2APFGBET6	student005@school.com	11	03/09/2021	Beginner	✓
student006	5MAOEJHD4	student006@school.com	11	17/09/2021	Beginner	✓
student007	4ALKEBFU8	student007@school.com	12	08/09/2021	Intermediate	✓
student008	9JHYTABG6	student008@school.com	13	09/09/2021	Expert	✓
student009	3EDASJHB8	student009@school.com	11	15/09/2021	Expert	✓
student010	2QDRCHYT7	student010@school.com	12	25/09/2021	Beginner	✓
student011	4SSJYTFV6	student011@school.com	12	29/09/2021	Intermediate	✓
student012	8ASLKIJH7	student012@school.com	13	25/09/2021	Expert	✓
student013	5CDENHYF8	student013@school.com	11	03/09/2021	Expert	✓
student014	9JHWGYTV5	student014@school.com	12	09/09/2021	Intermediate	✓
student015	7GHTYAKH7	student015@school.com	13	24/09/2021	Intermediate	✓
student016	3ASFGTRV9	student016@school.com	12	18/09/2021	Beginner	✓
student017	5HGFAWES4	student017@school.com	13	03/09/2021	Expert	✓
student018	2WQSAFRG6	student0108@school.com	12	07/09/2021	Intermediate	✓

– Copy the table structure shown below.
– List the field names from the gaming competition database in the table you have created. The first row has been completed for you.

Field name	Data type	Field length
Username	Short text	30

> Developers use tables like this to identify the data items or fields when they are designing a new database. This is known as a **data dictionary**.

– Place an asterisk (*) beside the field you think could be used as a primary key field. Write a sentence to explain why you selected this field.

3 Edit your table to show the data types and field lengths you would assign to each field. The first row in the table has been completed for you.

4 Use your new data dictionary to help you as you develop the gaming competition database further. In this part of the task, you are going to assign the correct data types and field lengths to the gaming competition database. Follow these instructions:
– Open the file **GamingComp.accdb** provided by your teacher.
– Open the table called `Registration Data`.

- Click to view the table called **Registration Data** in design view.
- Select the most appropriate data type for each field in the database by selecting the data type from the dropdown list beside each field name.

The drop-down list contains the list of all of the data types available in MS Access. We will not use all of these data types in this exercise.

Each time you select a field in data sheet view, additional properties associated with that data type will appear. When you select a text data type, you are able to edit the field length using the properties section.

- Edit the field size where appropriate.
- Set Username to be the primary key field. To do this, highlight the row containing the **Username** field and click on the **Primary Key** icon in the menu bar.
- Save the file.

Collecting user data

Learn

Before data can be added to a database, it must be collected in some way. Often this is done using a **data capture form**.

Data capture forms use labels, spaces, boxes (such as tick boxes) and a range of options for the user to select from. Sometimes example data is provided to make sure the correct data is collected in the correct format for each field in a database table.

> In MS Access, for example, form designers can use text boxes to add additional information to the form. The text boxes can be used to add example data or other instructions to help the user complete the form.

The example below is a data capture form, collecting personal details from users for a database:

Date laid out in a clear order

Personal details

First name [   ]   Surname [   ]

Date of birth [ ][ ] / [ ][ ] / [ ][ ][ ][ ]   Gender   Man/Woman/Prefer not   ← Options make
d d / m m / y y y y   to say (please circle)   user aware
                                                                                         immediately
                                                                                         that an answer
                                                                                         is expected

Other

What are your hobbies?

reading [ ]
walking [ ]
swimming [ ]
athletics [ ]   ← Range of possible
horse riding [ ]   answers is limited
computer games [ ]
music [ ]

Thank you for taking the time to complete this form.   ←   A polite way
                                                             of finishing
                                                             the form

Data capture forms can be used to collect data in many different ways. Some forms may be available only on a computer screen; others may be printed and sent out to be completed by hand. Some may be emailed out and data entered using a keyboard. No matter how the forms are completed, they must be easy to understand. This makes sure that the correct data is collected from the person providing it.

When forms are completed online, the data is returned to the database electronically and automatically added underneath the correct field heading in the database. When a form is completed on paper, the data must be manually entered by copying and typing the data into the database.

A well-designed data capture form should be **user-friendly**. To help with this, it is a good idea to ensure the form contains:

- clear instructions for the user to help them complete the form
- a description stating the purpose of the data collection
- the name of the organisation collecting the data
- a graphic or a logo to help explain the purpose of the form
- correctly sized boxes for each response, appropriate to the question
- a format that matches the database field headings
- examples to help the user complete the form
- options for the user to select a response from (a **multiple-choice format**) where appropriate.

KEYWORDS

data-capture form: a form designed to collect data for a specific task

user friendly: easy to use or understand

multiple-choice format: a question that provides a set of possible answers the user must choose from

Computational thinking – pattern recognition

- Examine the data capture forms below. Both are designed to collect data for a survey that is trying to understand students' favourite hobbies.
- Evaluate the effectiveness of each form. Copy and complete the table shown below. Use the criteria in the Learn box above.

Form 1

Data capture

This form will be used to record your details with our company. Complete this form by answering all questions using the boxes provided. Write all of your answers in capital letters.

Title

Forename

Surname

Address

Home Telephone Number

Mobile Telephone Number

Date of Birth

Are you interested in fashion?

What are your other interests?

Thank you for completing the form.

Form 2

CUSTOMER INFORMATION DATA CAPTURE FORM

This form will be used to help with our parent-survey records for mathematics and statistical analysis. Complete this form by answering all questions using the boxes provided.

Name
Title   Mr / Mrs / Miss / Ms / Dr (Please circle)
Forename   Surname

Address
House no / Name & Road
Town
County
Postcode

Contact details
Home   Mobile

Personal Details
Date of Birth   /   /
            d d   m m   y y y y

Other
Are you interested in fashion?   Yes / No (please circle)

What are your other interests? (please tick 2)
Reading   ☐
Walking   ☐
Swimming   ☐
Athletics   ☐
Horse riding ☐
Computer games ☐
Music   ☐

Thank you for taking the time to complete this form.

Form 1		Form 2	
Areas for improvement	**Examples of good design**	**Areas for improvement**	**Examples of good design**

133

Practise

1   Use what you have learned to design a user-friendly form that could be used to collect data for new competitors in the gaming competition.

Things to consider when designing your form include:
- Should you design a gaming competition logo or use the school logo?
- What title should you include on the form?
- What field headings are you collecting data for?
- Do all of these field headings need to link to data that must be provided by the competitors (for example, some forms include a section with the heading 'For office use only')?
- Should all of the data be included on the form?
- Should any of the fields contain a limit to the number of characters the person completing the form can include in their answer?
- Do any of the fields contain options the user could select from? How might you present these on the form?
- Should any additional guidance be provided to help users complete the form? What should this be and where should it be added?

> Think carefully. Did you set the field lengths to any of the fields in the table?

2   Ask a partner to review and evaluate the data capture form you have designed.
3   Make improvements to the design of your form based on the feedback provided by your partner.

Searching for the answers

Learn

Databases often hold large amounts of data. **Queries** are used to search a database and select data that can be used to answer questions for the user. For example, in the gaming competition database, a teacher might wish to search for students who have not yet paid their deposit for the trip.

Queries use **criteria** to search databases. The criteria are used to provide a set of **conditions** the data must meet for it to be selected when a search is carried out. For example, when searching a database for all of the students in Stage 7 in school, the condition is 'Stage = 7'.

When developers create a database, they need to know in advance the types of searches the database users will want to apply to the data they have. Database designers work with the database users to plan the queries they need.

Criteria for database queries can include text, numbers or **comparison operators**. A comparison operator is an operator that is used to compare something. When a comparison operator is applied to compare two data items, the outcome can only ever be **TRUE** or **FALSE**. Examples of comparison operators include >, <, =.

In the gaming competition database you have a field for age, so you could check the condition 'age>11'. If the competitor's age is 12, this would be **TRUE**, but if the competitor's age is 10 this would be **FALSE**.

Database queries select the correct data from a data table and present it to the end user. For example, here's the student data table from the gaming competition database:

StudentID	Surname	First Name	Stage	Class	DOB
1	Bhat	Aran	7	7T3	12/01/2010
2	Alarcos	Julia	7	7T2	09/04/2010
3	Arias	Gustav	7	7T5	01/06/2010
4	Gomez	Arianna	7	7T5	03/04/2010
5	Bhat	Aran	7	7T3	07/12/2010
6	Bekal	Genevieve	7	7T2	18/06/2010

Some example queries could include:

Query description	Table	Fields	Search criteria for query
List all the details of all the students in 7T2 who are going on the trip	Student table	Student ID Surname First name Stage Class DOB	Class = 7T2
List the name and DOB of all students in 7T3	Student table	First Name Surname DOB Class	Class = 7T3

KEYWORDS

query: a tool used in some applications to allow users to select useful data

criteria: a set of key words, rules or conditions used to search for data items

condition: something that is checked to determine whether it is true or false

comparison operator: a symbol that can be used to compare values, e.g. >, <, =

Practise

You will need a copy of the file **GamingComp.accdb** to complete this task.
Practise designing and creating a query using the table called Registration Data, saved in our gaming competition database. The table below shows the fields and the criteria used to search the registration data table. The query shows students who have not returned parental permission forms.

Query description	Table	Fields	Criteria
List all the details of all the students who have not returned parental permission forms	Registration Data	Username Password Email Age Date joined Gamer level Parental permission	Parental permission = NO

Follow these instructions:
- Open **GamingComp.accdb** provided by your teacher.
- Click on the `Create` tab. Select `Query Design` from the `Queries` group. This opens the query design window.

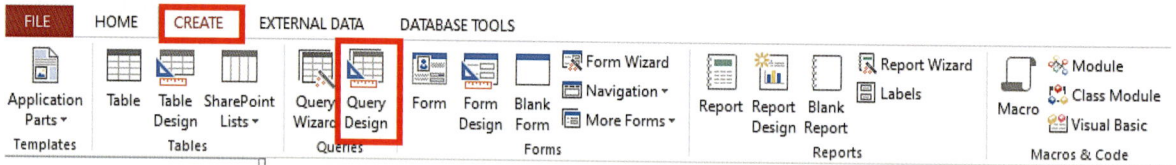

- Click on **Registration Data** and then click on **Add**.
- Click on each field in turn to add them to the query.

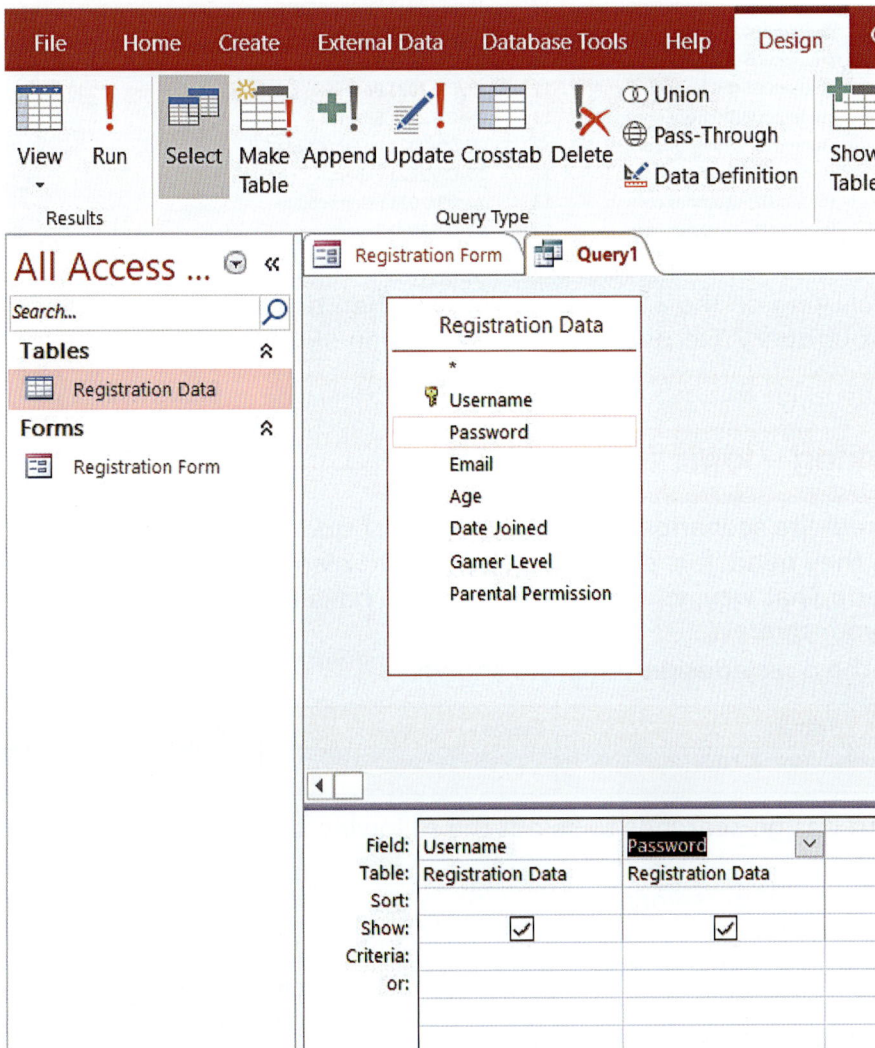

| File | Home | Create | External Data | Database Tools | Help | Design |

View Run | Select | Make Table | Append | Update | Crosstab | Delete | Union | Pass-Through | Data Definition | Show Table

Results | Query Type

All Access ...

Search...

Tables
Registration Data

Forms
Registration Form

Registration Form | Query1

Registration Data
*
Username
Password
Email
Age
Date Joined
Gamer Level
Parental Permission

Field:	Username	Password	∨
Table:	Registration Data	Registration Data	
Sort:			
Show:	☑	☑	
Criteria:			
or:			

- Enter F (for FALSE) into the **Criteria** row under the field **Parental Permission**.
- Select **Run** from the **Design** tab to carry out the actions in the query you have just created.

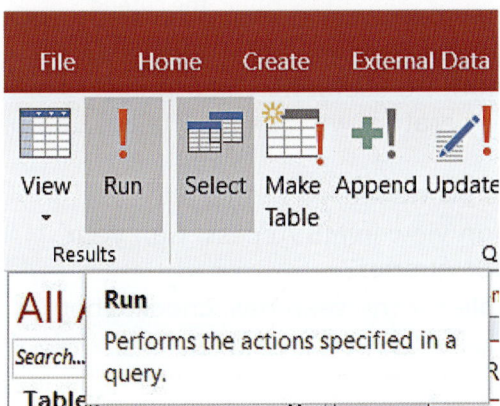

| File | Home | Create | External Data |

View Run | Select | Make Table | Append | Update

Results | Q

All A

Search...

Tables

Run
Performs the actions specified in a query.

● You should obtain the following results:

Username	Password	Email	Age	Date Joined	Gamer Level	Parental Perr
student002	3EDGFBNA6	student002@school.com	12	15/09/2021	Intermediate	✓
student004	4DFAECHY7	student004@school.com	11	07/09/2021	Expert	✓
student005	2APFGBET6	student005@school.com	11	03/09/2021	Beginner	✓
student006	5MAOEJHD4	student006@school.com	11	17/09/2021	Beginner	✓
student008	9JHYTABG6	student008@school.com	13	09/09/2021	Expert	✓
student011	4SSJYTFV6	student011@school.com	12	29/09/2021	Intermediate	✓
student012	8ASLKIJH7	student012@school.com	13	25/09/2021	Expert	✓
student015	7GHTYAKH7	student015@school.com	13	24/09/2021	Intermediate	✓
student017	5HGFAWES4	student017@school.com	13	03/09/2021	Expert	✓
*						

● Save your query by clicking on the `close` icon. You will then be asked to give your query a name. Call your query 'No permission' and click on `Save`.

Computational thinking – logic and evaluation

Databases that model real-life scenarios often require lots of queries to allow users to get the important data they need. It is always a good idea to plan your searches before you begin to create them. That way, you will make sure you have included all of the data that the user needs in your query.

1 Copy and complete the query design template shown.

Query description	Table	Fields	Criteria

Complete the table to design searches to select the following data from the gaming competition database:

– Output the username and password of everyone in the database whose gamer level is intermediate.

– Output the username only of everyone who is older than 10.

2 Open your database from the Practise task above. Examine the data stored in the gaming competition database.

> Remember: think carefully not only about the fields you wish to display in the query results, but also those you need to help you set the criteria.

– Can you think of any additional searches the organisers might find useful as they try to organise the competitions?

– Design some additional searches you think might be useful for the organisers of the competition. Try to use all of the comparison operators we looked at in the Learn box above.

– Create queries based on the designs you have produced.

– Ask a partner to examine your queries in design view in MS Access. Can your partner recreate a design table for each of your queries?

– When your partner has produced a design table for the searches, check whether yours matches it.

Highlighting the important data

Learn

Data models are often used to help organisers and managers make decisions. To help make decisions quickly, the important data must be easy find. To help with this, you can use a feature in MS Access called **conditional formatting** to highlight the really important areas. To do this, you need to set rules so that data that matches those rules is automatically highlighted.

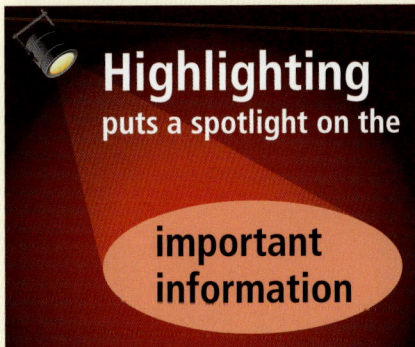

Highlighting puts a spotlight on the **important information**

> In MS Access you can use conditional formatting to highlight data on input forms and output reports.

KEYWORD

conditional formatting: formatting a data item that meets a specific rule

---

Practise

1   The gaming competition organiser wants to highlight the beginner level gamers when they are registering for the competition, as they would like to check that they are familiar with the rules of the competition.

Use conditional formatting in the Registration Form (this form has already been created for you) to highlight any students who are beginner level. This will help give the organisers a quick view of how many beginners they have in the competition.

- Open **GamingComp3.accdb** provided by your teacher.
- Open the item called **Registration Form** by double-clicking on it.
- Display the form in **design** view.
- Highlight the **control** (the text box) in the form where the user will enter the gamer level of the student.

– Click on the **Format** tab.
– Click on **Conditional Formatting** to display the conditional formatting rules manager.

> You can also right-click on the control and select **Conditional Formatting**.

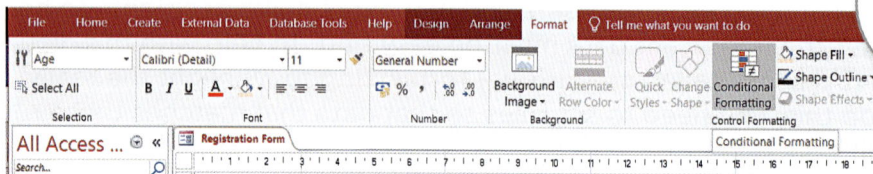

– In the conditional formatting rules manager, click on **New Rule** and set the rule for the gamer level field, as shown.

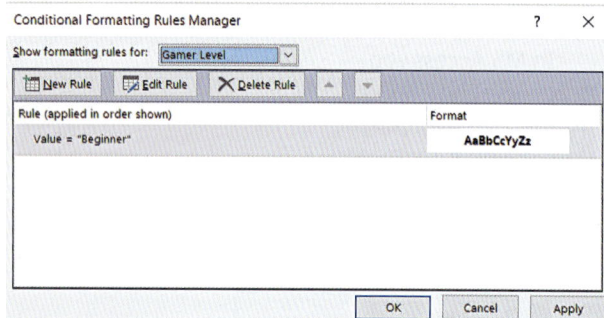

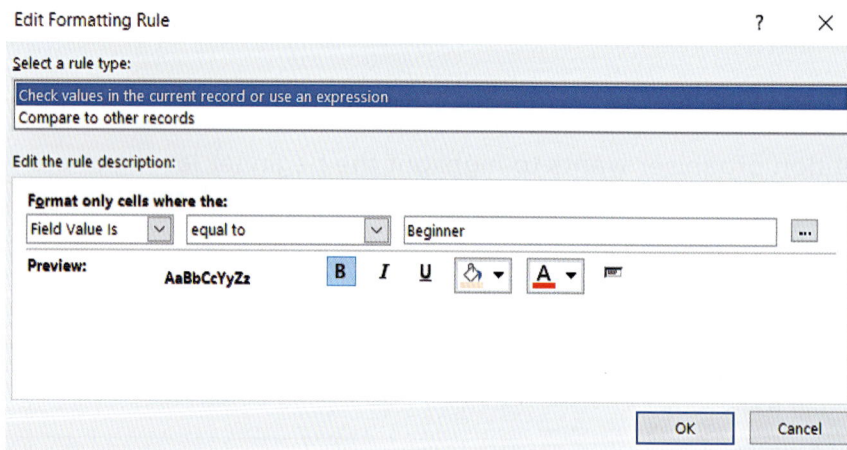

– Click **OK** in the **Edit Formatting Rule** screen and then click **OK** again to return to your form in design view.

2 Save your form and scroll through the records in your form to check that all beginner level registrations are highlighted.

> Change the format to suit your own form colour scheme.

KEYWORD

control: an element on a database input form, e.g. a text box or a label

Modelling methods: Software choices

Learn

Decision-making can be difficult when you have a lot of data to take into consideration. Computer applications such as spreadsheets and databases can help you make sense of large amounts of data. Databases and spreadsheets provide lots of useful tools that can be used to help us organise the data. They can also help us analyse the data and allow us to use it to solve problems. It can be difficult sometimes deciding which application to use!

Here's a comparison:

Database features	Spreadsheet features
• Organises data under field headings and in a table to make it easier to understand • Queries to allow us to search the data to answer questions • Forms to allow us to enter data in a user-friendly way • Primary keys to help identify one data item from another • Data types that can be used to change how data is presented • Conditional formatting to highlight data that meets certain criteria	• Stores data in individual cells • Labels to organise data and make it easier to understand • Data types to improve the formatting of data • Formulae to perform calculations and create links between different data items in a model • Conditional formatting to highlight data that meets certain criteria

> Database and spreadsheet applications can both use conditional formatting to highlight data that meets certain criteria.

Practise

1 Examine each of the scenarios listed below. With a partner, discuss the following questions:
   - What factors do you need to record for each scenario? For example, what data do you need to store?
   - List the field headings you would use to organise the data associated with each scenario.
   - List any queries or calculations you would need to help you to model each scenario.

   ### Scenario 1
   You are creating a data model to record seat bookings in a cinema.

   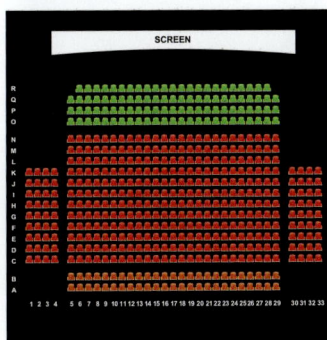

Scenario 2

You are creating a model to keep a record of student performance in a school swimming gala where an award is given to the team with most points.

2   Copy and complete the table below to help you decide which application you would use to model each scenario:

	Spreadsheet or database?	Give a reason for your answer
Cinema scenario		
Swimming gala scenario		

Should you use a spreadsheet or a database for the data model in each scenario? Think carefully. Do you need to perform a lot of calculations? Is the data mainly numbers? If the answer to either question is 'yes', then a spreadsheet may be better.

Go further

You have looked at how spreadsheets can be used to perform calculations on data. Database **models** can also be used to carry out calculations on data. One way of including calculations in a database model is by displaying data in a report and then adding a calculation to the report.

For example **database reports** can be used to produce data summaries with calculations. This helps to give the user of the data a quick overview of important facts and statistics.

The gaming competition organisers have asked you to help them extract some useful data from the competition database. They need a list of usernames and passwords with a count of the number of gamers in each of the levels (beginner, intermediate and expert). Follow these instructions:

1 Open **GamingComp.accdb**.
   - Create a query that contains the data the organisers need to help them to complete this task.
   - Save the query as **GamerLevel**.

2 Create a report to display the results of the query above in a way that will help the gaming competition organiser see how many gamers of each level they have in the competition. Follow these instructions:
   - Click on the **Create** tab and click on **Report Wizard**.

> Queries can be used to select data from a database table without adding criteria into the query design. Think carefully about the fields you need to help you to solve this problem.

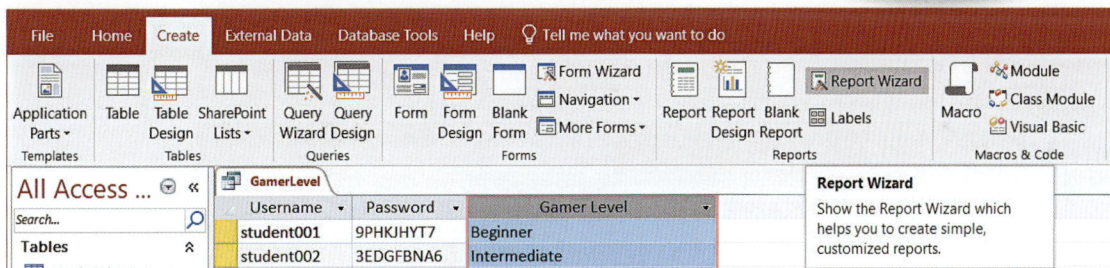

- Select the **GamerLevel** query from the **Tables/Queries** dropdown box.
- Click the double arrow to select all three fields.
- Click **Next**.
- Select **Group by Gamer Level** and click **Next** again.

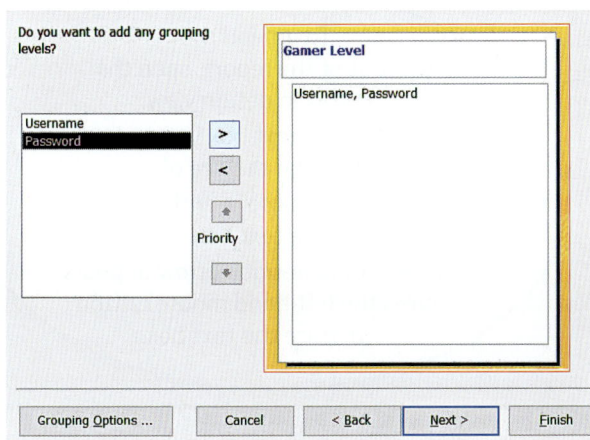

- Click **Next** again (as you are not sorting the data at this stage).
- Select **Stepped Layout** and click **Next**.
- Name the report **GamerLevel** and click **Modify the reports design**.
- Click **Finish**.
- Add additional calculations to the report in design view. Click on **Group & Sort** in the **Design** tab.

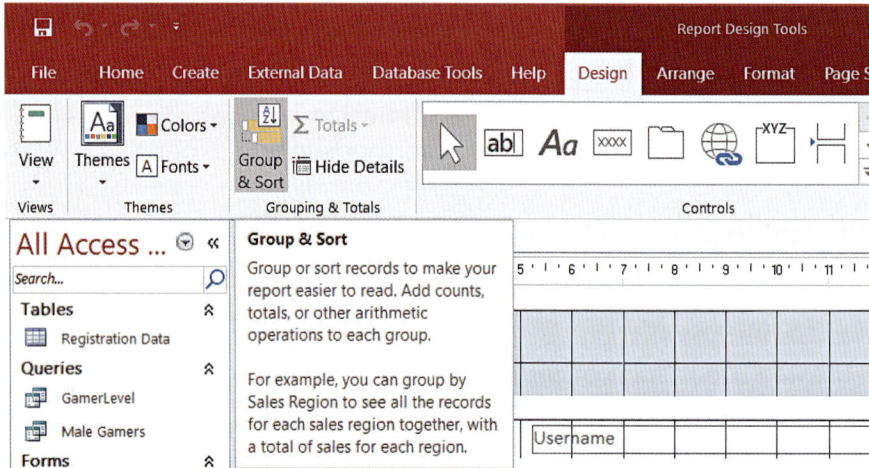

- Click on **More** in the **Group, Sort and Total** box, which appears at the bottom of the report screen, and select the options **Total On – Gamer Level**, **Type – Count Values** and **Show subtotal in group header**:

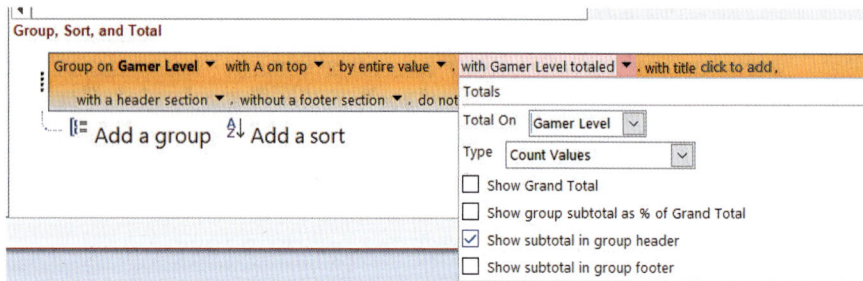

- Change the report to **Report View** to check the results.

3 Can you amend the layout of the report to include an additional text label to explain the totals that have appeared on the report? The data in the report should be displayed in three sections, grouped according to GamerLevel.

Use conditional formatting to highlight important data. For example, if the number entered for each gamer level is <6, use conditional formatting to highlight the number using a red background.

> To amend the layout of the report, open the report in design view:
> Click on any text box you wish to change the size of.
> Place your mouse over the side of the text box.
> When a double-sided arrow appears, press the left-hand mouse button to resize the text box.

KEYWORDS

model: a computer application that replicates a real-life environment, where data is changed to see what happens; simple models can be built in spreadsheet software

database report: a tool within a database used to output data for the user

Computational thinking – abstraction

During the gaming competition, the competition at each level can carry on only if there are more than five competitors at that level. Use what you have learned about conditional formatting in data-entry forms to amend the reports so that the number in the level is highlighted with a red background and black text if there are not enough entrants.

> Remember: before you can add conditional formatting, you will have to view the report in design view; you then need to select the `Format` tab. Think carefully about where on the report you need to apply the formatting.

Challenge yourself

Earlier in this unit, you used a spreadsheet to keep track of pupil payments into a school-trip fund. You then changed the cost of the trip and some of the payment figures to try to make sure that every student paid the trip balance in full.

Changing data in a model in this way is known as *What-If Analysis*. Spreadsheet applications such as MS Excel offer some built-in tools, such as What-if Analysis, to help organisations make decisions.

Another valuable tool offered by MS Excel is *Goal-Seek Analysis*.

- Use the internet to find out more about each of the tools listed below and how they can be used to analyse data in a spreadsheet application.
- Describe what the tools are designed to do. Say how you think the gaming competition organisers could use these tools in a spreadsheet to help them keep track of the funds they are raising for the school. Copy and complete this table.

Tool	What does this tool do?	How the competition organisers could use it
Goal-Seek Analysis		
What-If Analysis		

Final project

Some of the competitors in the gaming competition have asked the organisers whether they will have an opportunity to use simulations in the competition. The organisers have asked you to help them understand the difference between a model and a simulation.

1 Write a short paragraph to explain to the organisers what is meant by a *data model*. Explain the key features of a data model and the advantages and disadvantages of using one.
   - Use an example to show how data models are used in a real-life application you have studied in this unit.
   - Explain how a data model is used in this application to help make decisions.

2 Describe one application where simulations can be used to help model a real-life situation. What are the advantages of using a simulation in the real-life application you have selected?

Database task

The gaming competition organiser has created a data model in the form of a database to help keep track of the sales of both **merchandise** and **meet-and-greet** tickets. They have asked you to help them set up the database so that they can produce some useful data about how the sales have gone so far.

Before you can do this, however, you must amend the database design to ensure that:
- the correct data items have been assigned to each field
- a key field has been correctly assigned to the database table
- the field lengths have been amended so that the database does not take up too much space.

1 Open the file **Sales.accdb** provided by your teacher. Use this file to complete the following tasks:
   - Produce queries to list the student numbers of each person that has purchased baseball caps (as they would like to distribute these to the students at the end of the week).
   - Identify merchandise that has sold fewer than ten items. To do this, open the report called 'Sales'. Edit the report to highlight in red merchandise items where fewer than ten items have been sold.
   - Save your database.

2 Consider additional queries that might be useful to the organisers of the gaming competition. Design the queries using a table similar to the one used on page 135. If you have time, you should also create the queries.

3 Design a data capture form that would allow users to enter data into the table called Orders in the database called **Sales.accdb**.

Spreadsheet task

The organiser needs your help to set up a system that can enable them to make decisions such as:

- how much the meet-and-greet tickets should cost
- how much each T-shirt, sweatshirt and baseball cap should cost.

You have advised the organiser that a spreadsheet would be the best tool for this task.

- Review the key features of a spreadsheet, covered earlier in this unit.
- Write a sentence to explain why you feel a spreadsheet would be best for this task.

The organisers have created a spreadsheet to help them keep track of the data they have collected so far. They need your help developing some of the calculations in the spreadsheet.

3 Open the file **Final Project.xlsx** provided by your teacher.
   - Continue the development of the spreadsheet by adding the data and additional labels shown in the spreadsheet below. (Do not worry about shading your spreadsheet cells in the same way.)

	A	B	C	D	E	F	G	H	I
1	Income								
2	Item	Number Sold	Selling price	Income					
3	Baseball Cap	50	5						
4	T-Shirt (S)	67	6						
5	T- Shirt (M)	34	7						
6	T-Shirt (L)	22	8						
7	Hoody (S)	60	10						
8	Hoody (M)	45	12						
9	Hoody (L)	12	14						
10	Meet and Greet	120	7						
11			Total Income				Funds Raised		
12							Target	5,000	
13									
14	Expenses	Number Purchased	Cost	Expenses					
15	Celebrity Fee	1	500						
16	Hall Rental	1	100						
17	Baseball Cap	200	3						
18	T-Shirt (S)	150	3.5						
19	T- Shirt (M)	100	4						
20	T-Shirt (L)	100	4.5						
21	Hoody (S)	150	5.5						
22	Hoody (M)	100	6.5						
23	Hoody (L)	100	8						
24			Total Expenses						
25									

- Use what you have learned about spreadsheet applications and formulae to add the correct formulae to the cells outlined in red. The spreadsheet cell colours provide a hint as to which cells can have a formula copied and pasted.
- Use conditional formatting to colour the funds green when **Funds Raised > Target** and red when **Funds Raised < Target**.
- A second celebrity gamer will appear; their appearance fee is $300 and 25 tickets have been sold so far. Update the spreadsheet to include this additional information.
- Save your spreadsheet.

> Programmers often write programs that use different arithmetic operators. In this task, think like a programmer to decide on the structure of the formula you need to use in each cell. What other cell references do you need to use? Are there any MS Excel functions you can use? How do you lay out your formula? Remember to make sure that you include all parts of the formula in the correct place. Just like in programming, spreadsheet formulae need to follow a specific layout. Think carefully about this layout before you create your formula.

KEYWORDS

merchandise: items that can be bought at events

meet and greet: an event where members of the public are able to meet famous individuals

arithmetic operator: +, –, *, / and other symbols that can be used for arithmetic calculations

Evaluation

Database task evaluation

1 Ask a partner to review your completed database. Ask them to comment on the following:
   - Will the data-entry form you have designed be user friendly and easy to complete?
   - Have you selected an appropriate field as a primary key field in your database table?
   - Do your queries use the correct criteria with the correct operators (for example < and >) to answer all of the questions outlined by the gaming competition organiser?
   - Have you made effective use of conditional formatting to highlight the data the competition organisers requested?

2 Based on the feedback provided by your partner, make a list of recommendations to improve your database.

Spreadsheet task evaluation

3 Ask a partner to review your completed spreadsheet. Ask them to comment on the following:
   - Have you correctly used conditional formatting in your spreadsheet?
   - Can your partner make any further recommendations for how the spreadsheet could be improved?

4 Based on the feedback provided by your partner, make a list of recommendations to improve your spreadsheet.

What can you do?

Read and review what you can do.
- ✔ I can explain what is meant by a data model.
- ✔ I can identify a range of real-life scenarios where data models and simulations are used.
- ✔ I can describe how spreadsheet and database applications can be used to model real-life scenarios.
- ✔ I can evaluate the layout of a data capture form to decide if it is an effective model and is easy to use.
- ✔ I can write rules for applying conditional formatting in a database application to highlight important data in an input form.
- ✔ I can write rules for applying conditional formatting in a spreadsheet to highlight important data.
- ✔ I can explain why a primary key is needed in a database table.
- ✔ I can identify an appropriate field to use as the primary key in an existing database table.
- ✔ I can amend the structure of a database to include a primary key.
- ✔ I can use criteria such as > or < to search a pre-existing database for useful information.
- ✔ I can describe how data is used to model scenarios in a range of industries.

How often have you used a **digital device** to help you make a decision at home or at school?

In a small group, make a list of examples where you have used digital devices in this way, for example:

- Using the TV listings screen to select a program to watch
- Looking at your phone's calendar to decide when you are free to visit a friend's house
- Asking a **digital assistant** what the weather will be like to help decide on a suitable activity for the weekend.

Have you ever considered how the devices we use in these situations are able to operate the way we need them to? All digital devices require a software application to enable users to interact with them and to allow users to make a decision, solve a problem or complete a task.

In this unit, you will examine how digital devices use components called *logic gates* to help make decisions. You will look at the different types of software used by digital devices and some of the complex programs used to help users in real-life scenarios. You will also explore how some of these software applications work and how they store data in the form of text, images, sound and numbers.

KEYWORDS

digital device: a piece of physical equipment that uses digital data

digital assistant: an electronic device that can be used to help a user complete tasks such as switching on other appliances, controlling heating systems, searching the internet for information or organising music play lists

Learning outcomes

In this unit, you will learn to:

- explain the difference between systems software and application software
- explain what AI means
- describe how AI enables a computer to use information from its surroundings to produce an output
- evaluate the design of a device or an AI system
- explain how AI works in a range of applications
- explain how AI helps automate the completion of tasks in some industries
- explain how image recognition is used in some AI applications
- describe how an analogue image is converted into digital format
- explain what a binary number is and how it represents different data
- explain what a logic gate is and describe what is meant by Boolean logic
- explain how AND, OR and NOT logic gates work in a circuit.

Warm up

Many of the devices you interact with on a daily basis use **artificial intelligence** (AI). But what is AI?

In pairs, discuss the following questions:

- What do you think is meant by the term *artificial intelligence*?
- What does the word *artificial* mean?
- How do we decide whether something is intelligent? Discuss how you would describe intelligence in a person.
- How can you use your answers to the question above to help you decide whether a digital device is intelligent?

> You may want to discuss the meaning of *intelligence* first!

In this unit, you will explore how digital devices use AI to help us with daily decision-making. You will find out how software and hardware work together to create an 'intelligent' device and how these devices help to **automate** actions.

KEYWORDS

artificial intelligence: an area of computing that focuses on creating intelligent computers that can mimic the way humans think and make decisions; a computer system able to perform tasks normally done using human intelligence, such as understanding speech

automate: to reduce human interaction and leave the running of a device to use sensors to determine the output

SCENARIO

Your school has decided to introduce the use of an AI system to help students learn independently. The teachers have produced a very basic design and have jotted down some ideas about how the system will collect and use some data and how the system will operate. They have asked you to evaluate the design and make some recommendations on how to improve the design to make sure that the AI system they are planning on creating can:

- help increase student learning
- make learning enjoyable
- help reduce teacher workload.

Before you can fully evaluate the AI system the school is designing, you need to learn more about AI computer systems.

DID YOU KNOW?

Many people think of AI as being related to robots, but a lot of digital devices and systems in modern homes now use AI. Some examples include smart heating systems, digital assistants and smart fridges. All of these devices use technology known as smart technology.

Do any devices in your home use smart technology?

KEYWORD

smart technology: *SMART* means 'Self-Monitoring, Analysis and Reporting Technology'; technologies that use AI to support their operation

Do you remember?

Before starting this unit, you should be able to:

✔ identify the difference between analogue and digital data
✔ explain why analogue data needs to be digitised to be processed by a digital device
✔ explain some ways in which robots can operate without human interaction
✔ identify some of the advantages and disadvantages of using robots to complete a range of tasks.

Applications and systems software

Learn

All digital devices need **software**. *Software* is the term used to describe the program or instructions that tell a digital device how to complete a task. Software can fall into two main groups:

- Systems software
- Applications software.

Systems software is the software that helps the user run a digital device. Types of systems software include the **operating system** and utility programs. The operating system is the part of the systems software we are most familiar with and it is the most important piece of systems software. One of the main tasks carried out by the operating system is providing a **user interface** between the user and the computer. It allows the user to interact with the computer hardware and other programs or applications stored on the computer. Without the operating system, the computer **hardware** would be useless.

Applications software is software that is used to carry out **user-related tasks**, such as creating a presentation or a party invitation or making a video call. Examples of applications software include apps on your mobile phone, word-processing applications, image-editing applications, internet web browsers and spreadsheet applications.

All of the digital devices we use in our homes require both systems software and applications software to operate correctly.

Some of devices you use in everyday life now require applications software that can include **artificial intelligence** (AI) to allow you to interact with them fully. For example, when asking 'What will the weather be like?' to a **digital assistant**, the microphone records what you are saying and sends it to a cloud-based service that is able to extract key words from what you have asked in order to interpret your request. In this instance, an audio response detailing today's weather forecast is sent back to the device and played through its speaker so that you hear the forecast.

KEYWORDS

software: aspects of a computing device that you *cannot* touch; the programs that run on a device

systems software: software that runs the hardware and software, i.e. the operating system

operating system: the systems software that manages hardware and software on a device

user interface: the way that users and computer systems communicate

hardware: aspects of a computing device that you *can* touch; the physical components of a device

applications software: applications for general or specific tasks

user-related tasks: tasks that are to be carried out by the user of a digital system

artificial intelligence: an area of computing that focuses on creating intelligent computers that can mimic the way humans think and make decisions; a computer system able to perform tasks normally done using human intelligence, such as understanding speech

digital assistant: an electronic device that can be used to help a user complete tasks such as switch on other appliances, control heating systems, search the internet for information or organise music play lists

DID YOU KNOW?

Applications packages such as the Google App Suite, or MS Office, where the applications are part of a larger package, all have similar interfaces, and these are known as integrated applications.

KEYWORD

integrated applications: applications packages such as the Google App Suite, or MS Office, where the applications are part of a larger package and all have similar interfaces

Practise

1 In pairs, discuss the differences between applications software and systems software. Explain why you think computer systems need both types of software.

2 Open the file **Software Knowledge Organiser.docx** provided by your teacher.

 - Complete the knowledge organiser with your own definitions of applications software and systems software.
 - Add examples of applications software and systems software that you have used on a device.
 - Complete the table to show the differences between applications software and systems software.

3 Produce a table with the headings:

 - applications software
 - operating systems.

 Underneath the headings list some examples of applications software and operating systems that you are familiar with.

Use representations of the software icons or images to show the applications operating to help illustrate your table.

AI around us

Learn

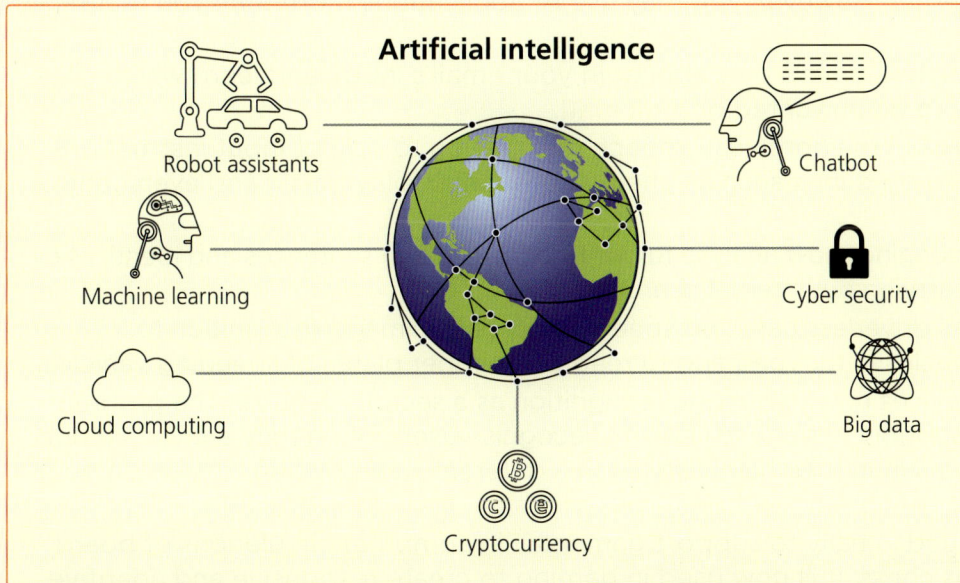

Artificial intelligence

- Robot assistants
- Machine learning
- Cloud computing
- Chatbot
- Cyber security
- Big data
- Cryptocurrency

Artificial intelligence (AI) is technology that allows a digital device to act or think in a way that is similar to a human. This can include tasks such as speech recognition, image recognition, self-drive cars, smart assistants, **search engines** and even social-media monitoring.

The key feature of AI applications today is that the devices designed to use AI are also designed to continue to learn from experiences in the same way humans do. This means that the way an AI device responds to a situation or output may change (improve) over time as the device learns from past interactions.

Devices with AI applications, such as **digital assistants**, become easier to interact with over time, for example:

- The user's voice patterns are more easily recognised over time and instructions understood more clearly.
- Recommendations are made regarding music the user likes to listen to or things the user might like to buy.
- Home locations are identified in the user's car-navigation system and alerts regarding the duration of their journey home are sent automatically when the user starts a journey.

> In pairs, name five devices in the home that use AI. Write a sentence about how a user's interactions with these AI devices may improve over time.

You may think of AI as being related to robots and specialised digital devices used to automate boring tasks, such as deleting unwanted emails, checking the weather or searching the internet. However, you may use AI applications more than you realise, for example:

- **Spam filters** analyse emails that appear in your email's inbox and learn which ones are most likely to be unwanted or **junk mail**.
- Digital assistants in the home use speech recognition to collect input instructions to allow users to do things such as check the weather, play music and even control home heating.
- Internet search engines now analyse full written (or spoken) sentences and identify key words before carrying out internet searches.
- Devices such as driverless cars and speed cameras use image recognition to recognise obstacles in the road and to read the number plates of speeding vehicles.
- Many digital devices now use image recognition as a security feature. The programs developed to support this are still able to recognise users when they are (or are not) wearing glasses, when their hair is styled in a different way or when they are in poor lighting.
- AI was developed initially to support gameplay in computer simulations of board games, such as chess. It is now used in gaming to create responsive and adaptive behaviours in **NPCs** (non-player characters) in computer games. These are characters in the background of a game who are able to interact with the game player.

AI affects the way you live your life, how you work, how you shop and even how you spend your free time. The devices that use AI are improving all the time and researchers are investigating how to develop AI systems that can detect and respond to human emotions.

KEYWORDS

search engine: a website designed to search for content on other websites

digital assistant: an electronic device that can be used to help a user complete tasks such as switch on other appliances, control heating systems, search the internet for information or organise music play lists

spam filter: a computer program that detects junk mail and removes it from an email inbox

junk mail: unwanted emails, sent from organisations to many users at one time

NPC: non-player character; a character in the background of a computer game that the game player can interact with

Practise

1 In a group, make a list of the range of applications you have used at home or in school that use AI to support user interaction.

Describe the tasks you have completed with each device and explain how AI was used to complete the task, for example using a digital assistant to tell you a joke.

2 Identify one device that uses **image recognition**, for example to gain access to a mobile phone. Think about how you use this device and consider how you do not need to look exactly the same each time for the device to recognise your image. Identify the range of ways your appearance can be altered while the AI is still able to recognise you and provide you with access to your device.

3 Some computer games use AI to make gameplay more interesting for the user. For example, as a user becomes more experienced in a game, the game becomes more difficult. Identify an example of a game you have played that uses AI to control user interactions or experiences.

- How was AI used to change your gaming experience in the game you have selected?

- How might AI and image recognition be used to support user interactions in the AI system the school is hoping to develop? Make a list of possible ideas.

KEYWORD

image recognition: computers identifying similarities in lines, colours, textures and shapes of an image in an attempt to identify objects

AI in industry

Learn

AI helps in many areas of industry.

Large amounts of data are collected about individuals daily. For example, data is collected from terms you have used to search the internet, images you have viewed or downloaded, films you have watched and even the URLs of websites you have visited. This data is used by AI systems to build a data model to represent you: your preferences (likes and dislikes). AI systems then use this data to carry out a range of tasks automatically without the need for a human telling them to, for example by automatically targeting you with further suggestions for websites, films and products to buy.

AI relates to the processing of data to make a decision, and also to the control of physical machines to manufacture a new product. When computer systems operate in this way we say they are **automated**. Use of data and systems like this can apply to a wide range of industries and applications; some of these are shown in the table below:

> Think about the various ways in which cookies collect data about users' online activities, the products they are interested in or even local events that might be of interest to them.
>
> AI is able to analyse this data at high speed and select appropriate advertisements for users. Advertising cookies collect information about users from their digital devices.

AI in industry	How AI is used
Businesses ordering products	Sales predictions: AI applications can help businesses make predictions. The data about past sales is stored in large databases and analysed quickly using AI to make predictions about future sales. This means that they order the correct level of goods and there is no waste.
Business and finance	**Fraud** detection: By analysing **consumer** purchases over time, AI applications can quickly pick up unusual activity on a customer's bank card and send a text to the user to alert them. Often this task is automated.
Bookings and online enquiries	**Chatbots**: Chatbots are AI systems that users can interact with in a conversation-like way. One can ask questions and the other will provide answers. These are often used to interact with users online when they first make enquiries about something such as a holiday booking. The user types a question into the chatbot. The chatbot then decides whether the user needs to speak to a human assistant, if it cannot answer the question.
Manufacturing	Many products are now designed using software applications. The applications then use product input to design a computer program to manage the **manufacturing** process of a product without human intervention, for example adding the contents to canned food products and sealing the tin, or putting together the parts to make a new product such as a car or a toy.
Advertising	AI applications can collect data about users from their personal digital devices. This is done using **text files** called **cookies**. Using this data, advanced AI applications can automatically target advertisements for each user the next time they open up a social-media application. For example, how many times have you heard an adult at home say that they were only just talking about something or had just searched for an item online when all of a sudden they start receiving electronic advertisements for that same item?
Healthcare	AI applications are often used for diagnosing illness, research and development of medicines, and remotely treating patients. AI is changing the medical profession. AI applications can collect data about a patient's heart rate, using, for example, **smart watches**, and use this data to alert doctors to problems with a patient's health.

The use of AI applications offers many pros to numerous areas of our lives and industry today. However, there are also some cons, for example:

AI pros	AI cons
• Reduction in errors: for example, using AI in weather forecasting has reduced errors in forecasting and increased accuracy. • Available 24 hours a day: for example, AI can be used automatically to monitor standards of production in manufacturing industries without any breaks. • Increased speed of decision-making: for example, self-driven cars use AI to monitor and react faster to changes in the environment around them than a human driver can. • Helps with research and development in almost all areas of life: for example, AI can be used to predict patterns in health trends and allow for decisions to be made about the location of health centres and hospitals to meet the changing needs of society.	• Expensive to develop: AI applications software is complex and expensive to produce, as are any devices linked to the AI application (they can also be costly to maintain). • Unemployment: AI systems can perform tasks more quickly than humans, and they can work 24 hours a day and do not make mistakes. Some people are concerned that these advantages of AI systems will lead to job losses. • No emotional connection: many people are worried that using AI to make decisions means that decisions are made on facts only and do not take into account people's feelings. For example, AI systems will make recommendations regarding treatment hospital patients should or should not get without considering the patients' personal circumstances.

KEYWORDS

automated: when task is carried out automatically, without human intervention, and based on input and the processing of a set of program instructions

fraud: deceiving someone for financial or personal gain

consumer: an individual purchasing a product or service for their own use

chatbot: software that simulates a human-like conversation via text messages

manufacturing: the process of creating something

text file: a file that contains data in text format only, with no additional images or formatting

cookie: a text file that holds small pieces of data about a user

smart watch: a wearable computer in the form of a watch

trend: a pattern that shows behaviour or data moving in a general direction

DID YOU KNOW?

Devices that are able to respond to human emotions are said to have artificial empathy. If AI devices can be developed to respond appropriately to human emotions, this could have a huge impact on medical and social-care provision in society.

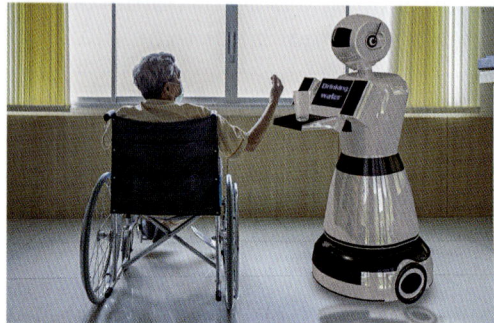

KEYWORD

artificial empathy: the ability of digital devices to respond to human emotion

Practise

1 Use the internet to conduct some research into how automation is used in AI applications. Open the PowerPoint template **AI Around Us.pptx** provided by your teacher.
   – Add information to this template to show how automation is used in:
     – manufacturing
     – retail (shops).
   – For each AI application, consider the pros and cons of using AI in each area. Add your ideas to the template.
2 Research the use of AI applications and automation in medicine. Complete the additional slides on the file to show your findings.
   Present your findings to a small group.

Collecting the input

Learn

When designing any new digital device, developers need to think carefully about:
- how data will be supplied to the device **(INPUT)**
- how the data will be processed **(PROCESS)**
- how results will be sent to the user **(OUTPUT)**.

The diagram below shows how an AI system such as a digital assistant is used to control a lightbulb, represented in terms of INPUT, PROCESS and OUTPUT.

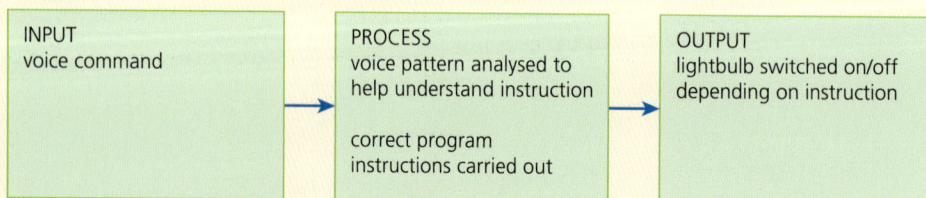

INPUT voice command	PROCESS voice pattern analysed to help understand instruction / correct program instructions carried out	OUTPUT lightbulb switched on/off depending on instruction

AI devices use a range of methods to collect data from the environment for processing, for example touchscreen keyboards or a microphone for entering queries into an internet search engine. Data can also be collected using devices known as **sensors**.

You can see examples of AI systems everywhere today. Many towns, for example, have AI cameras that can be used to detect a build-up of traffic and use this information to amend traffic-light sequences, or that use facial recognition to alert emergency services to the possibility of a crime being committed.

You may have access to AI systems on a daily basis. For example, photos in a mobile phone collect data that can be used to provide information on the local area, such as the location of a bank, restaurant or parking.

Some examples of sensors include:

Sensor	Data it collects	Possible uses
Temperature	Measures change in temperature in the environment	Intelligent body-temperature measurement systems in hospitals, airports and other crowded areas use AI to monitor the temperature of multiple people at the same time. They can combine data collected from the temperature sensor with **facial-recognition algorithms** to identify and then automatically contact individuals who are potentially ill. This can help prevent the spread of illness.
Proximity	Detects the presence of a nearby object	In noisy industrial areas such as construction sites, proximity sensors can be fitted to moving vehicles such as forklifts or trucks. Staff working in the area wear a special tag that vibrates to warn them of an approaching vehicle, helping to prevent accidents.
		Driverless cars use proximity sensors to detect the presence of obstacles in the road. Data feedback to the car's AI system helps calculate the location and size of the object so the system can decide whether the car needs to swerve to avoid the obstacle or whether it has time to stop.
Infrared	Measures the amount of heat being given off by an object	AI is combined with data from infrared sensors on drones. This creates a complex AI system that can fly over remote areas or areas with a lot of trees to collect information about animals being studied, for example to count how many of an endangered species there are in the area.

Sensor	Data it collects	Possible uses
Humidity	Measures the level of water content in air	AI-assisted heating, ventilation and air-conditioning control systems collect data using humidity sensors and use this data to help maintain a comfortable environment inside buildings.
Touch	Measures how much force is being applied to the surface of an object	New technologies are being developed to help provide AI systems, such as those combined with robots, with a sense of touch, similar to humans'. Data is collected using cameras and a gel-like substance inside the sensor. The sensor can be placed at the end of a robotic hand. The data collected helps the system detect how much pressure it is placing on an object to make sure it isn't damaging it when picking it up.

KEYWORDS

sensor: a device that is able to gather data from its surroundings to record or respond from

facial-recognition algorithm: a program that collects data about someone's facial features

proximity: a measure of how close two objects are to each other

infrared: a type of light that is invisible to the human eye but is useful for electronic devices such as remote controls

humidity: the amount of water in the air

DID YOU KNOW?

If you press a button on a TV remote control that is pointed towards the front camera on a mobile phone, you will be able to see a red or purple flash on the image or screen of your camera; this is the infrared light. Infrared sensors can be used to detect the presence of individuals in dark environments, which means that they can be combined with AI security systems to detect intruders, sound alarms and trigger additional security responses.

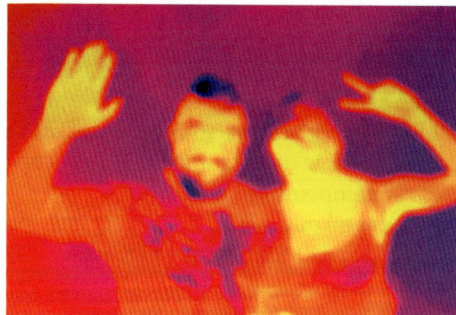

Practise

1 Take a look again at the AI systems in the table on page 158. Choose an example and, with a partner, think carefully about the input, processing and output of that system. Create a diagram to show INPUT, PROCESS and OUTPUT for the AI system you have selected. Look back to the Learn box on page 160 for an example diagram.

2 Use the internet to carry out research into the sensors below. Copy and complete the table.

Sensor	Data it collects	Examples of AI systems where this sensor is used	Improvements/additional uses
pressure			
colour			
smoke/gas			
tilt			

> Think of devices or applications you see every day to help you complete this task.

- With a partner, discuss each of the examples you have found.
- Can you think of any other ways in which each AI system can be used or any improvements that could be made to the examples so that the system could be used to help carry out another task? Add your ideas to the table.

> **KEYWORD**
>
> **tilt:** a measure of the degree to which an object is raised or lowered from a flat surface

Designing your own AI system

Learn

Many of our homes currently contain a wide range of devices that are activated using sensors. Some of the most popular are linked to digital assistants that collect input from home users in the form of voice-activated instructions.

Homes with devices linked to digital assistants in this way are known as *smart homes*. As you've explored in earlier units, devices in a smart home are interconnected via the digital assistant to the internet. This allows users in the smart home to do such actions as monitor temperature, switch on and off a burglar-alarm system and switch lights on and off. This can all be done via a smartphone, tablet, laptop or game console.

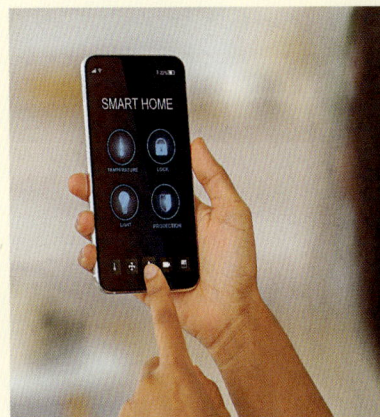

Practise

1   Use what you have learned about sensors; AI; and input, output and processing to design an AI system. The system should help you to complete a daily task or something else of your choosing.

Before you design your AI system, you need to think about these questions:

- What type of **input** should the AI system collect? What sensors will it need?
- What do you want the AI system to do? What **processing** will it do?
- What type of **output** will the AI system provide? Will it need a screen to display results of processing? Will it be able to move? Will it need speakers?

Some examples of AI devices you might want to consider include:

- a robot toy that can be taught tricks and provide company but that also needs to be fed virtually
- an AI system that could be used with virtual-reality glasses to allow you to visit and move around new locations, for example exploring space.

2   Create a sketch of your device. As part of your design you should identify:
- the purpose of your device
- the input and output devices your device will have
- how you would interact with the device
- what the device will be used for
- what sensors the device will require and what they would be used for.

3   Ask a partner to evaluate your AI device and give feedback on ways to improve your design.
- Can your partner think of any additional sensors, processing or output you could add to your AI system?
- Can your partner think of any additional applications for your AI system?
- Make improvements to your design based on your partner's feedback.

Representing data: Images

Learn

Data used in AI systems can be represented in different ways. You saw earlier how data is collected for AI systems using different types of sensors and even cameras.

Before **digital cameras**, like those on mobile phones, film cameras were used to take photographs. Photographs were taken by exposing to light a special plastic **film** coated in chemicals to create an image. The plastic film was then sent off to a photography laboratory where it was developed in a darkroom and the pictures printed onto photographic paper. Cameras that used film to produce images in this way were called **analogue cameras**, and they were said to produce **analogue images**.

> Analogue images were not available straight away. You had to send your film to a lab where it was developed.

Binary numbers

Remember: all data represented inside a computer is stored in **binary** format. Data stored in binary format is represented using 1s and 0s. A single **binary digit** (1 or 0) is called a **bit**. All data stored in a digital device, for example numbers, characters, images, sound, must be stored in this format. When data is collected by AI systems it is often not in digital format and it must be converted into 1s and 0s before the AI system can process it.

Converting analogue images to digital format

AI systems that use images as input need to ensure that the images collected are in digital format. For example, an AI system that uses image recognition may need to convert an image from analogue format into digital format before the image can be processed. One way of representing images used in digital applications is through the use of **bitmap graphics**.

Bitmap graphics

Bitmap graphics (or *raster images*) are stored as tiny dots called **pixels** (short for 'picture element'). The pixels are organised on a grid on screen. Each pixel has its own group of binary digits that is used to represent its colour. For example, in an image where the only colours used are black and white, each pixel could be represented using only 1 bit, for example 1 = black and 0 = white.

The number of pixels making up an image is measured in pixels per inch (**ppi**). This value is the image's **resolution**. The higher the resolution, the better the quality of the image and the bigger the file size needed to store the image. This is due to a higher resolution meaning more pixels and therefore more data.

Analogue images are often provided in the form of a printed copy. Before the image can be converted to digital format it needs to be input into the digital system using a scanner, although most people now prefer to take a photograph of the image with the camera on their mobile phones.

To convert an analogue image to digital, the image is divided into pixels and details about each pixel are stored.

In the example below, each pixel is only coloured black or white. This means that each pixel can be represented by just 1 bit, **0** or **1**. This image is said to have **colour depth** of 1, as only 1 bit is used to represent each pixel.

As the image is made up from 100 pixels (10 pixels wide × 10 pixels high), it will need 100 bits to store it.

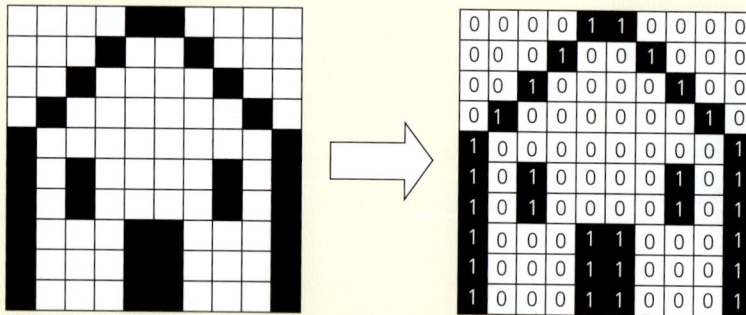

Once the analogue file is converted into pixels, it can be displayed on screen and the file can be saved and used for further processing. The image below shows how a high-quality image is represented in digital format.

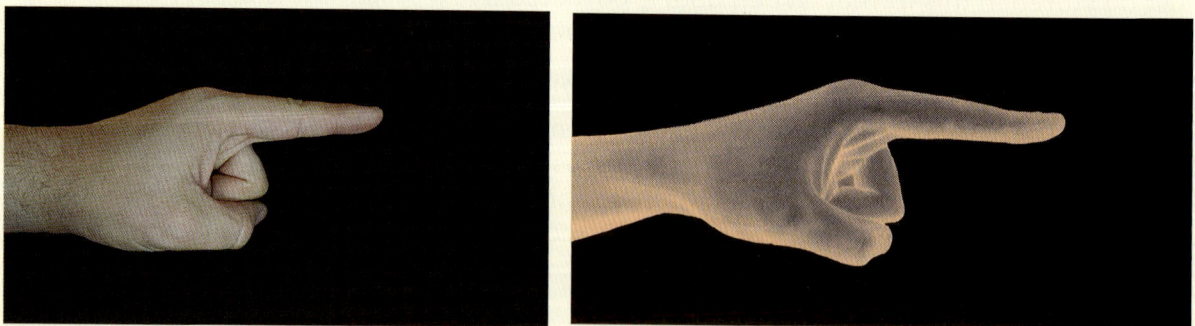

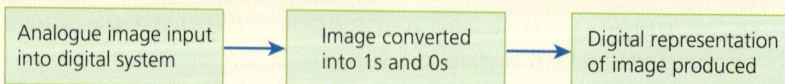

Analogue image input into digital system → Image converted into 1s and 0s → Digital representation of image produced

Colour images

The bitmap grid showing the house on page 166 contains 100 pixels. Each pixel has a colour depth of 1 so this image needs 100 bits to store it:

$$(10 \times 10) \times 1 = 100 \text{ bits}$$

The number of pixels high multiplied by the number of pixels wide

Colour depth

If you want the image to be represented in colour, you need to use more bits for each pixel to allow you to represent more colours. Bitmap image files can get very large; this means that they can take up a lot of memory when they are being processed.

If you want to store an image with more than two colours, you need to include additional bits, for example if you had a colour depth of two (this means you have 2 bits representing each pixel) you could represent four colours:

- 00 = white
- 01 = black
- 10 = green
- 11 = red

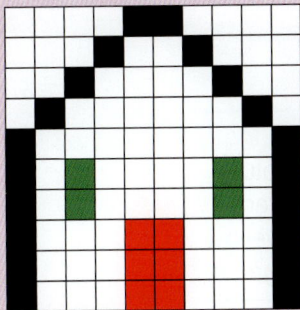

The calculation for the image above is $(10 \times 10) \times 2 = 200 \text{ bits}$

KEYWORDS

digital camera: a camera that captures photographs and stores them in the form of digital data

film: a plastic strip coated in light-sensitive crystals, inserted into analogue cameras and used to store images

analogue camera: a camera that used photographic film to take pictures

analogue image: an image created using an analogue camera and film

binary: a number system that uses combinations of two digits (0 and 1) to represent all numbers; used to represent data in computer systems

binary digit: 1 or 0

bit: short for 'binary digit'; a single bit of data, either a 0 or a 1

bitmap graphic: digital image produced using a grid of pixels

pixel: short for 'picture element', the small element displayed on a computer screen

ppi: 'pixels per inch'; the number of pixels in a square inch of screen

resolution: the total number of pixels on a screen

colour depth: a measure of the number of bits used to represent colour in individual pixels in an image

Practise

1 Describe in detail to a partner how analogue images are digitised.

2 Open the file **Bitmap Practice.docx** provided by your teacher.
   Use the key provided in the document to help you complete the bitmap image represented. The image has a colour depth of two. A copy of the bit pattern for this image is shown below.

```
00 00 00 00 00 00 00 00 00 00 00 00 00 00 00 00 00 00 00 00 00 00
00 00 00 00 00 00 00 00 00 01 01 00 00 00 00 00 00 00 00 00 00
00 00 00 00 00 01 01 01 00 01 01 01 01 01 01 00 00 00 00 00
00 00 00 00 00 01 01 01 01 01 01 01 01 01 01 00 00 00 00 00
00 00 00 00 00 01 01 01 01 01 01 01 01 01 01 00 00 00 00 00
00 00 00 01 01 01 01 01 10 10 10 10 01 01 01 01 01 00 00 00
00 00 00 01 01 01 01 01 10 10 10 10 01 01 01 01 01 00 00 00
00 00 00 01 01 01 01 01 10 10 10 10 01 01 01 01 01 00 00 00
00 00 00 01 01 01 01 01 10 10 10 10 01 01 01 01 01 00 00 00
00 00 00 00 00 01 01 01 01 01 01 01 01 01 01 00 00 00 00 00
00 00 00 00 00 01 01 01 01 01 01 01 01 01 01 00 00 00 00 00
00 00 00 00 00 01 01 01 01 01 01 01 01 01 01 00 00 00 00 00
00 00 00 00 00 00 00 00 00 01 01 00 00 00 00 00 00 00 00 00 00
00 00 00 00 00 00 00 00 00 11 11 00 00 00 00 00 00 00 00 00 00
00 00 00 00 11 00 00 00 00 11 11 00 00 00 00 00 00 00 00 00 00
00 00 00 00 00 11 11 00 00 11 11 00 00 00 00 11 00 00 00 00
00 00 00 00 00 11 11 11 00 11 11 00 00 11 11 00 00 00 00 00
00 00 00 00 00 00 11 11 11 11 11 00 11 11 11 00 00 00 00 00
00 00 00 00 00 00 00 11 11 11 11 11 11 11 00 00 00 00 00 00
00 00 00 00 00 00 00 00 00 11 11 11 11 00 00 00 00 00 00 00 00
```

Key:
00 = blue
01 = red
10 = yellow
11 = green

3 Use the file **Your Bitmap.docx** provided by your teacher to create your own image in binary format.

   - The colour depth for the image should be no larger than two.
   - Include a colour key.
   - Ask a partner to colour the image for you.
   - Complete the calculation to show how many bits you would need to store your image with a colour depth of two:

     (_____ × _____) × _____ = _____

> Do not make your image too complex, or include too many colours. Remember: you are coding your image using 1s and 0s. It can be easy to make a mistake.

Vector graphics

Learn

Digital images can be store in **vector graphic** format. Vector graphics are made up of shapes placed on the screen. When vector graphics are being created, this is done using instructions about where each part of the image should be placed on the screen. The instructions also describe the part of the image by providing details such as its colour or the length of a line that is used. Vector graphics do not hold information regarding every pixel on the screen display in the same way that bitmap images do. As a result, they take up less memory. This is important if you need to store lots of images for processing at a later stage.

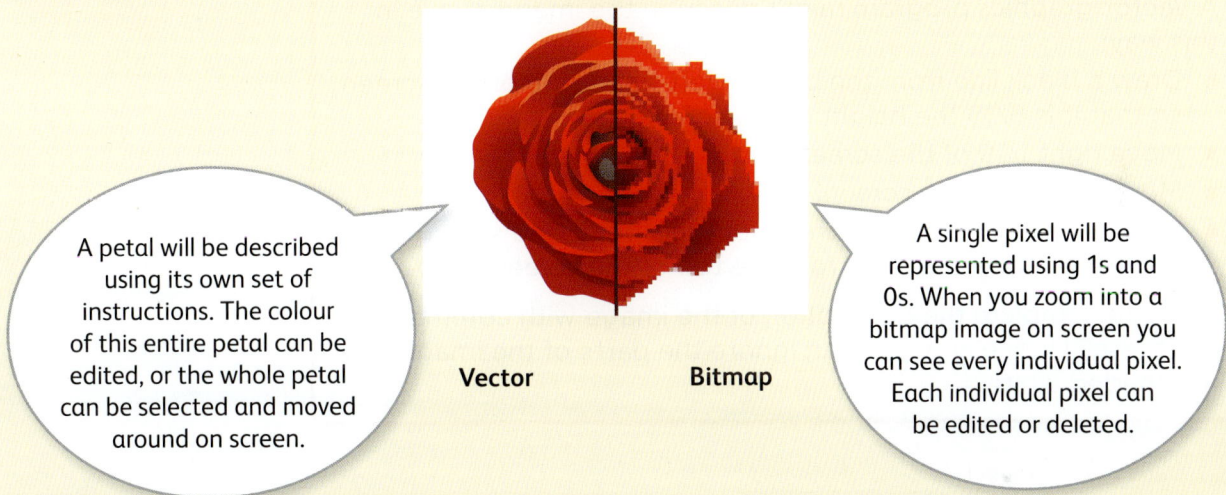

A petal will be described using its own set of instructions. The colour of this entire petal can be edited, or the whole petal can be selected and moved around on screen.

Vector   **Bitmap**

A single pixel will be represented using 1s and 0s. When you zoom into a bitmap image on screen you can see every individual pixel. Each individual pixel can be edited or deleted.

The image above helps show the difference between how vector and bitmap images are created. The vector graphic is made up of multiple objects combined on screen to create the image of a flower. Each part of the image is represented using a set of instructions that describes that part of the image. When analogue images are converted into digital format, the computer program used to store the image will identify each individual component in the image and generate a set of instructions to describe that part of the image. These instructions are stored and used to recreate the image when it is used for processing.

> **KEYWORD**
>
> **vector graphic:** digital image made from a series of objects placed on a computer screen

Computational thinking – algorithms

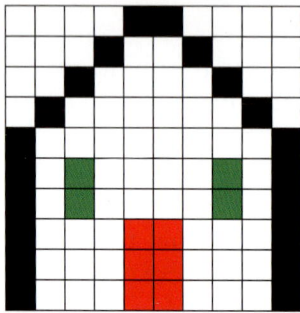

A vector-graphics program might describe the image above in this way:

- Draw a black line from the bottom left-hand side of the screen so that it is 6/10 the height of the screen.
- Move right 1/10 of the screen.
- Move up 1/10 of the screen.
- Draw a black line that reaches from this point and stop when you have reached 5/10 across the top of the screen.

Can you complete the description of the image with commands like these? Notice how you can ignore the parts of the image that are shaded white.

Practise

1 Draw a simple image on a piece of squared paper. An example is shown below.

   a Describe your image to a partner using vector image commands. Ask your partner to try to recreate the image on paper. Remember to include descriptions about line length, shape descriptions and shape positions on the page when describing your image.

   b Compare the image you created to your partner's drawing. This will give you an idea of how complex the instructions about vector graphics must be to ensure that the image is recreated accurately each time the image is opened.

2 Think about how difficult it might be if you had to describe this image pixel by pixel.

   – How much longer might this take?

   – Which approach, vector or bitmap, provides more detail to support processing by an AI system?

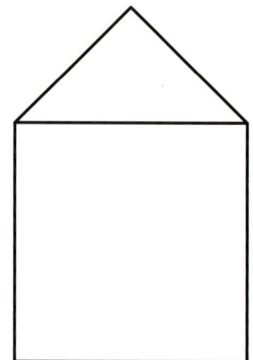

Representing data: Sound and text

Learn

Many AI devices use cameras and digital images to provide information to the **processor** to help the device decide what actions it should take next. The processor is the part of the computer that carries out instructions provided by computer programs. Think about driverless cars, for example.

Self-driven cars use sensors such as speakers, cameras and even radar. These work together to act like the human brain and eyes to help the car get a clear idea of its environment and examine its surroundings.

Using the camera and information about its surroundings, the processor in the car can detect details in road signs, for example the speed limit in its current location.

Using microphones, self-driven cars can detect sirens from emergency vehicles, or odd engine noises that might indicate that a repair is needed. But, how do processors input and process text and sound?

Data such as sound and text must be converted into digital format before it can be stored on a computer. For example, sound creates an analogue signal which is entered into a computer via a microphone. Computers cannot store analogue data so the sound wave must be converted into binary format using an analogue to digital convertor.

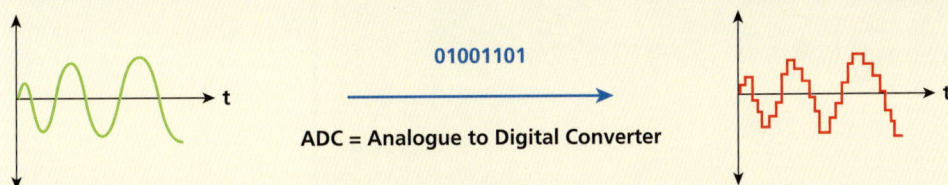

01001101

ADC = Analogue to Digital Converter

Sound is input into systems, such as AI systems, in analogue format. Before the sound can be processed it needs to be converted into digital format.

Instructions can be programmed into AI systems using typed text. When you type instructions or data into a computer via a keyboard, it must be stored in binary format. Each time you type a letter or number on a keyboard on any digital system, a group of binary digits is sent to the systems processor. Each set of binary digits is used to recreate the word-processed document, spreadsheet or database that you are creating.

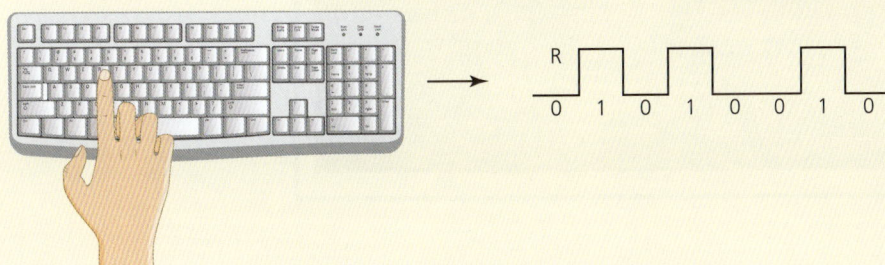

R
0 1 0 1 0 0 1 0

Each key pressed on a keyboard creates a unique binary pattern

For example, if you type the word **HELLO**, the following group of binary digits is created:

Character	H	E	L	L	O
Binary	01001000	01100101	01101100	01101100	01101111

Practise

1   Driverless cars are an example of an AI system that uses cameras and microphones to collect input from their environment. Use the internet to carry out research into other AI applications that use cameras and microphones in the same way. Make a list of these applications and describe how they use each image and sound input.

2   Open the file **ASCII Conversion Chart.docx** provided by your teacher.

   –   Use this chart to write a message to a partner.

   –   Swap messages and try to work out what your partner's message says.

KEYWORD

processor: the part of a computer that carries out instructions

DID YOU KNOW?

Mars rovers and driverless cars use the same AI technology to help them decide when help is needed from humans if they are unable to work out how to get around an obstacle.

Introduction to logic gates

Learn

Digital devices process data using **logic gates**. Logic gates are used by processors to analyse inputs, make decisions and produce an output. Input to and output from **logic circuits** is provided using electricity. Electricity can be either **ON** or **OFF**, which makes it ideal for representing binary digits **1** or **0**.

Logic gates can have one or two binary inputs that are processed to produce a single output signal:

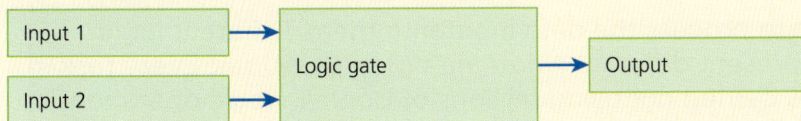

Input 1		
	Logic gate	→ Output
Input 2		

A logic gate can combine two inputs, process the inputs and produce a single output.

Where complex decisions need to be made, the output from one logic gate can be used as the input into another logic gate. When this happens, an **electronic circuit** is created:

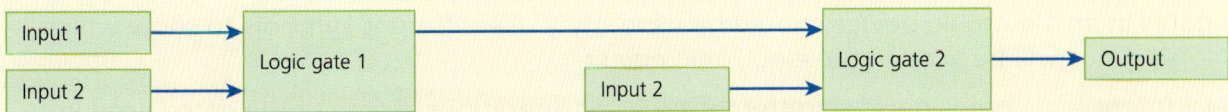

Input 1				
	Logic gate 1		Logic gate 2	→ Output
Input 2		Input 2		

The output produced from a logic gate will depend on the type of logic gate being used as well as the combination of ON/OFF (or 1/0) inputs.

Logic gates can be found in many digital devices in the home. You will find a logic gate in any device that uses an electronic circuit to process data.

Some examples of digital devices where logic gates are required include:

- Burglar alarms
- Door bells
- Street lights
- TV remote controls
- Automatic lights on cars.

> Logic gates are said to be the building blocks of digital circuits as the electronic circuit inside a digital device is made up from multiple logic gates.

Practise

1. As a class, make a list of the devices you use at home and at school that require electronic circuits to support the processing of data.
2. Look back to the Scenario on page 152 at the start of this unit. Discuss with a partner: Will the AI device you design need to use electronic circuits and logic gates? Explain your answer.

KEYWORDS

logic gate: a physical device or circuit that processes one or more input signals to produce a single output signal

logic circuit: a combination of logic gates used to carry out complex operations

electronic circuit: a route that electricity can flow around

Types of logic gate

Learn

Boolean logic

Conditions are statements that can be true or false. AND and OR can be used to combine a number of conditions. **Boolean logic** is used to compare the statements in the condition and a **Boolean value** of true or false is returned after every comparison.

Logic gates use Boolean logic to process the data input into them. Different logic-gate types are designed to represent different **Boolean logic operations**. Every task carried out by the processor is carried out using millions of Boolean logic operations.

In a digital device, electronic circuits can contain a number of different types of logic gate. Each logic gate has a name that helps to describe how different inputs will determine the possible outputs. When hardware designers are planning how the logic gates in an electronic device should be used, they use different symbols to show which logic gates will be used in the electronic circuit.

Different logic gates perform different types of operations. Some of the gates used in electronic circuits include **AND** gates, **OR** gates and **NOT** gates.

Rules for gate operation		
AND gate	**OR gate**	**NOT gate**
• AND gates have two inputs (each of which can be 1 or 0) • The AND gate will only output 1 if both inputs are a 1	• OR gates have two inputs (each of which can be 1 or 0) • The OR gate will output 1 if either of the two inputs is 1	• NOT gates have only 1 input (which can be 1 or 0) • Output from the NOT gate will always be the opposite of the input

Understanding AND gates

AND gates have two inputs. Each input can be only ON/OFF or TRUE/FALSE. The output from the AND gate will depend on the combination of the two inputs.

Think about how you make decisions when you have two important factors to consider.

For example, imagine trying to work out whether you can have a cheese sandwich for lunch. You can have a cheese sandwich only if:
- A there is bread in the cupboard AND
- B there is cheese in the fridge.

You analyse these two factors in the same way in which the AND gate produces an output.

Lunch decisions using an AND gate

Input A	Input B		Output Z
Is there bread?	Is there cheese?	Explanation	Can I have a cheese sandwich?
0	0	bread = FALSE cheese = FALSE	FALSE I cannot have a cheese sandwich.
0	1	bread = FALSE cheese = TRUE	FALSE I cannot have a cheese sandwich.
1	0	bread = TRUE cheese = FALSE	FALSE I cannot have a cheese sandwich.
1	1	bread = TRUE cheese= TRUE	TRUE I can have a cheese sandwich.

Often the inputs to logic gates are given labels using letters of the alphabet, for example the inputs could be labelled A and B and the output could be labelled Z.

You can have a cheese sandwich only when you have both bread and cheese: the output can only be TRUE when both inputs are TRUE.

Understanding OR gates

OR gates also have two inputs, each of which can be either ON/OFF or TRUE/FALSE. The output from the OR gate will depend on the combination of the two inputs.

You often use the same principles as OR gates to help make a decision.

For example, imagine trying to decide whether you will play online at the weekend. You have two friends who you normally play online with, so you will play online if:

- Friend A is online OR
- Friend B is online.

Online gaming decisions using an OR gate

Input A	Input B		Output Z
Friend A is online	Friend B is online	Explanation	Can I play online?
0	0	A online = FALSE B online = FALSE	FALSE I cannot play online.
0	1	A online = FALSE B online = TRUE	TRUE I can play online.
1	0	A online = TRUE B online = FALSE	TRUE I can play online.
1	1	A online = TRUE B online = TRUE	TRUE I can play online.

You will also happily play online if both friends are online!

Understanding NOT gates

The NOT gate is the simplest of all gates. It has only one input and it always produces an output that is the opposite of the input received.

Our behaviour in real life is sometimes similar to the way in which a NOT gate operates. For example, imagine trying to decide whether you should turn on an alarm system in your home:

- If you are in the house (1), the alarm system will be switched OFF (0).
- If you are not in the house (0), the alarm system will be switched ON (1).

KEYWORDS

condition: something that is checked to determine whether it is true or false

Boolean logic: a form of algebra where all values are reduced to either true or false

Boolean value: a data type that has one of two possible values: true or false

Boolean logic operations: operations based on the terms AND, OR, NOT

AND gate: a logic gate that accepts two inputs and will output a 1 (or TRUE) value only if both inputs are a 1

OR gate: a logic gate that accepts two inputs and will output a 1 (or TRUE) value when either of the inputs is a 1

NOT gate: a logic gate that accepts only one input; the output will always be the opposite of the input

Practise

1   Open the file **Using Logic Gates.xlsx** provided by your teacher. Open the tab AND Gates on the file.
    - Complete Part 1 to test your understanding of how an AND gate operates.
    - Complete Part 2 by describing a problem that requires you to consider two important factors before you make the decision.

      > The two factors will become Input A and Input B into your logic gate.

    - Complete the table with the explanations in a similar way to the 'Lunch decisions using an AND gate' table in the Learn box above.
    - Explain your output in the Output column. What did Z equal? What does this mean your decision will be?
    - Save your files.

2 Open the tab `OR Gates` on the file.

Complete Part 1 and Part 2 of this task using a decision you might make in the same way as an OR gate operates.

3 Open the tab `NOT Gates` on the file.

Test the NOT gate model using a problem with only one question that has a TRUE/FALSE answer and where the outcome must be the opposite of the answer to your question.

> Another name for a NOT gate is an *inverter* because it inverts the input (changes it to the opposite).

4 Look back to the Scenario on page 152 at the start of the unit. The AI system being developed by the school is expected to include a login system. Discuss with a partner which of these gates you would use to help manage student logins to the system.

Go further

In Unit 7.2, you looked at Smart solutions in the home. In this unit, you've explored how AI can be used in the wider community, in our streets, towns, cities and even in space.

1 Design one area of a smart city to show how AI could be used. Choose from:
   - health care
   - a typical manufacturing organisation found in a city
   - a typical business advertising their products.

AI can be used in a city to:
- detect pedestrians in the roads/crossing roads/on the footpaths
- detect and prevent crime
- track traffic on the city's roads
- automate a process in a manufacturing company
- automate a process in the city's health system
- advertise a typical business located in the city
- plan journeys for residents/delivery drivers/taxis
- automate hotel check-ins/flight check-ins/supermarkets check-outs.

2 In your design, give examples of how sensors might be placed to support the AI system.

3 Explain how information will be collected, processed and then used to generate output.

4 Explain how automation with AI can support the operation.

5 Decide whether image recognition could be used in your system, and if so explain how it will be used.

Challenge yourself

You have learned how logic gates can be used to help computers make decisions. For complex decision-making, a number of logic gates can be combined together to make a logic circuit.

1 Consider how two logic gates could be combined together to manage user access to a simple digital device such as an air-conditioning system in the home. The system uses inputs from temperature sensors in the home but it can also be switched ON/OFF by the homeowner using an app on their mobile phone:

> The access system on the alarm follows these simple rules to determine whether the air-conditioning unit should be switched ON or not:
> - The air conditioning system will be switched on if the temperature in the house is >20 °C; it will be switched off when the temperature is <20 °C).
> - The air-conditioning system will operate only if the homeowner has switched the power on.

2 Copy the table below and place the following descriptions and gates under the correct headings to help you decide which are INPUT, PROCESS or OUTPUT.

| AND | Air-conditioning system ON | Temperature <20 | Temperature >20 | OR |

INPUT	PROCESS	OUTPUT

3 Draw a diagram like the one on page 173 to place the descriptions and gates in the correct order to help you understand how this system operates.

> Match the inputs to the correct gates to show how the system will switch ON if the temperature is >20 °C and OFF if it is <20 °C, AND if the owner has switched the power to ON.

4 There are more than three different types of logic gates. One additional example is the **Exclusive OR** gate.
- Use the internet to find out more about the Exclusive OR logic gate.
- Write a description of how the Exclusive OR logic gate operates.
- Draw the symbol used to represent an Exclusive OR logic gate.
- Design a problem that can be solved using an Exclusive OR gate. The problem should have two input questions where the answers can be only TRUE or FALSE.

Final project

Part 1

Look back to the Scenario on page 152 at the start of this unit. Your school has provided the template deisgn below that shows an outline of the AI system required. The device will include a **virtual reality** headset and will run on a hardware platform such as a PC or a portable tablet, or a mobile phone.

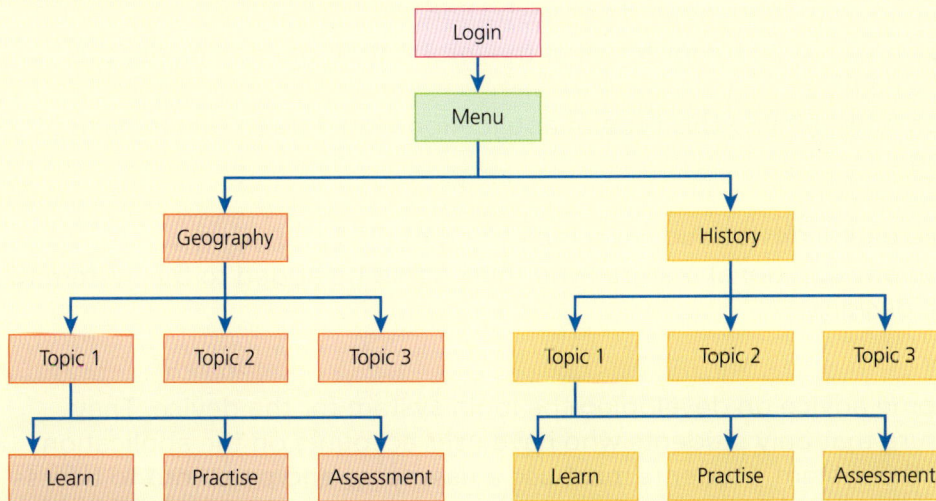

The school plan to trial the system in two subject areas, geography and history, before expanding the application to include other subjects, such as science and mathematics.

The application will have a login screen and allow students to select a subject area from a menu. Each subject is divided into a series of topics and each topic is contains a Learn, Practise and an Assessment area.

In geography the school would like to use:
- digital text books with:
  - videos, images and text to help student learning
  - interactive quizzes and games in the learn section
- a method of helping students keep track of where they left off in each topic area
- virtual-reality smilations to allow students to visit different countries
- image recognition to help students identify different geographic items such as rock types
- practice questions with automated feedback for each question to help students' understanding of difficult questions
- assessments with multiple-choice questions.

1 The school is unsure whether the software they are developing is applications software or systems software.

a Write a short paragraph to explain which it will be. Include examples of each type of software to illustrate your answer.

b Evaluate the template design and make recommendations on the type of devices the school would need to collect input from the users. Write a paragraph about how well you think the design would:
  - use student input to help student learning, for example would it be enjoyable to use, and why?
  - help teachers with marking and adminstration.

c How difficult it would be to collect all of the information needed to suit the school curriculum?

d Comment on how suitable this type of application would be to run on each of the following:
  - a PC
  - a portable digital device such as a tablet or a mobile phone.

e Comment on any additional features you think could be added to the system to improve the design.

Part 2

The school needs some advice on developing the login system for the device. They woud like to make sure that only students who have user accounts on the application are able to log in to the system. Students must use a username and password to access the system.

2 The school have asked you to design a login system using either an AND, OR or NOT gate to help with this process. Students can speak either their username or their password into the system.

a Explain to the school how the letters and numbers used to represent a password can be stored using binary digits.

b Explain how the analogue voice pattern of a username could be converted into digital.

c Draw a diagram to show how the login system could work using a logic gate.

d Design a simple logo for the history section in the software system.

e Open the file **Your Bitmap.docx** provided by your teacher.
Use the 10 × 10 digital grid to design a suitable logo. You should use a colour depth of two to represent your image.

Part 3

The principal would like to find out about how AI could be used in other areas around the school.

3 Write a short paragraph explaining your ideas, how they would work and how they would benefit the students and staff at school.

KEYWORD

virtual reality: computer-generated simulation of a three-dimensional image or environment; can be interacted with by a person using special electronic equipment, such as a helmet with a screen inside or gloves fitted with sensors

Evaluation

Ask a partner to review the work you have completed in Parts 1, 2 and 3 of the Final project above. Your partner should comment on:
- the type of devices you have recommended for the collection of data for use with the geography section of the computing system
- the accuracy of your logic-gate design
- the accuracy of your logo design
- any additional features you thought could be added to the system
- your ideas on how AI could be developed in other subjects studied at the school.

What can you do?

Read and review what you can do.
- ✔ I can explain the difference between systems software and application software.
- ✔ I can explain what AI means.
- ✔ I can describe how AI enables a computer to use information from its surroundings to produce an output.
- ✔ I can evaluate the design of a device or AI system.
- ✔ I can explain how AI works in a range of applications.
- ✔ I can explain how AI helps automate the completion of tasks in some industries.
- ✔ I can explain how image recognition is used in some AI applications.
- ✔ I can describe how an analogue image is converted into digital format.
- ✔ I can explain what a binary number is and how it represents different data.
- ✔ I can explain what a logic gate is and describe what is meant by Boolean logic.
- ✔ I can explain how AND, OR and NOT logic gates work in a circuit.

Get started!

Lights can be used for many things, for example to send messages, entertain or attract attention. Many advertising signs use **light sequences** to help get your attention and ensure you see and read the advert. These can be both physical signs and online adverts.

Have you considered the sequence of lights you see on a **light display**? Discuss these questions with a partner:

- Where have you seen lights that have a changing sequence?
- How does the change in lights help convey a message or generate a feeling?

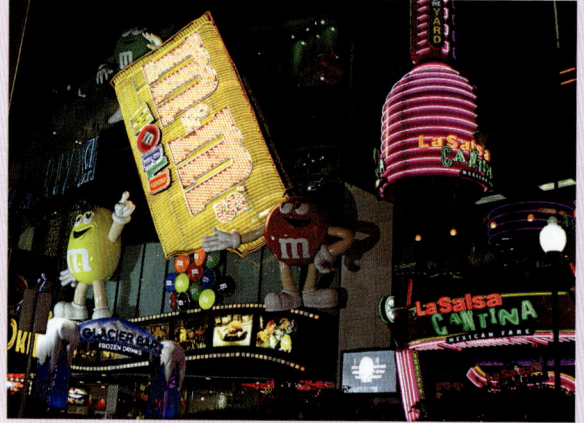

In everyday life, you encounter situations where you use **pattern recognition** and **sequences** to help solve a problem.

For example, in the past, watching a parent or sibling brush their teeth helped you to learn the patterns for doing the task correctly: putting on the toothpaste, brushing the teeth using movement of the toothbrush, rinsing the brush.

You've also learned how to complete tasks in a particular order (the sequence needed to complete the task), for example following a series of instructions to make your favourite meal, or following a map to get from one place to another. The sequence is as important as the instructions themselves.

In this unit, you will explore how sequencing and pattern recognition are important tools when planning and creating working programs. You will look at how the micro:bit displays an image using LED lights, and how to plan and create a program to control the micro:bit display in MicroPython.

KEYWORDS

light sequence: the order lights are displayed in

light display: a visual show using lights

pattern recognition: looking for a pattern and then using that pattern to solve a problem

sequence: the specific order of instructions

Learning outcomes

In this unit, you will learn to:
- follow, edit and explain an algorithm using a flowchart
- follow and explain the logic of AND, OR and NOT in a flowchart and MicroPython program
- explain and use selection statements IF, THEN and ELSE in a flowchart
- predict the outcome of a flowchart that uses selection
- create an algorithm as a flowchart using sequence and selection statements
- explain, edit and correct an algorithm represented as a flowchart that uses sub-routines
- evaluate a software prototype to help debug and improve it
- explain the purpose of a project plan
- evaluate the design of a micro:bit solution
- develop programs using multiple inputs and outputs on the micro:bit
- develop a MicroPython program for the micro:bit that displays a sequence of LED lights
- apply a test plan to check that a program works as expected
- explain how errors have occurred in a flowchart and MicroPython program
- identify and fix errors in a MicroPython program
- explain how pattern recognition can be used to plan, create and debug programs.

Warm up

In pairs, think about a sequence of lights that you may see daily: traffic lights!

Write the answers to these questions.
- Traffic lights are an automated solution for which task?
- What is the sequence of traffic lights in your country?
- What does each light represent?
- Why is the sequence specific across the country?
- What might happen if the sequence of lights changed without warning?

Create a diagram in colour to show the different steps of the traffic-light sequence where you live. Annotate parts of your diagram to explain how the light sequence works and the different meanings.

In pairs, make a list of anywhere else you see lights in a sequence for safety purposes. Discuss how it is important for the sequence to remain correct and what could potentially happen if the sequence was not correct.

SCENARIO

Your school has found that when students are working on projects with headphones they are sometimes unable to hear the school's break-time buzzer when it sounds. The school wants you to develop a **prototype** for a visual alarm that will display a light pattern when the buzzer sounds. This will help alert students to break time when they are wearing headphones.

The micro:bit allows a sequence of instructions to be seen visually on the **LED (light emitting diode) display**. You will create a prototype of the visual alarm using a micro:bit. It will output a sequence of lights when activated.

You should consider the following:

- How to represent the school's break-time buzzer
- What the visual alarm will display
- Where the micro:bit should be placed around the classroom and the level of sound needed to activate it
- Which micro:bit input will activate the visual alarm: shake, sound detector or button.

You will first create a **flowchart** to show the **algorithm** of the sequence of instructions needed to solve the problem. You will need to test your flowchart with a range of possible inputs and document your outcomes by applying a **test plan**. You will then create a program of your flowchart on the micro:bit using MicroPython.

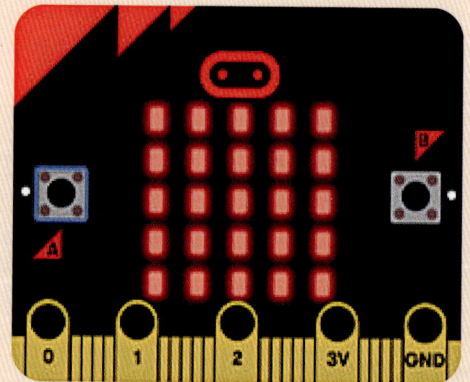

KEYWORDS

prototype: a sample, model or first release of a product, such as a program or device, built to test a concept or process

LED (light emitting diode) display: a flat panel that uses lights as pixels on a digital display; the output of light on the micro:bit with 25 individual LEDs

flowchart: a diagram showing the sequence of actions in a computer program; a graphical representation to show the steps to solve a problem

algorithm: a sequence of steps or instructions to solve a problem

test plan: a structured approach to testing whether your solution works as expected; a document that describes the areas of a program to be tested – includes details of the tests to be applied to each area of the program, including test data and expected results

---

DID YOU KNOW?

The LED display on the micro:bit is made up of 25 individual LED lights that can be programmed individually or combined to create an image.

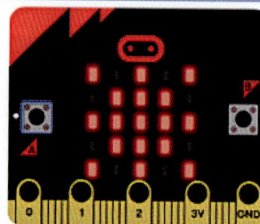

Do you remember?

Before starting this unit, you should be able to:
- ✔ create a simple algorithm using flowchart symbols
- ✔ identify flowchart symbols
- ✔ connect the micro:bit to a computer
- ✔ create a basic program using MicroPython
- ✔ identify the inputs and outputs available on the micro:bit
- ✔ understand how sensors can be used as an input on the micro:bit
- ✔ break a problem down into individual steps
- ✔ explain how sequence and selection can be seen in a flowchart and basic program
- ✔ develop programs for a micro:bit with MicroPython using an input and an output.

Before starting this unit you will need to access MicroPython on a computer through online software.

To access MicroPython:
- Open your chosen web browser software.
- Go to https://python.microbit.org

You will also need the following physical computing devices:
- Micro:bit
- USB cable
- Optional battery pack for micro:bit.

You will also need access to https://app.diagrams.net to complete some of the flowchart tasks.

Prototyping

Learn

To develop a fully working software product, a designer first creates a project plan for the software-development process. A **prototype** is developed as part of this process.

The aim of a prototype is to develop a basic solution that includes all of the elements needed in the final solution. This helps to find and fix errors in the programming and in the product's look and feel. The requirements for the project are tested and **user feedback** is gathered to enable improvements to be made before the final solution is created.

The type of prototype created depends on the type of project.

For example, hardware products, such as car manufacturing, require a physical prototype (a model of the car). By creating a physical prototype, the designer can be clear on materials to use, costs and the quantities of any parts required to create the final product.

When developing software, the prototype is a working model of the software solution (program). This prototype is used to gather user feedback on how the software looks and any aspects that don't work, as well as any thoughts on improvements that could be made.

Prototyping is an important stage for new software development as releasing new software with **bugs** in it will not give a good impression (and people will stop using it). When new software is released, it is expected to be a fully working software option.

Game development uses prototyping. The environment and characters need to be created in a partial or full software prototype. The design process incorporates developing the software prototype, using it to gather user feedback and testing the final program before it moves into **full release**. Designers look at any developments that are required to the software prototype to make the product a perfect final solution.

There are two types of prototyping linked with software development: evolutionary and throwaway prototyping.

Evolutionary prototyping

This is the development of a full prototype of the software that is given to users to gather feedback. Once feedback has been received, improvements are made and a new prototype created. This process is repeated until the original prototype has evolved into the completed solution.

An example of an evolutionary prototype is a full new game for users to use and test. Users play the game and give feedback based on how the game works, what they think of the challenges, how to use it, characters, scenes, and so on. Once all the feedback is gathered, the game is redeveloped and a new software prototype released to test again.

Throwaway prototyping

This is the development of small sections of the final software solution, and is given to users to gather their feedback. The feedback is incorporated and the small-section prototype is thrown away. The benefit of this type of prototyping is that feedback is incorporated as the solution is developing and the risk of creating a full solution that needs lots of improvements is reduced. Smaller sections mean that smaller improvements need to be made as the solution is developed.

An example of a throwaway prototype in game development would be a particular section or world that is released for users to play and test in order to give feedback. The feedback is then used, the old prototype thrown away and a new one is released for testing.

KEYWORDS

prototype: a sample, model or first release of a product, such as a program or device, built to test a concept or process

user feedback: gathering feedback from users of the product to aid development

bug: an error in the program that stops it working correctly

full release: in game development, the final full game released to users

Practise

1 Explain to a partner the purpose of a software prototype in a software-development project.

2 Evaluate the following throwaway software prototype. It has been created for a light sequence on the micro:bit. The prototype is moving from a large square to a small square to a clear screen.
   - Open the file **LightSequence1.py** provided by your teacher.
   - Connect the micro:bit to the device with the USB cable.
   - Send the program to the micro:bit to test it.
   - Discuss these questions with a partner:
     Can the images be recognised easily?
     Are the images displayed for long enough to be seen clearly?
     Do the images flow smoothly from one to another?
     What improvements would you make?

3 Evaluate the following evolutionary software prototype. It has been created for two light sequences on the micro:bit. The software prototype displays:
   a large diamond, small diamond then clear screen if the B button is pressed
   a large square, small square and then clear screen if the A button is pressed.
   - Open the file **LightSequence2.py** provided by your teacher.
   - Connect the micro:bit to the device with the USB cable.
   - Send the program to the micro:bit to test it.
   - Discuss these questions with a partner:
     Does the correct light display show when the A or B button is pressed?
     Can the images be recognised easily?
     Are the images displayed for long enough to be seen clearly?
     Do the images flow smoothly from one to another?
     What improvements would you make?

4 What are the advantages and disadvantages of the two types of prototyping in software development? Discuss your ideas with a partner.

5 Which type of software prototype will you use when creating your visual alarm light sequence: evolutionary or throwaway? Explain your reasons to a partner.

Pattern recognition

Learn

Pattern recognition is about looking for a pattern and using it to solve a problem. Problems come in all shapes and sizes, from creating a program to continuing a pattern that has been started.

For example, look at the pattern below. To replicate the pattern across the remaining grid, you first need to identify the pattern:

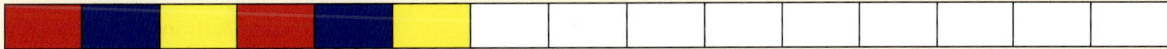

Then, you use pattern recognition to complete the grid:

Another way to explore pattern recognition is to look at the similarities between two problems or two examples of the same code in different software. Think about when you moved from **block-based programming** to **text-based programming**. You looked for patterns to help you to understand how the blocks translated into text.

For example, look at this MakeCode block to **show** a heart icon:

The MicroPython code to do the same action is:

```
display.show(Image.HEART)
```

A pattern is found in the wording **show** and **heart**, which features in both types of code.

Compare this code showing MakeCode and MicroPython:

```
if button_a.is_pressed():
    display.show(Image.HAPPY)
```

When the A button is pressed, the output for both programs is that a happy face is displayed on the micro:bit.

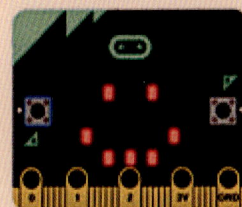

There are some similarities in the code:

- MakeCode: The outer block is an input that is looking to see whether the A button is pressed. MicroPython: The same is happening on the first row of code

  `if button _ a.is pressed ():`

- Look at the code that is within the input block in MakeCode. Can you see a similarity with the **indented** line of code in the MicroPython example?

- Some words in MakeCode and MicroPython are similar: `button a pressed`.

> By looking for similarities, you can develop your understanding of programming and become more confident writing program code in MicroPython.

Pattern recognition can also be useful when using just one programming language.

For example, look at this MicroPython code, which outputs a happy face when the A button is pressed.

```
if button_a.is_pressed():
    display.show(Image.HAPPY)
```

You can use this code to add to the program, so that a different icon is displayed when the B button is pressed. You can do this by copying and editing the code that you already have.

Using the patterns seen in the code, you can identify that the area to change is the reference to the A button (this needs to change to the B button). The image displayed can also be edited (and you can see a pattern of using capitals for the image to be used), for example:

```
if button_a.is_pressed():
    display.show(Image.HAPPY)
if button_b.is_pressed():
    display.show(Image.SAD)
```

There are also patterns in the flowcharts for the program above, where you need to have a happy face displayed when the A button is pressed, and a sad face when the B button is pressed. These flowcharts represent the program running for each of the micro:bit buttons:

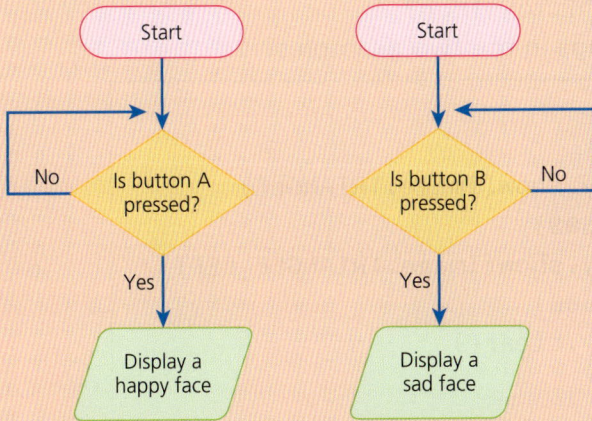

In the flowcharts, you can see the similarities in the decision block, asking whether the A button or the B button is being pressed. You can also see that each program has an output based on **if** the button has been pressed.

Showing the flowcharts side by side helps you to see the similarities and the patterns between the two.

KEYWORDS

pattern recognition: looking for a pattern and then using that pattern to solve a problem

block-based programming: programming using drag-and-drop blocks; a popular block-based language is Scratch

text-based programming: programming that requires the programmer to type text, e.g. Python

indentation: moving the line of code in to represent the code that will run if the condition is met

Practise

1 Look at the examples of MakeCode and MicroPython below. Discuss with a partner the patterns you can see:
   - Where are the similarities between the code?
   - What words are used in MakeCode and MicroPython?
   - Are there any words with similar meanings in the two examples?

```
display.show(Image.TRIANGLE)
sleep(500)
display.show(Image.TRIANGLE_LEFT)
sleep(500)
display.clear()
```

2 Look at this flowchart and discuss the questions below with a partner.
   - What patterns you can see?
   - What sequence is being displayed?
   - Use the patterns you see to extend the flowchart to display the same images in the same sequence again.

3 Open the file **LightSequenceChallenge.py** provided by your teacher.
   - Look at your flowchart from the previous activity and add the MicroPython code to extend the light sequence.
   - Connect the micro:bit to the device with the USB cable.
   - Send the program to the micro:bit to test it.

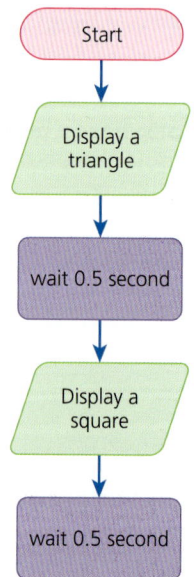

Patterns between text-based programming languages

Learn

You looked in the previous theme at patterns between block-based programming in MakeCode and text-based programming in MicroPython. You can also look for patterns between text-based languages, such as MicroPython and Python. For example:

To output text in Python you use the **print()** function:

```
print("Hello World")
```

To output text in MicroPython you use the **display.scroll()** function:

```
display.scroll("Hello, World")
```

Both lines of code have the text to be output encased in brackets and defined by using quotation marks. The quotation marks tell the computer that the content inside the quotation marks is a string, a series of characters like a text output.

You can also look for patterns in flowcharts. Look at this example. Can you predict what will happen?

- Following the flowchart from top to bottom helps you to understand what is expected to happen.
- The flowchart symbols also help you to understand what is expected to happen as you can see the output shape and the process shape.
- What else can you see that can help you to predict the outcome of the flowchart?

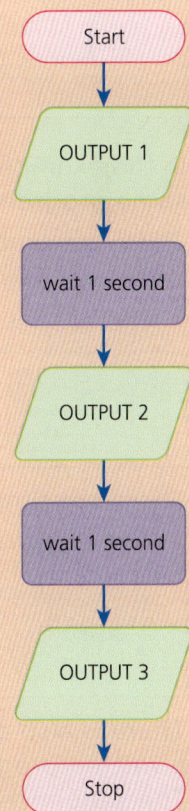

Start
↓
OUTPUT 1
↓
wait 1 second
↓
OUTPUT 2
↓
wait 1 second
↓
OUTPUT 3
↓
Stop

The flowchart above has been created as a program in Python and MicroPython in this table:

Flowchart	Python	MicroPython
Start → OUTPUT 1 → wait 1 second → OUTPUT 2 → wait 1 second → OUTPUT 3 → Stop	```import time

print(1)
time.sleep(1)
print(2)
time.sleep(1)
print(3)``` | ```from microbit import *

display.scroll(1)
sleep(1000)
display.scroll(2)
sleep(1000)
display.scroll(3)``` |

> When transferring 1 second into MicroPython it is represented in milliseconds. There are 1000 milliseconds in a second. Therefore, half a second would be 500 milliseconds.

> Remember that **from micro:bit import *** means import everything to do with the micro:bit and MicroPython so that you can write the program. The use of the * means 'everything'.

In the example above, you can see that there are different ways of representing the same program that outputs the numbers 1, 2, 3 with a 1 second wait in between them.

There are similarities between the delay that is added for 1 second between each output.

- The word *sleep* is seen in both Python and MicroPython.
- 1 second is the same as 1000 milliseconds.

wait 1 second	`time.sleep(1)`	`sleep(1000)`

There are similarities between the output that will display the numbers 1, 2 or 3.

- The number to be output is written within brackets in Python and MicroPython.

OUTPUT 3	`print(3)`	`display.scroll(3)`

There is also an overall pattern in the way the program is displayed as a flowchart or as a written program: they are in order, in a sequence that is run from top to bottom. The sequence is important: if the sequence is wrong, the program output will not be as expected.

Practise

1 The flowchart below uses a **variable** to store an individual value, an **integer**. An integer is a whole number. Defining the data type is important: if the program does not know it is an integer, it will not be able to perform a calculation.

   – Look at the flowchart. What will be the output?

   – What will be the output if the integer stored in the variable **number** is changed to 5?

2 The flowchart above can be used to create a program in Python and MicroPython.

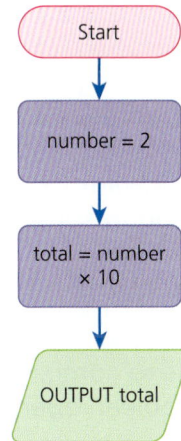

   Look at the Python and MicroPython programs in the table below and write down the patterns you see.

Python	MicroPython

`number = 2`
`total = number * 10`
`print (total)`
	`from microbit import *`
	`number = 2`
	`total = number * 10`
	`display.scroll(total)`

```
Start

number = 2

total = number
        × 10

OUTPUT total
```

It is important to note the two uses of * in the MicroPython program:

import* means import everything so that you can program with the micro:bit.

However, within the program, the * is an **arithmetic operator** and is the symbol for multiplying.

3 Open the file **CalculationProgram.py** provided by your teacher.

   – Connect the micro:bit to the device with the USB cable.

   – Send the program to the micro:bit to test it.

   – Copy and apply the test plan below to predict the outcome and then test the actual outcome.

Test number	Data entered	Expected outcome	Pass/fail
1	number = 5	number * 10	
2	number = 3		
3	number = 6		
4	number = 7		

4 Using the same program, set the variable **number** to 5 and edit the arithmetic operator to copy and apply the following test plan:

Test number	Data entered	Expected outcome	Pass/fail
1	total = number + 10		
2	total = number – 10		
3	total = number * 10		
4	total = number / 10		

5 How did pattern recognition help you to complete these tasks? Explain to a partner.

KEYWORDS

string: data that is made up of letters, numbers or any characters on the keyboard

variable: a named memory location used to store data of a given type during the program execution; a variable can change value as the program runs

integer: whole number

arithmetic operator: +, –, *, / and other symbols that can be used for arithmetic calculations

The logic of AND/OR/NOT

Learn

In programming there may be times when multiple inputs are required to activate the output, for example you may want to start a light sequence with a button and a sound sensor. This would allow the program to be started if the button is pressed **and** the sensor detects a sound alarm.

> When an input is used it has two possible states: **true** or **false**. If the A button is used on the micro:bit, it can be **pressed (true)** or **not pressed (false)**.

As you explored earlier in Unit 7.5, **Boolean operators** allow us to combine more than one input. There are three main Boolean operators: AND, OR and NOT. Here's a recap:

The **AND** Boolean operator requires **both** inputs to be **true** to activate the output. Look at this flowchart for a micro:bit program:

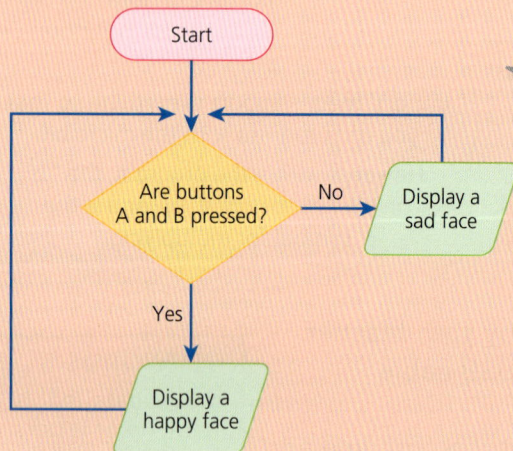

> The use of **selection** to check whether the outcome of the question **Are buttons A AND B pressed?** is being used in this flowchart. If the answer is yes (true), **then** a happy face is displayed. **Else** the answer is no (false), then a sad face is displayed.

- What would happen if either the A or B button was pressed on its own?
- What must happen for the happy face to be displayed?

Here is the MicroPython code for the flowchart:

```python
if button_a.is_pressed() and button_b.is_pressed():
    display.show(Image.HAPPY)
else:
    display.show(Image.SAD)
```

> The word AND is placed between the two sections of code that check to see whether each button is pressed. The program is still showing the use of selection. If the A and B buttons are pressed, **then** a happy face is displayed; **else** a sad face is displayed.

The **OR** Boolean operator requires **either or both** inputs to be **true** to activate the output.

Look at this flowchart:

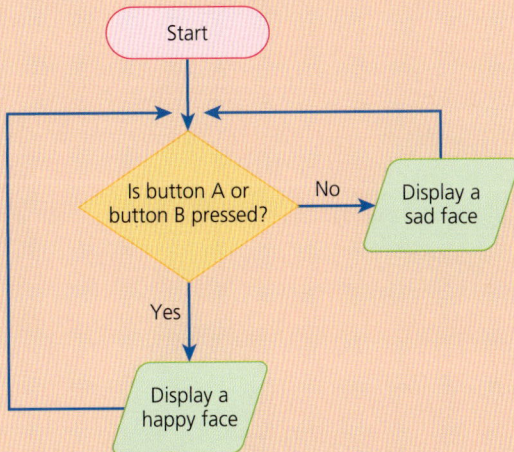

- What would happen if either the A or B button was pressed on its own?
- What would happen if both the A and B buttons were pressed at the same time?
- What must happen for a sad face to be displayed?

Here is the MicroPython code for the flowchart:

```python
if button_a.is_pressed() or button_b.is_pressed():
    display.show(Image.HAPPY)
else:
    display.show(Image.SAD)
```

The word OR is placed between the two sections of code that check to see whether either or both buttons are pressed.

The **NOT** Boolean operator will return **the opposite to the input**. For example, if the **A button is pressed (true)**, then the output would be **false**, as it is the opposite to the input.

Look at this flowchart:

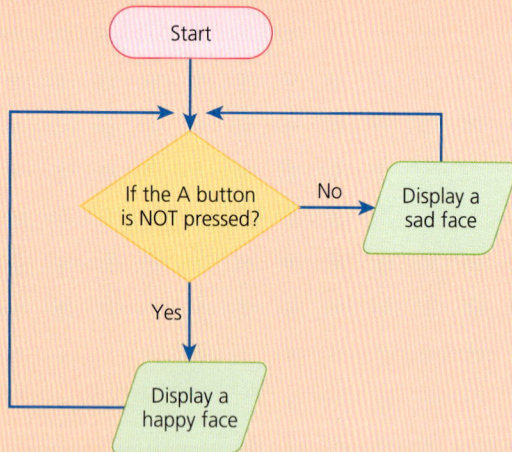

Start

If the A button is NOT pressed? → No → Display a sad face

Yes

Display a happy face

- What would happen if the A button was pressed?
- What would happen if the B button was pressed by accident?
- What must happen to display a happy face?

Here is the MicroPython code for the flowchart:

```
if not button_a.is_pressed():
    display.show(Image.HAPPY)
else:
    display.show(Image.SAD)
```

The word NOT is placed before the code to check whether the A button is not pressed.

If the A button **is NOT pressed (true)**, then a happy face is displayed. If the A button **is pressed (false)**, then a sad face is displayed.

Normally, you would expect that when a button is pressed, it generates true. With the NOT Boolean operator, false is generated: the opposite to the input.

Do you remember that code that may be used more than once in a program can be written as a **sub-routine**? A sub-routine is a section of code that is placed separately from the main code and run by using the sub-routine name.

A sub-routine uses this shape in a flowchart:

The sub-routine shape starts the sub-routine and is given a name. By adding this name to the main flowchart, the program knows to run the sub-routine code.

Look at this example. The sub-routine shape has been shaded to help you to see it.

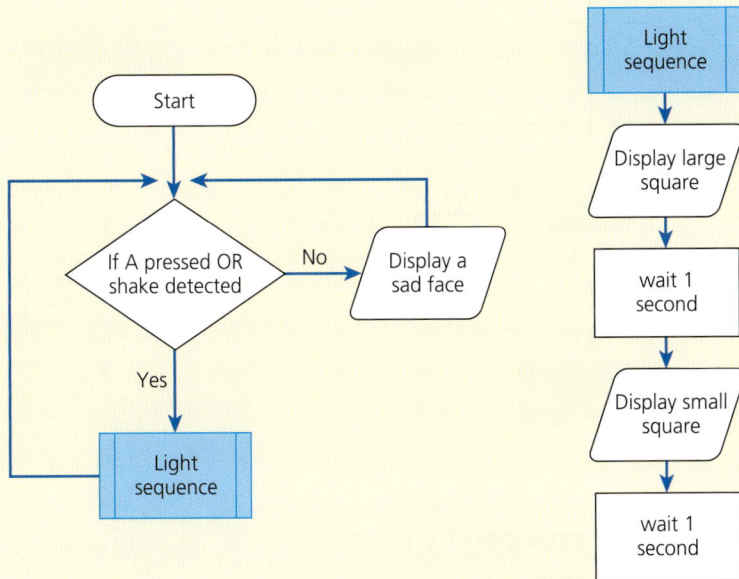

The flowchart will run the sub-routine **if** the A button is pressed **OR** movement on the micro:bit is detected; **else** a sad face is displayed.

The sub-routine runs when the name **Light sequence** is reached in the main flowchart. The sub-routine is **display a large square**, **wait for 1 second**, **display a small square**, **wait for 1 second**.

KEYWORDS

Boolean logic operations: operations based on the terms AND, OR, NOT

AND gate: a logic gate that accepts two inputs and will output a 1 (or TRUE) value only if both inputs are a 1

selection: a programming construct with more than one possible pathway; a condition is tested (using a question or criterion) before deciding which pathway to follow (the output)

OR gate: a logic gate that accepts two inputs and will output a 1 (or TRUE) value when either of the inputs is a 1

NOT gate: a logic gate that accepts only one input; the output will always be the opposite of the input

sub-routine: mini program inside a program that can be completed or repeated when requested

Practise

1 Look at this flowchart with a sub-routine.

   a In pairs, follow the flowchart and explain how it works.

   b What input will allow the sub-routine to run?

   c How would a sad face be displayed?

2 Use the software **draw.io** to create, view and edit flowcharts:

   a Open a web browser and the URL **https://app.diagrams.net**

   b Open the file **SubroutineActivity.drawio** provided by your teacher.

   c Look at the selection used in this program. What will activate the sub-routine?

   d How will a clear screen be displayed?

   e The sub-routine should display a large heart followed by a small heart. However, there is an error and the sub-routine is not running at all. Can you find the error and edit the flowchart? Double-click on the text within a shape to edit the wording.

3 Open the file **ANDprogram.py** provided by your teacher. The program displays the word 'Boolean' when the A **AND** B buttons are pressed. Create a flowchart using **draw.io** to represent this program.

4 Open the file **ORprogram.py** provided by your teacher. The program displays the word 'Boolean' when the A **OR** B button is pressed. Create a flowchart using **draw.io** to represent this program.

5 Open the file **NOTprogram.py** provided by your teacher. The program displays the word 'Boolean' when the B button is **NOT** pressed**.** Create a flowchart using **draw.io** to represent this program.

6 Discuss these questions with a partner:

   – How could you use a sub-routine to help plan a light sequence for a visual alarm on the micro:bit?

   – Think back to the Scenario on page 184 at the start of this unit. How could you use more than one input to activate your visual alarm?

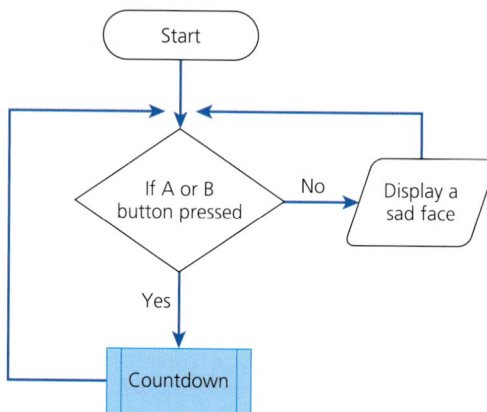

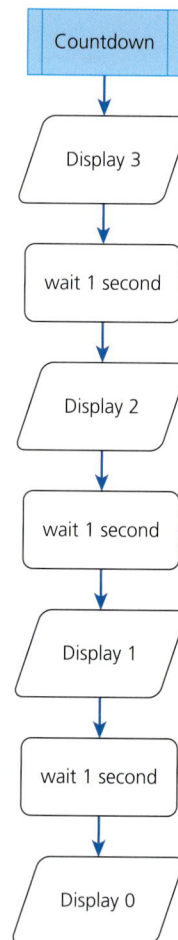

Flowchart:

Start → If A or B button pressed — No → Display a sad face
If A or B button pressed — Yes → Countdown

Countdown sub-routine:
Countdown → Display 3 → wait 1 second → Display 2 → wait 1 second → Display 1 → wait 1 second → Display 0

Project plans and test plans

Learn

Before a program for a prototype is created, a project plan is written. Part of the plan will map out what the program needs to include. To do this, the program is broken down into smaller problems to solve. For example, to create a program where an alarm activates when a button on the micro:bit is pressed, the following questions could be asked:

- Which button will be the input?
- What will be the alarm sequence?
- What will need to happen if the alarm is not activated?

Remember: a project plan lays out a software-development project from start to finish. The plan is essential to ensure that the software is created (and runs) as expected, and is released on time.

To recap, some areas of a project plan include:

what the software being developed is expected to do

what individual sections are required

what inputs and outputs are required

how to test it

how to use the outcome of the tests to improve the final product.

These individual problems can be explored using a flowchart:

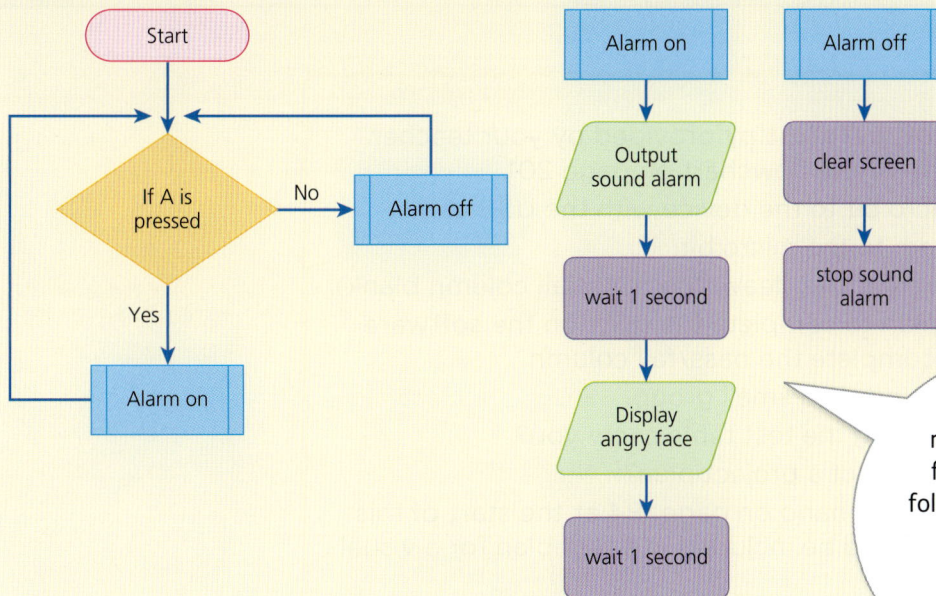

The use of sub-routines makes the flowchart easier to follow and understand. It also splits the flowchart into smaller sections to test.

A **test plan** can be used at this time to check the flowchart against what you expect to happen. This is an important stage in a project plan, before starting to write the program code.

Here is an example test plan for the flowchart above:

Test number	Data entered	Expected outcome	Pass/fail
1 A button activates the alarm	Button A pressed	alarm activates alarm sequence starts	Pass (no action)
2 Alarm sequence	Button A pressed	sound 1 second angry image 1 second	Pass (no action)
3 Alarm turns off after sequence is completed	Button A pressed	alarm sequence displays clear screen sound stops	Pass (no action)
4 Alarm off	No buttons pressed	the display is clear no sound	Pass (no action)

Once an algorithm on a flowchart works as expected, it can be used to write the program. Then, the same test plan can be used to check that the program runs correctly.

KEYWORD

test plan: a structured approach to testing whether your solution works as expected; a document that describes the areas of a program to be tested – includes details of the tests to be applied to each area of the program, including test data and expected results

Practise

1 Open the file **PrototypeToTest.py** provided by your teacher. This is the program for the flowchart on page 201.
   - Connect the micro:bit to the device with the USB cable.
   - Send the program to the micro:bit.
   - Copy the test plan above (leave the pass/fail column blank).
   - Apply the test plan to complete the tests on the software prototype and complete the pass/fail column.
2 Discuss these questions in a small group:
   - What did completing the test table show you?
   - What is the purpose of a project plan?
   - Think back to the Scenario on page 184 at the start of this unit. What tests could be included in a test plan for a visual alarm?

Identifying errors and debugging

Learn

In the previous theme, you examined the importance of test plans to help find and fix errors in the flowchart and the program code. A programming error can also be identified through **debugging** the code. Debugging is about finding any errors in the code and fixing them.

> Look back to Unit 7.1 page 29 for a recap about debugging and more information about errors in program code.

A **sequence** is a set order of instructions or events. In programming, the sequence of the programming code determines the output. If the sequence is wrong, it can cause an error or an incorrect output. In the example below, a particular sequence of colours needs to be repeated. Can you spot the error in the sequence?

To solve the error above you look for the pattern in the sequence of colours, for example the sequence is red, blue, yellow repeated. Using **pattern recognition**, you can see that the error is two blues next to each other.

You can also apply pattern recognition to debugging program code. For example, patterns can be used to check the sequence in a flowchart, by following the flow from top to bottom and looking at the flowchart shapes.

In the flowchart shown on the right, the pattern is an **output** followed by a **process**. The sequence is:

- display a large square
- wait 0.5 second
- display a small square
- wait 0.5 second
- display a chessboard
- wait 0.5 second.

> If there was an error in the sequence, such as the shapes in the wrong order, it would be obvious in the flowchart.

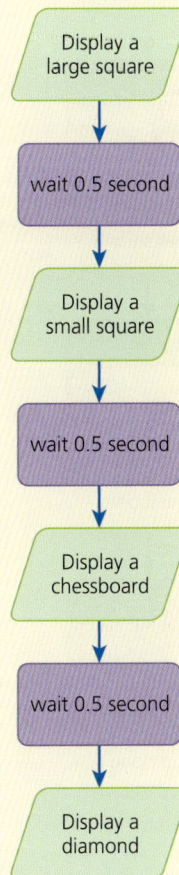

You can also add to a sequence by identifying and continuing the pattern; in the example above, the next instruction in the flowchart would be an output followed by the process. You then add the specific information about what is to be displayed and the time to wait.

Display a
large square

↓

wait 0.5 second

↓

Display a
small square

↓

wait 0.5 second

↓

Display a
chessboard

↓

wait 0.5 second

↓

Display a
diamond

Here is the MicroPython code for the flowchart above. The pattern and sequence are visible but there is an error in the code. Can you spot it?

Comparing the flowchart to the MicroPython can reveal where a pattern or sequence has been added incorrectly. To do this, line up the flowchart with the lines of code:

```
from microbit import *

display.show(Image.SQUARE)
sleep(500)
display.show(Image.CHESSBOARD)
sleep(500)
display.show(Image.SQUARE_SMALL)
sleep(500)
display.show(Image.DIAMOND)
sleep(500)
```

Flowchart	MicroPython
	`from microbit import *`
Display a large square	`display.show(Image.SQUARE)`
wait 0.5 second	`sleep(500)`
Display a small square	`display.show(Image.CHESSBOARD)`
wait 0.5 second	`sleep(500)`
Display a chessboard	`display.show(Image.SQUARE _SMALL)`
wait 0.5 second	`sleep(500)`
Display a diamond	`display.show(Image.DIAMOND)`
	`sleep(500)`

The highlighted sections show where the errors in the sequence are. These lines of MicroPython code are not the same as the flowchart. Once the errors have been found, you can rearrange the sequence to fix the program.

When debugging, you should also check for other errors that may cause the program not to run as expected. If you have checked the sequence and know that this is not the cause of the error, then you can look at the program code itself for errors in the way it has been typed in.

When there are errors in the program code, the micro:bit will display a sad face and then, if applicable, it will scroll across the display in the line the error is on. If this happens when you try to run a program, you know that the error lies in the code itself. Some areas to check are:

- Does the program start with **from microbit import** *?
- Are brackets opened and closed when used?
- Is there a colon at the end of an **if** statement line?
- Are there capitals where there should be, such as the image to be displayed, e.g. HAPPY?
- Does the **string** to be displayed have quotation marks around it?
- Are code words spelled correctly?

KEYWORDS

debug/debugging: the process of identifying and removing errors from a computer program

sequence: the specific order of instructions

pattern recognition: looking for a pattern and then using that pattern to solve a problem

output: a visible or audible outcome on a device through, for example, the display, monitor, speakers, headphones

process: the function within a computing device where an instruction in a program is carried out, such as a calculation or display

string: data that is made up of letters, numbers or any characters on the keyboard

Practise

1   In a program, the sound sensor on the micro:bit is used to play a tune and display a tick if a loud sound is detected; else it will display a clear screen.

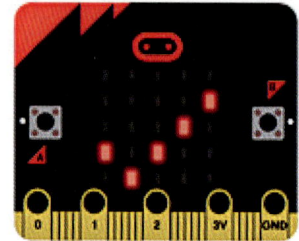

This flowchart has been created as part of the project plan for the program:

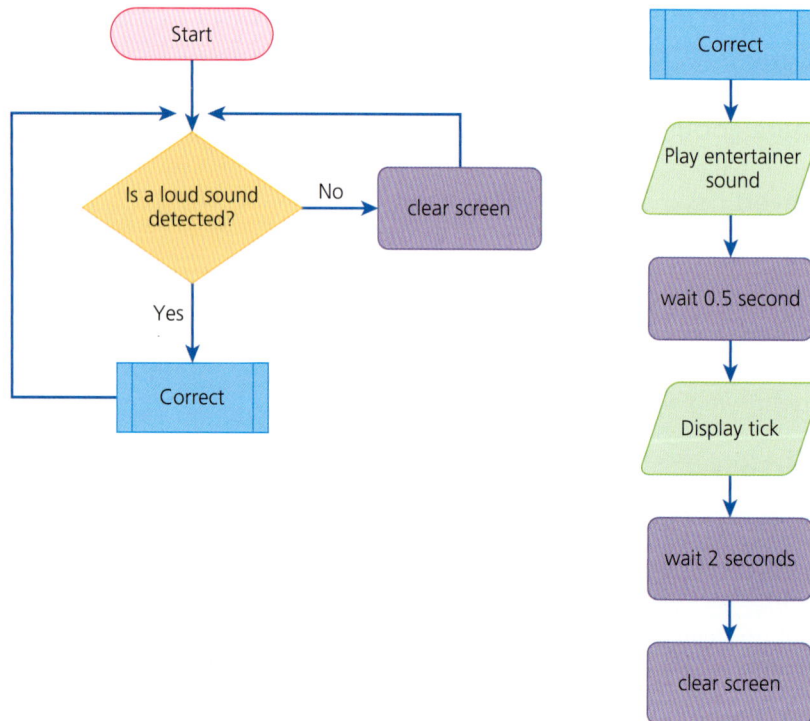

- Open the file **DebugProgram.py** given to you by your teacher.
- Connect the micro:bit to the device with the USB cable.
- Send the program to the micro:bit to test it.
- Use the checklist below to identify and debug any errors.

> Also remember to check the program against the flowchart above!

Debug possibilities checklist:
- Does the program start with **from microbit import ***?
- Are brackets opened and closed when used?
- Is there a colon at the end of an **if** statement line?
- Are there capitals where there should be, such as the image to be displayed, e.g. HAPPY?
- Does the string to be displayed have quotation marks around it?
- Are code words spelled correctly?

- Send the program to the micro:bit again to test your debugging.

2 Once you have your program running, copy and apply the test plan below to check that the program works as expected.

Test number	Data entered	Expected outcome	Pass/fail
1 Loud sound activates the program	Loud hand clap	the output of sound and display is run	
2 Output sequence is correct	Loud hand clap	music plays wait ½ second display a tick wait 2 seconds clear screen	
3 Clear screen on start	N/A	when no sound detected the display is clear	

3 Explain to a partner why debugging is important.
  - What would happen if you did not test a program before releasing it?
  - Give examples of errors that can be introduced when programming in MicroPython.

Sequences and lights

Learn

As well as displaying an image, the micro:bit can also turn on and off individual **LED lights**. There are 25 individual LED lights that can be programmed to do this.

Displaying lights on the micro:bit

You can create a sequence of lights in a specific pattern using the individual LED lights. To turn on one individual LED at the centre of the micro:bit display:
- open the MicroPython online platform on your web browser
- type in the program code shown below in the correct format expected in MicroPython.

```
from microbit import *

display.show(Image(
    "00000:"
    "00000:"
    "00900:"
    "00000:"
    "00000:"))
```

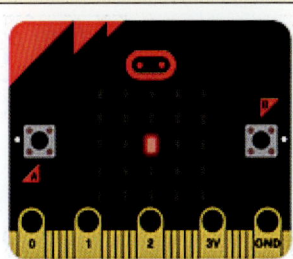

> In MicroPython, each individual LED can be switched **on with the number 9** or **off with the number 0**.

- Connect the micro:bit to the device with the USB cable.
- Send the program to the micro:bit to test that the centre LED is turned on.
- What would you need to change in the programming to turn on the top-left LED only?

Using a grid to create a pattern of lights

How could you use the visual pattern on this grid to find the pattern and create the program code?

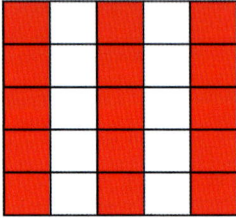

- First, break the pattern down into **on** and **off** LED lights on the grid, using **0 for off** and **9 for on**:

9	0	9	0	9
9	0	9	0	9
9	0	9	0	9
9	0	9	0	9
9	0	9	0	9

- Using the grid as a guide, add the 0 or 9 in the relevant spaces in the program code:

```
from microbit import *

display.show(Image(
    "90909:"
    "90909:"
    "90909:"
    "90909:"
    "90909:"))
```

You can see a pattern in the way the program code is written as the numbers are laid out in the same 5 × 5 pattern. This is the same as the LED display on the micro:bit and you can see the pattern to replicate it in the code.

- Run the program to check the pattern against the grid. The code above looks like this on the micro:bit and follows the pattern correctly:

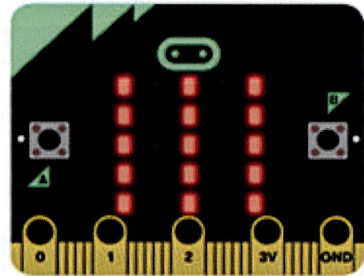

You can create a pattern of ON/OFF lights using the numbers to represent whether the LED is on (9) or off (0). Adding colour to a grid can help you to see the pattern that the numbers represent:

9	9	9	9	9
0	0	0	0	0
9	9	9	9	9
0	0	0	0	0
9	9	9	9	9

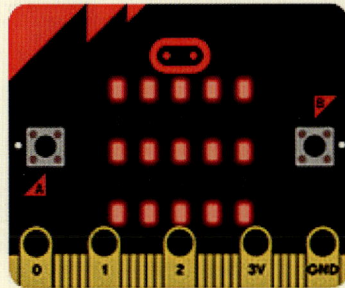

• Open the MicroPython online platform on your web browser.
  – Type in the program code shown below in the correct format expected in MicroPython.

```
from microbit import *

display.show(Image(
    "99999:"
    "00000:"
    "99999:"
    "00000:"
    "99999:"))
```

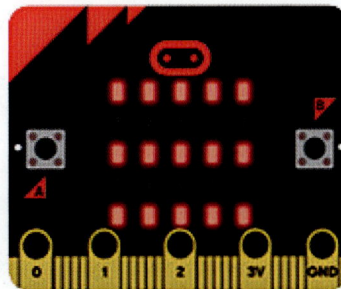

There is a visual pattern seen with an LED light being on and the number 9 being in its place. You can also see patterns in the way MicroPython is written:

Each light can be turned on or off individually. To code these, values for the lights in each row are written between quotation marks, with a colon immediately after the value for the last light in the row.

The open brackets must be closed at the end of the code relating to the LED lights.

• To test the program works as expected, connect the micro:bit to the device with the USB cable.
• Send the program to the micro:bit to test that the three rows of LEDs are turned on.

KEYWORD

LED (light emitting diode) display: a flat panel that uses lights as pixels on a digital display; the output of light on the micro:bit with 25 individual LEDs

Practise

1 Open the file **LEDlights1.py** provided by your teacher.
  – Edit the program to turn on the bottom-right LED.
  – Connect the micro:bit to the device with the USB cable.
  – Send the program to the micro:bit to test it.

2 Using the file above, edit the file to carry out the following:

Program edit 1	Program edit 2
	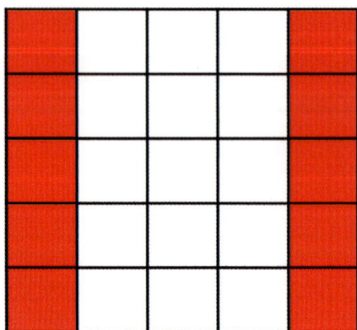
• Edit the program to turn on the LED shown in the image above. • Connect the micro:bit to the device with the USB cable. • Send the program to the micro:bit to test it.	• Edit the program to turn on the LED shown in the image above. • Connect the micro:bit to the device with the USB cable. • Send the program to the micro:bit to test it.

3 Open the file **Pattern1Debug.py** provided by your teacher. There is an error when you run this program.
  - Connect the micro:bit to the device with the USB cable.
  - Send the program to the micro:bit to see the error.
  - Edit the program to match the LEDs displayed for Pattern 1 below.
  - Send the program to the micro:bit to test it.

4 Open the file **PatternStart.py** provided by your teacher.
  - Connect the micro:bit to the device with the USB cable.
  - Send the program to the micro:bit to see the error.
  - Edit the program to match the LEDs displayed for Pattern 2 below.
  - Send the program to the micro:bit to test it.
  - Continue to edit the program to display Patterns 3 and 4 below.

Pattern 1

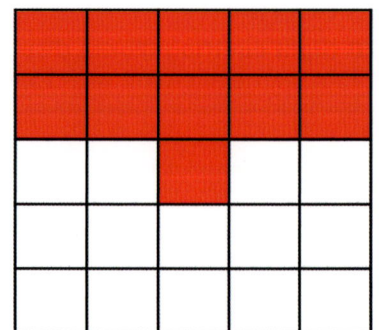

Pattern 2

Pattern 3

Pattern 4

Creating a moving sequence of lights

Learn

In the previous theme, you created a single image output on the micro:bit's LED display. The LED lights were turned **on by using 9** and turned **off by using 0**.

By combining more than one image output, you can create a moving image output.

Creating a moving image

A moving image is created by combining more than one image output into one program. For example, to turn on only the LED lights on the left-hand side of the display followed by turning on only the LED lights on the right-hand side of the display, you need two image outputs following each other in the program:

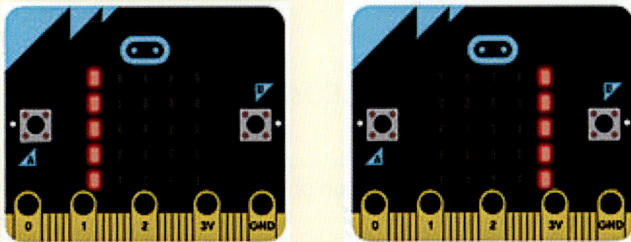

Follow these steps to create a moving image:
- Plan the program sequence through a flowchart first, for example:

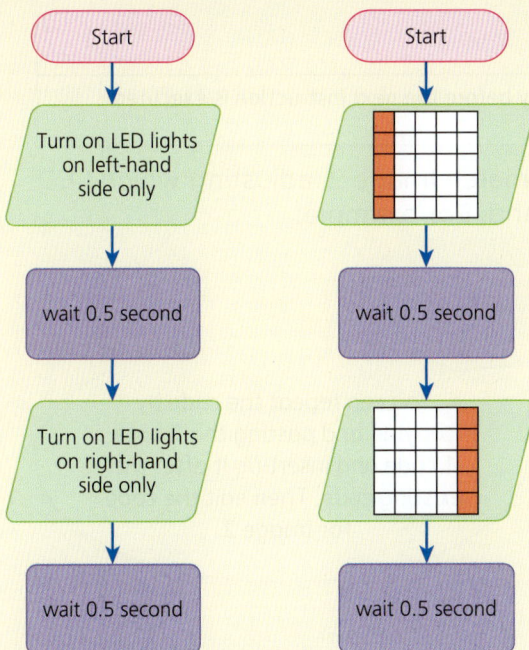

These flowcharts show which LED lights must be switched **on** or **off** in the program.

The flowchart on the right contains a **visual representation** (grids) of the LED display to help demonstrate the pattern in the sequence.

- Using the flowchart, identify the pattern of where the 9 or 0 needs to be placed. Create a grid for each image output, for example:

9	0	0	0	0
9	0	0	0	0
9	0	0	0	0
9	0	0	0	0
9	0	0	0	0

0	0	0	0	9
0	0	0	0	9
0	0	0	0	9
0	0	0	0	9
0	0	0	0	9

Image 1: lights on the left are lit   **Image 2: lights on the right are lit**

- Write the program code for the grids:
  - First code the lights for Image 1.
  - Use the grid to see the pattern for replicating the correct LEDs to turn on with a 9. For example:

`display.show(Image(`
 `"90000:"`
 `"90000:"`
 `"90000:"`
 `"90000:"`
 `"90000:"))`
	Program code for one instance of turning on or off the LED lights.
	 The LED display in the micro:bit is 5 × 5
	 The code has the same pattern 5 × 5

`sleep(500)`	Code to leave a delay before the next instruction is executed.

  - Repeat the code for Image 1 and edit it to match Image 2, adjusting which LED lights are turned on after the sleep command. For example:

```
from microbit import *

display.show(Image(
    "90000:"
    "90000:"
    "90000:"
    "90000:"
    "90000:"))
sleep(500)
display.show(Image(
    "00009:"
    "00009:"
    "00009:"
    "00009:"
    "00009:"))
sleep(500)
```

You can repeat the code by copying and pasting the Image 1 code and inserting it after the existing code. Then edit the code for Image 2.

- Connect the micro:bit to the device with the USB cable.
- Send the program to the micro:bit to test it.

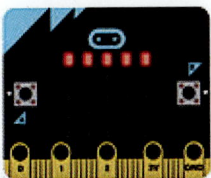

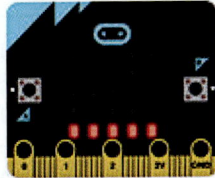

> It will display a line of lights along the left-hand side of the micro:bit and, after half a second, the lights will go off and the lights on the right-hand side will be displayed. Then, the program will stop and the final image output will stay displayed.
>
> What would you need to add to clear the screen at the end of the program?

Practise

1 In the example above, the program displayed a moving image using two **vertical** lines.
   - Look at the flowchart below. It creates a similar pattern of images using two **horizontal** lines. Discuss with a partner what the program will do.
   - Identify the pattern of where the 9s or 0s need to be placed. Copy and complete a grid for each image output.

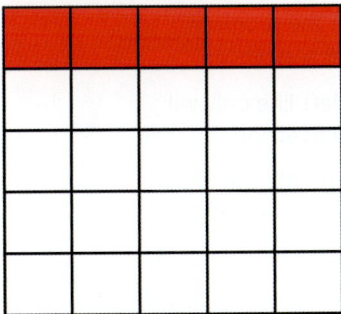

Image 1: lights on the top row are lit   **Image 2: lights on the bottom row are lit**

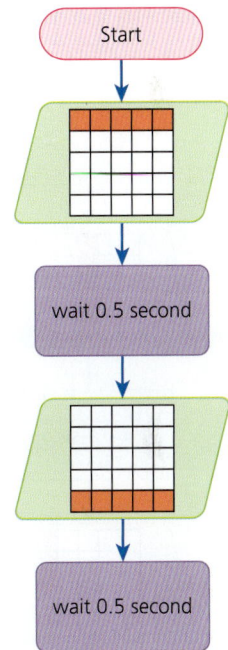

Start

wait 0.5 second

wait 0.5 second

2 Open the file **HorizontalPattern.py** provided by your teacher.
   - Using your grids for help, edit the code to create a new moving sequence of Image 1 followed by Image 2.
   - Connect the micro:bit to the device with the USB cable.
   - Send the program to the micro:bit to test it.

KEYWORDS

visual representation: a way of seeing the image that will be displayed visually on a digital device, such as a micro:bit

vertical: a line from top to bottom

horizontal: a line from side to side

3 Discuss with a partner:
   - What are the advantages of using more than one image in a light sequence?
   - Think back to the Scenario on page 184 at the start of this unit. Will using more than one image help to alert others in a visual alarm?

Extending a light sequence

Learn

Now that you can program two individual images of different LED lights turning on and off, you can extend this to add more to the sequence.

Adding images to a sequence

Follow these steps to add images to a sequence:

- First, plan the program sequence through a flowchart. For example:

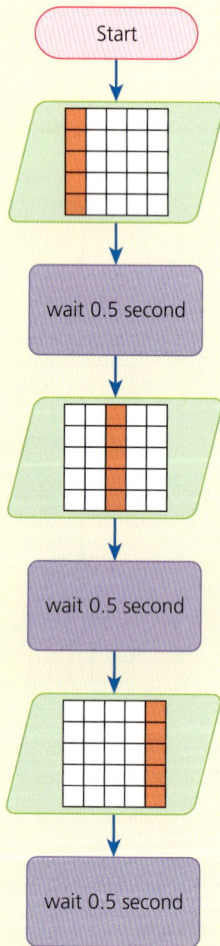

The pattern of the program will be a light sequence:

- Image 1: The left line only will be lit for 0.5 second
- Image 2: The middle line only will be lit for 0.5 second
- Image 3: The right line only will be lit for 0.5 second.

- Using the flowchart, identify the pattern of where the 9s or 0s need to be placed. Create a grid for each image. Here's the grid for Image 2 in the flowchart above:
- Write the program code for the grids. Edit the program code to display the new image followed by the sleep command, for example:

0	0	9	0	0
0	0	9	0	0
0	0	9	0	0
0	0	9	0	0
0	0	9	0	0

```from microbit import *```
 	
 ```display.show(Image(```
 `    "90000:"`
 `    "90000:"`
 `    "90000:"`
 `    "90000:"`
 `    "90000:"))`
 `sleep(500)`
	This is the first image in the sequence:

```display.show(Image(```
 `    "00900:"`
 `    "00900:"`
 `    "00900:"`
 `    "00900:"`
 `    "00900:"))`
 `sleep(500)`
	This is the new second image:

```display.show(Image(```
 `    "00009:"`
 `    "00009:"`
 `    "00009:"`
 `    "00009:"`
 `    "00009:"))`
 `sleep(500)`
	This is the third image in the sequence:

> The code must be in the same sequence as the flowchart shows. In this example, the new section of code will be in between the existing Image 1 and Image 3 code. You can edit the code by copying and pasting the Image 1 code and inserting it before the Image 3 code. Then edit the pasted code for Image 2.

- Connect the micro:bit to the device with the USB cable.
- Send the program to the micro:bit to test it. The lights will now look as though they are moving from one side to the other.

Practise

1 Create a program for these LED patterns on the micro:bit:

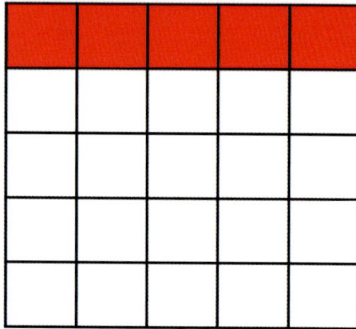 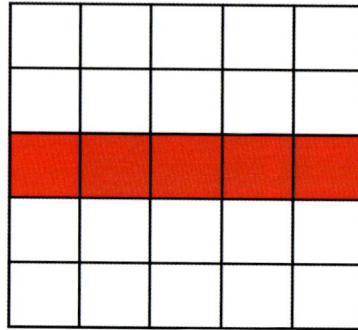 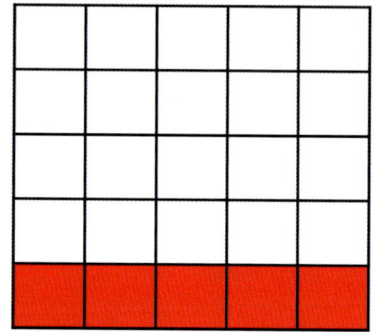

Image 1   Image 2   Image 3

 - First, draw the flowchart for the program.
 - Using the flowchart, identify the pattern of where the 9s or 0s need to be placed. Create a grid for each image.

2 Open the file **Sequence1Debug.py** provided by your teacher.
 - Connect the micro:bit to the device with the USB cable.
 - Send the program to the micro:bit to test it.

3 There are some errors in the program, so the lights are not displaying as expected.
 - Edit the code to correct the errors.
 - Send the program to the micro:bit to test that that it works correctly. It should show the following output:

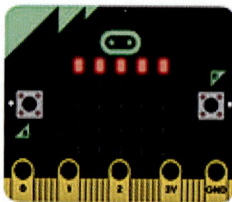 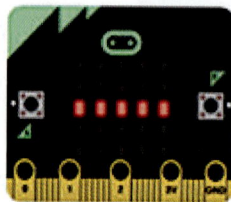 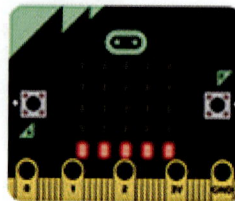

Light brightness

Learn

You have seen that the micro:bit can be used to turn on and off individual LED lights by using the numbers 0 and 9. But what about the numbers between 0 and 9?

The brightness of the LED can also be controlled. If **0 is off** and **9 is fully on**, the numbers in between represent different levels of brightness of the LED. Numbers 1–8 can be added to determine how bright the red LED light is going to be when switched on.

0	1	2	3	4	5	6	7	8	9

You can use the brightness of the LED light to generate an image or sequence. For example, the pattern on the grid below shows how the brightness can be used to create a new image. The pattern shows different levels of brightness. The numbers tell the program how much to turn that LED on by, which represents the brightness of the LED.

9	4	1	0	0
9	4	1	0	0
9	4	1	1	1
9	4	4	4	4
9	9	9	9	9

The pattern of the numbers on the grid creates this program:

```
from microbit import *

display.show(Image(
    "94100:"
    "94100:"
    "94111:"
    "94444:"
    "99999:"))
```

Programming the light brightness

Follow these steps to create a program to display an image that starts with a low brightness, then changes to full brightness and finally shows a clear screen:

- Plan the pattern using a grid, for example:

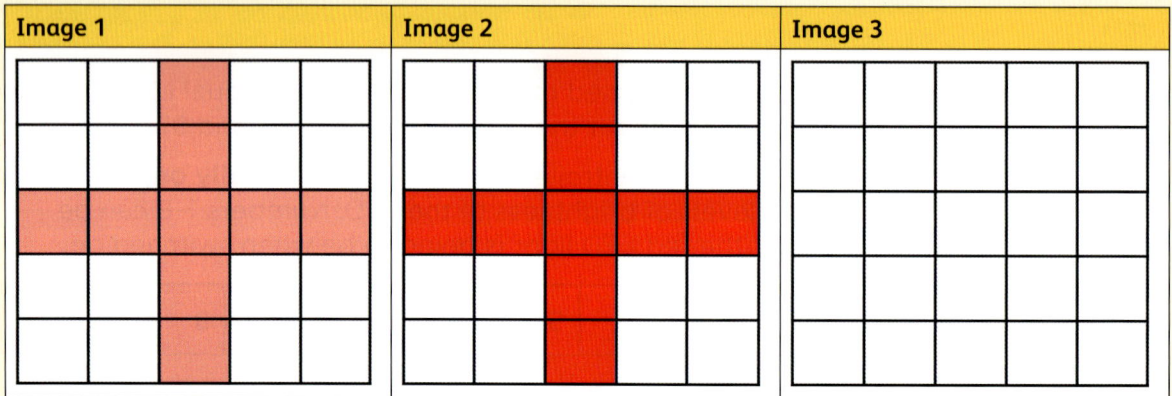

Image 1	Image 2	Image 3

- Plan the program sequence through a flowchart, for example:

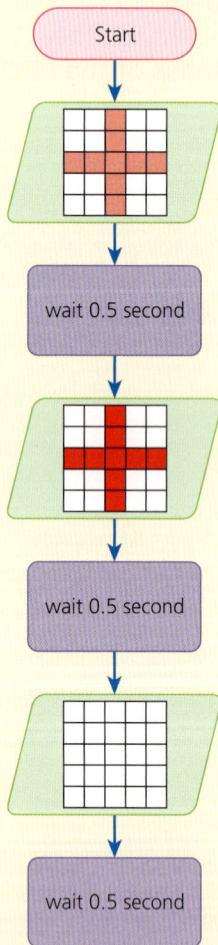

This flowchart shows that the first image to be displayed will be a plus sign (+) and that the brightness will be low. Next, the brightness of the plus sign is increased to full brightness. Finally, the LED lights are all off.

- Using the flowchart, identify the pattern of where the numbers need to be placed. Create a grid for each image with the numbers to represent the brightness and on and off. When the flowchart shows a reduced brightness, the number 4 could be used as this is about half the full brightness, for example:

0	0	4	0	0
0	0	4	0	0
4	4	4	4	4
0	0	4	0	0
0	0	4	0	0

0	0	9	0	0
0	0	9	0	0
9	9	9	9	9
0	0	9	0	0
0	0	9	0	0

0	0	0	0	0
0	0	0	0	0
0	0	0	0	0
0	0	0	0	0
0	0	0	0	0

● Write the program code for the grids. Repeat and edit the program code to display each image followed by the sleep command. The delay is important as it gives the image time to show before the next image is displayed, for example:

The third image in the sequence has no LED lights on. This still needs to be programmed and represented with a 0 for all LED lights on the display. By having this in the sequence, the display will be cleared at the end of the program.

```python
from microbit import *

display.show(Image(
    "00400:"
    "00400:"
    "44444:"
    "00400:"
    "00400:"))
sleep(500)
display.show(Image(
    "00900:"
    "00900:"
    "99999:"
    "00900:"
    "00900:"))
sleep(500)
display.show(Image(
    "00000:"
    "00000:"
    "00000:"
    "00000:"
    "00000:"))
sleep(500)
```

219

Practise

1 Open the file **Flowchart plan.docx** provided by your teacher.
Complete the plan for the following sequence of images.

Image 1	Image 2	Image 3

2 Open the file **SequenceStart.py** provided by your teacher.
  – Use your flowchart to edit the code to create a program that makes the letter **P** appear through increasing the brightness in the image sequence.
  – Send the program to the micro:bit to test that it works correctly.

3 The images below are for a new light sequence.
  – Predict what the output will be on the micro:bit display.

5	0	0	0	0
5	0	0	0	0
5	0	0	0	0
5	0	0	0	0
5	5	5	5	5

9	0	0	0	0
9	0	0	0	0
9	0	0	0	0
9	0	0	0	0
9	9	9	9	9

  – Open the file **Sequence2Debug.py** provided by your teacher.
  – Connect the micro:bit to the device with the USB cable.
  – Send the program to the micro:bit to test it.
  – Identify the errors that have been made when creating the program code. Find and fix the errors.
  – Send the edited program to the micro:bit to test it.

> Remember to look for patterns by checking the lights that should be **on** or **off** to find and fix the errors.

4 What is good about being able to control the brightness of the LED lights? Think back to the Scenario on page 184 at the start of the unit. How will using brightness help your visual alarm light sequence? Discuss your ideas with a partner.

Go further

At the start of this unit, you looked at the use of software prototypes; below is a prototype designed as part of a loading screen for a game on the micro:bit.

The following sequence has been planned, but needs to be created as a program. Then the program needs to be tested and evaluated.

Image 1	Image 2	Image 3

1 Open the file **GoFurther.py** provided by your teacher.
   - Connect the micro:bit to the device with the USB cable.
   - Send the program to the micro:bit to test it.
   - Edit the code to create the light sequence shown in the plan above.
   - Send the program to the micro:bit to test that it works correctly. Apply this test plan:

Test number	Data entered	Expected outcome	Pass/fail
1 LED lights displays 1st image	N/A		
2 LED lights displays 2nd image	N/A		
3 LED lights displays 3rd image	N/A		

2 Can you edit the code to include changing the brightness of the LED lights displayed?

3 Evaluate the program. Discuss with a partner:
- What was good about the loading sequence?
- What could you do to improve the loading sequence?

Challenge yourself

Your challenge is to create a light sequence to spell out the letters in your name.

1 Create a flowchart to represent the sequence the program needs to follow to spell out your name.

Using the flowchart, identify the pattern of where the 9s or 0s need to be placed for each letter. Create a grid for each image output, for example:

0	9	9	9	0
0	9	0	9	0
0	9	9	9	0
0	9	0	0	0
0	9	0	0	0

2 Open the file **ChallengeYourself2.py** provided by your teacher.
- Edit the code to match your flowchart.
- Add to the program sequence if more letters are required.
- Connect the micro:bit to the device with the USB cable.
- Send the program to the micro:bit to test it.

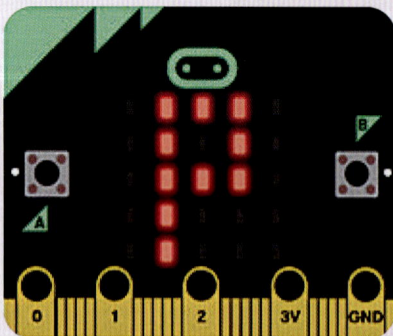

- Debug as required.

Final project

Look back to page 184 to remind yourself of the Scenario at the start of this unit.

1 Write a short paragraph to explain the meaning and purpose of a prototype.

2 You are now going to create a prototype on the micro:bit for a visual alarm, to ensure that all students know when the break-time buzzer sounds.

The micro:bit will be placed around the classroom and should be activated by the micro:bit sound sensor.

You should consider the following:
- how the program will be activated (for example, how to represent the school's break-time buzzer)
- what light sequence and brightness the visual alarm will display – a word or an image
- how the sound sensor will be used as part of the program to activate the visual alarm.

First, plan your visual alarm:

a Create a flowchart to show the micro:bit input used and the light sequence as a sub-routine.

b Using the flowchart, identify the pattern of where the numbers need to be placed for the images. Create a grid for each image with the numbers to represent the brightness and on and off.

c Open the file **Final project test plan.docx** supplied by your teacher. Complete this test plan to match your flowchart. Test your flowchart by applying this plan.

3 When you are sure that your flowchart fully covers the requirements of your visual alarm prototype, write the program in MicroPython:

a Open the file **FinalProjectStartingCode.py** supplied by your teacher. Edit the file to create your program.
- Connect the micro:bit to the device with the USB cable.
- Send the program to the micro:bit to test it.

b Test your program against your flowchart to make sure that the sequence works as expected.

c Check and correct any errors.

Evaluation

1 Swap programs with a partner and test the flowchart and the visual alarm. Comment on the following:
- Does the flowchart match the sequence on the micro:bit?
- Did the input(s) used activate the alarm?
- Did the visual alarm program work as expected?
- Now open your own program and look at the code. Reflect on what could be improved in your visual alarm. Think about the following:
  - Could the image fade in and out to help alert students?
  - Could the delay be slower or quicker to allow the light sequence to be viewed clearly?

2 Based on the evaluations, make a list of recommendations to improve your visual alarm.

What can you do?

Read and review what you can do.

✔ I can follow, edit and explain an algorithm using a flowchart.

✔ I can follow and explain the logic of AND, OR and NOT in a flowchart and MicroPython program.

✔ I can explain and use selection statements IF, THEN and ELSE in a flowchart.

✔ I can predict the outcome of a flowchart that uses selection.

✔ I can create an algorithm as a flowchart using sequence and selection statements.

✔ I can explain, edit and correct an algorithm represented as a flowchart that uses sub-routines.

✔ I can evaluate a software prototype to help debug and improve it.

✔ I can explain the purpose of a project plan.

✔ I can evaluate the design of a micro:bit solution.

✔ I can develop programs using multiple inputs and outputs on the micro:bit.

✔ I can develop a MicroPython program for the micro:bit that displays a sequence of LED lights.

✔ I can apply a test plan to check that a program works as expected.

✔ I can explain how errors have occurred in a flowchart and MicroPython program.

✔ I can identify and fix errors in a MicroPython program.

✔ I can explain how pattern recognition can be used to plan, create, and debug programs.

Glossary

404 error an error sent to a web browser if the DNS could not find the web server

absolute cell referencing a cell reference that will not be updated as part of a formula if the formula is copied and pasted into another cell

accelerometer a sensor to detect movement

address bar allows the user to type in a URL to go to a chosen website, via DNS

administrator a person who is responsible for managing a network

algorithm a sequence of steps or instructions to solve a problem

algorithm tracing the process of following the flow of a flowchart using a specific input

analogue camera a camera that used photographic film to take pictures

analogue image an image created using an analogue camera and film

analyse examine something in detail to ensure you fully understand it

AND gate a logic gate that accepts two inputs and will output a 1 (or TRUE) value only if both inputs are a 1

applications software applications for general or specific tasks

arithmetic operator +, −, *, / and other symbols that can be used for arithmetic calculations

artificial empathy the ability of digital devices to respond to human emotion

artificial intelligence an area of computing that focuses on creating intelligent computers that can mimic the way humans think and make decisions; a computer system able to perform tasks normally done using human intelligence, such as understanding speech

automate to reduce human interaction and leave the running of a device to sensors that determine the output

automated when a task is carried out automatically, without human intervention, and based on input and the processing of a set of program instructions

bandwidth the amount of data that can be transmitted within a certain amount of time

BIDMAS an acronym to help you remember the order of operations when completing mathematical calculations; a program will carry out the calculation in the following order: brackets, indices, division, multiplication, addition, subtraction

binary a number system that uses combinations of two digits (0 and 1) to represent all numbers; used to represent data in computer systems

binary digit 1 or 0

bit short for 'binary digit'; a single bit of data, either a 0 or a 1

bitmap graphic digital image produced using a grid of pixels

block-based programming programming using drag-and-drop blocks; a popular block-based language is Scratch

Bluesnarfing a method that hackers use to access the data on a device with Bluetooth

Bluetooth a method for computing devices to communicate with one another using radio waves

Boolean logic a form of algebra where all values are reduced to either true or false

Boolean logic operations operations based on the terms AND, OR, NOT

Boolean value a data type that has one of two possible values: true or false

brute-force attack a type of cyber-attack that a hacker can make on a computer – it attempts to guess a password by using a large bank of words and phrases; it keeps trying different combinations until it finds the correct password

bug an error in a program that stops it working correctly

built-in functions carry out a set of tasks or operations using data specified by the user; the function will output a result for the user

byte a group of 8 bits of data, often used to represent a single character in a computer, e.g. 01010011

case sensitive able to distinguish between capital and small letters

casting the process of ensuring data is set to the correct data type

cell an area where a row and column intersect and data can be entered

cell range a group of cells in a spreadsheet, identified by naming the first and last cells in the group, e.g. A1:A5

cell reference a combination of letters and numbers used to identify individual cells in a spreadsheet

cellular data a method for computing devices to communicate with one another using radio waves

central processing unit (CPU) the processor in a computing device that executes all instructions

chatbot software that simulates a human-like conversation via text messages

cipher text a message once it has been encrypted

colour depth a measure of the number of bits used to represent colour in individual pixels in an image

comments text entered by a programmer to improve the readability of code; they start with the # symbol in Python

comparison operators symbols used to compare values, e.g. >= meaning greater than or equal to

computer models computerised representations of real-life situations created using software or specialised software applications

computer networks groups of computers connected together

computer programs the instructions used to tell a computer system how to complete a task

computing device any device that follows the input, process, output model

condition something that is checked to determine whether it is true or false

conditional formatting formatting a data item that meets a specific rule

connectivity the method that devices use to connect to each other to form a network

consumer an individual purchasing a product or service for their own use

control an element on a database input form, e.g. a text box or a label

cookie a text file that holds small pieces of data about a user

corrupted binary code can be lost or scrambled if an error occurs

criteria a set of keywords, rules or conditions used to search for data items

data raw facts and figures; computers understand only binary data, which is 0s and 1s

data-capture form a form designed to collect data for a specific task

data dictionary a table used to identify key data items and their key features (such as data type and field length) when designing a database

data sheet view a method of viewing content in MS Access that allows the user to edit data

data type the different ways in which data can be stored, e.g. integer, string, decimal number

database a computer application that is used to organise data that can then be stored, processed and accessed electronically

database report a tool within a database used to output data for the user

debug/debugging the process of identifying and removing errors from a computer program

decompose break down into smaller parts

design view a method of viewing content in MS Access where the layout of the database can be changed

digital assistant an electronic device that can be used to help a user complete tasks such as switch on other appliances, control heating systems, search the internet for information or organise music play lists

digital camera a camera that captures photographs and stores them in the form of digital data

digital device a piece of physical equipment that uses digital data

digitised image a computer representation of an image, often in file formats such as JPEG, GIF, PNG or TIFF

display window where the content is displayed when downloaded from a web server

DNS (Domain Name System) a system used to translate a URL to an IP address

domain name an easy-to-remember name for a website, e.g. www.hoddereducation.com

electrical interference when lots of electrical devices are operating in a small area, the electrical and radio waves can cause other devices to work incorrectly

electronic circuit a route that electricity can flow around

encryption a process that scrambles data so that it cannot be understood by unauthorised users; only the device that the data is sent to is able to decrypt the data using a key

evolving changing and improving

execute another word for running a program

facial-recognition algorithm a program that collects data about someone's facial features

factors the key data items represented in a data model

field heading a word or phrase used to describe the contents of a field in a database

fill handle a square that appears in a spreadsheet cell to let the user know that the contents can be copied and filled into the cells the user drags the fill handle into; when you hover over it the plus sign appears, which is what you click on and drag to replicate the contents

film a plastic strip coated in light-sensitive crystals, inserted into analogue cameras and used to store images

fixed budget a fixed amount of money available to complete a task

float another name for the data type *real*; it is short for 'floating point number', which is a decimal number

flowchart a diagram showing the sequence of actions in a computer program; a graphical representation to show the steps to solve a problem

formula a combination of numbers, mathematical symbols, cell references and functions used to process data in a spreadsheet

formula bar an area in a spreadsheet window where a formula can be entered

formulae mathematical calculations expressed with letters

fraud deceiving someone for financial or personal gain

full release in game development, the final full game released to users

functionality the range of operations that can be run on a computing device

general-purpose application software that can be used for more than one purpose

gesture a specific movement on the micro:bit

graphical user interface also known as a *GUI*; used to interact with a computer using icons and menus

graphics the use of images to illustrate a real-world situation

hacked when somebody accesses a system when they are not supposed to; this is often illegal

hackers people who may try to access data that they are not allowed to access

hard disk drive a hardware device that is used to store digital data

hardware aspects of a computing device that you *can* touch; the physical components of a device

higher-level DNS another DNS that is used for checking large lists of URLs and IP addresses

home network a network of devices that can be found in a household

horizontal a line from side to side

humidity the amount of water in the air

image recognition computers identifying similarities in lines, colours, textures and shapes of an image in an attempt to identify objects

indentation moving the line of code in to represent the code that will run if the condition is met

infographic a chart or a diagram that represents information in a visual way

infrared a type of light that is invisible to the human eye but is useful for electronic devices such as remote controls

input a physical input into a computing device, e.g. keyboard, mouse, microphone, button

input function a function that Python uses to capture string data from users

integer whole number

integrated built into

integrated applications applications packages such as the Google App Suite, or MS Office, where the applications are part of a larger package and all have similar interfaces

Integrated Development and Learning Environment (IDLE) an environment used to program in Python

interactive mode the Python shell allows commands to be entered and run immediately

interface a visual way of interacting with software

interference what happens when something interrupts the transmission of a signal; this could be a physical obstruction such as a wall, or other radio waves

interpreter the feature of Python that translates the Python code into language that the computer can understand, line by line

IP (Internet Protocol) address an address assigned to each device on a network that is unique to the network

junk mail unwanted emails, sent from organisations to many users at one time

labels headings used in a spreadsheet application to aid the understanding of data

LED (light emitting diode) display a flat panel that uses lights as pixels on a digital display; the output of light on the micro:bit with 25 individual LEDs

library a list of all programming commands that are available under the library name

light display a visual show using lights

light sequence the order lights are displayed in

logic circuit a combination of logic gates used to carry out complex operations

logic gate a physical device or circuit that processes one or more input signals to produce a single output signal

machine code the language that a computer uses to carry out instructions

machine learning computer systems that are able to learn and adapt by analysing patterns in data

manufacturing the process of creating something

meet and greet an event where members of the public are able to meet famous individuals

merchandise items that can be bought at events

messaging service software that allows users to send and receive text messages between devices

MicroPython: the version of Python used with the micro:bit

model a computer application that replicates a real-life environment, where data is changed to see what happens; simple models can be built in spreadsheet software

multiple-choice format a question that provides a set of possible answers the user must choose from

naming convention a specific way of writing a variable name; the two main ways are called *snake_case* and *camelCase*

navigation buttons back, forwards and refresh buttons are included to help navigate pages; all browsers also have bookmark features for saving pages

neural network a type of machine learning designed to mimic the way the human brain works

NOT gate a logic gate that accepts only one input; the output will always be the opposite of the input

NPC non-player character; a character in the background of a computer game that the game player can interact with

operating system the systems software that manages hardware, software and resources on a device

OR gate a logic gate that accepts two inputs and will output a 1 (or TRUE) value when either of the inputs is a 1

output a visible or audible outcome on a device through, for example, the display, monitor, speakers, headphones

padlock icon shows in the address bar if the page is sent via HTTPS and is secure

pattern recognition looking for a pattern and then using that pattern to solve a problem

pedometer a device that estimates the distance travelled on foot by recording the number of steps taken

physical computing device a small microprocessor that can be programmed using block or text-based programming languages

pixel short for 'picture element'; the small element displayed on a computer screen

plaintext a message before encryption or after decryption; a message that can be read easily

portable something that can easily be moved around

power surge computer hardware can be damaged by a temporary increase in power, often caused by lightning

ppi 'pixels per inch'; the number of pixels in a square inch of screen

preset program a program that has already been created for the user

primary key a value that is unique for every record in a database

print statement a Python statement used to output text or values onto the screen

process the function within a computing device where an instruction in a program is carried out, such as a calculation or display

processor the part of a computer that carries out instructions

protocol set of rules for how data is sent between devices

prototype a sample, model or first release of a product, such as a program or device, built to test a concept or process

proximity a measure of how close two objects are to each other

Python shell the Python interactive mode, where commands can be typed directly

query a tool used in some applications to allow users to select useful data

real any number with a decimal point, such as 1.2 or 56.8

relative cell referencing a cell reference that will be updated as part of a formula if the formula is copied and pasted into another cell

resolution the total number of pixels on a screen

script mode Python's text editor, which allows programmers to enter a list of commands and they are executed together

search engine a website designed to search for content on other websites

selection a programming construct with more than one possible pathway; a condition is tested (using a question or criterion) before deciding which pathway to follow (the output)

sending the program downloading the MicroPython program file to the micro:bit to run

sensor a device that is able to gather data from its surroundings to respond to or record

sequence the specific order of instructions

server a hardware device that stores and manages files and services for a network

simulation a computer model that can predict the outcome of a real-world system or scenario

simulator software to simulate a real-world application

smart device a device that utilises sensors and is connected to other devices

smart technology *SMART* means 'self-monitoring, analysis and reporting technology'; technologies that use AI to support their operation

smart watch a wearable computer in the form of a watch

software aspects of a computing device that you *cannot* touch; the programs that run on a device

spam filter a computer program that detects junk mail and removes it from an email inbox

spreadsheet a computer application that uses rows and columns to organise data and carry out calculations using that data

SSL (Secure Sockets Layer) technology for keeping a connection between devices secure through encryption

SSL certificate a digital certificate that confirms that a website is genuine and allows it to use an encrypted connection using SSL

streaming watching or playing media over a computer network; playback can be started before all of the data has downloaded

string data that is made up of letters, numbers or any characters on the keyboard

sub-routine a mini program inside a program that can be completed or repeated when requested

syntax the structure of the code used in a programming language

systems software software that runs hardware and software, i.e. the operating system

test plan a structured approach to testing whether your solution works as expected; a document that describes the areas of a program to be tested – includes details of the tests to be applied to each area of the program, including test data and expected results

text file a file that contains data in text format only, with no additional images or formatting

text-based programming programming that requires the programmer to type text, e.g. Python

thermostat a device that has a built-in sensor to detect changes in temperature

tilt a measure of the degree to which an object is raised or lowered from a flat surface

transmission distance how far data can be sent using the transmission method

trend a pattern that shows behaviour or data moving in a general direction

Uniform Resource Locator (URL) used to locate a file on a web server on the internet

unique only one exists; there are no duplicates

URL Uniform Resource Locator; the address of a web page

usability considering how a user will interact with a program

user: person who will use a program

user feedback gathering feedback from users of the product to aid development

user interface the way that users and computer systems communicate

user friendly easy to use or understand

user-related tasks tasks that are to be carried out by the user of a digital system

value a number that can be used in a programming language

variable a named memory location used to store data of a given type during program execution; a variable can change value as the program runs

vector graphic digital image made from a series of objects placed on a computer screen

verify to check that something is correct

vertical a line from top to bottom

virtual reality computer-generated simulation of a three-dimensional image or environment; can be interacted with by a person using special electronic equipment, such as a helmet with a screen inside or gloves fitted with sensors

virus software designed to cause damage to computer systems

visual representation a way of seeing the image that will be displayed visually on a digital device, such as a micro:bit

web browser a software application that allows users to locate, access and display information on the world wide web

web server a server that provides access to web pages stored on them

Wi-Fi a method for computing devices to communicate with one another using radio waves

Wi-Fi access point a hardware device that allows devices to connect to a network using Wi-Fi

Index

Acknowledgements

The Publishers would like to thank the following for permission to reproduce copyright material.

Photo credits

p. 8 © Rawpixel.com/stock.adobe.com; p. 9 © phanasitti/stock.adobe.com; p.10 © Michael Cavotta. License: CC BY-NC-ND 4.0; p. 23 © Evgeniy Shkolenko/123RF.com; p. 39 © heijotheone/stock.adobe. com; p. 45 t © Ninja SS/Shutterstock.com, m © Phil's Mommy/Shutterstock.com, b © Alex/stock. adobe.com; p. 48 © Nadezda Murmakova/Shutterstock.com; p. 49 © Gargantiopa/Shutterstock.com; p. 62 © SpicyTruffel/stock.adobe.com; p. 63 © Micro:bit Educational Foundation microbit.org; p. 70 © bloomicon/stock.adobe.com; p. 75 © alliya2000/stock.adobe.com; p. 78 © vectorpouch/stock. adobe.com; p. 82 © jamesteohart/stock.adobe.com; p. 83 t © Rawpixel.com/stock.adobe.com, m © fizkes/stock.adobe.com, b © Debby Wong/Shutterstock.com; p. 85 © terovesalainen/stock.adobe. com; p. 87 t © koblizeek/stock.adobe.com, b © Ferid Huseynli/Shutterstock.com; p. 88 l © Nasarudin/ stock.adobe.com, r © Panchenko Vladimir/Shutterstock.com; p. 89 © .shock/stock.adobe.com; p. 106 Matthew Field, www.photography.mattfield.com, available under Creative Commons licence CC BY 2.5, creativecommons.org/licenses/by/2.5/; p. 107 © Colin Temple/Shutterstock.com; p. 108 © Ekaterina Belova/stock.adobe.com; p. 109 © Apichon_tee/stock.adobe.com; p. 112 © Rudzhan/ stock.adobe.com; p. 113 t © karandaev/stock.adobe.com, b © ziiinvn/stock.adobe.com; p. 114 © irissca/stock.adobe.com; p. 141 © Maxim Grebeshkov/stock.adobe.com; p. 142 © Andrey_Kuzmin/ Shutterstock.com; p. 150 © Andrey Popov/stock.adobe.com; p. 151 © phonlamaiphoto/stock.adobe. com; p. 152 © NicoElNino/stock.adobe.com; p. 153 © bht2000/stock.adobe.com; p. 154 © Koshiro/ stock.adobe.com; p. 160 © PaO_STUDIO/Shutterstock.com; p. 161 l © Have a nice day/stock.adobe. com, r © Kaspars Grinvalds/stock.adobe.com; p. 162 © ft2010/stock.adobe.com; p. 163 © Prostock-studio/stock.adobe.com; p. 164 © Ft2010/stock.adobe.com; p. 165 © chamillew/stock.adobe.com; p. 166 l © SIVStockStudio/Shutterstock.com, r © Vinko93/Shutterstock.com; p. 169 © Sunny_nsk/stock. adobe.com; p. 171 © scharfsinn86/stock.adobe.com; p. 172 © Corona Borealis/stock.adobe.com; p. 176 © Brian Jackson/stock.adobe.com; p. 177 © elenabsl/stock.adobe.com; p. 182 © Eric Glenn/ Shutterstock.com; p. 183 © Candice Willmore/Shutterstock.com; p. 184 t © Tom Wang/stock.adobe. com; p. 186 © Sushiman/stock.adobe.com.

Text credits

The following brands mentioned in this book are trademarks or registered trademarks:

- Android
- Apple iPod
- BBC micro:bit
- Bluetooth
- Python
- Quick, Draw!
- Google
- Google Apps
- MakeCode
- MicroPython
- Scratch
- Wi-Fi
- Microsoft Access
- Microsoft Excel
- Microsoft Office
- PowerPoint
- Windows

Apple product screenshot(s) reprinted with permission from Apple.

BBC micro:bit images and screenshots © Micro:bit Educational Foundation microbit.org

Google, Google Apps and Quick, Draw! are trademarks of Google LLC and this book is not endorsed by or affiliated with Google in any way.

MicroPython copyright © 2013-2022 Damien P. George, https://github.com/micropython/micropython/blob/master/LICENSE

Microsoft product screenshot(s) used with permission from Microsoft.

Python copyright © 2001-2022 Python Software Foundation; All Rights Reserved.

Scratch is developed by the Lifelong Kindergarten Group at the MIT Media Lab. See http://scratch.mit.edu.

Every effort has been made to trace all copyright holders, but if any have been inadvertently overlooked, the Publishers will be pleased to make the necessary arrangements at the first opportunity.

Although every effort has been made to ensure that website addresses are correct at time of going to press, Hodder Education cannot be held responsible for the content of any website mentioned in this book. It is sometimes possible to find a relocated web page by typing in the address of the home page for a website in the URL window of your browser.